D0712708

Tolstoy's
Major Fiction

Edward Wasiolek

Tolstoy's
Major Fiction

THE UNIVERSITY OF CHICAGO PRESS

CHICAGO AND LONDON

The University of Chicago Press, Chicago 60637
The University of Chicago Press, Ltd., London

83 82 81 80 79 78   9 8 7 6 5 4 3 2 1

Edward Wasiolek is Avalon Foundation Distinguished Service Professor and Chairman of the
Department of Slavic Languages and Literatures,
and Chairman of the Committee on Comparative Studies in Literature, the University of
Chicago. He is the author of *Dostoevsky: The
Major Fiction*; coauthor of *Nine Soviet Portraits*;
editor of *"Crime and Punishment" and the
Critics*; editor and translator of *The Notebooks
for "Crime and Punishment"* and *The
Notebooks for "The Brothers Karamazov"*; and
editor of *The Notebooks for "The Idiot," The
Notebooks for "The Possessed," The Notebooks
for "A Raw Youth,"* and *The Gambler*.

Library of Congress Cataloging in Publication Data

Wasiolek, Edward.
  Tolstoy's major fiction.

Bibliography: p.
  Includes index.
  1. Tolstoĭ, Lev Nikolaevich, graf, 1828–1910
—Criticism and interpretation.   I. Title.
PG3410.W3   891.7'3'3   77–81732
ISBN 0-226-87397-8

For Emily, Mark, Karen, Eric,
and the Grindstone years:
Tolstoy would have understood

Prince Andrey to Pierre: "Nothing is forever."

If one goes by reality there are no games. And if there are no games—what is left? (From *Childhood*)

Contents

1 Introduction

There are good books on Tolstoy, both in Russian and English, and Eikhenbaum's three-volume work on Tolstoy, as well as his earlier *The Young Tolstoy*, written in the twenties, are among the best.[1] The three-volume work is a massive source study, but there is nothing of the dreariness that attends many such works. Eikhenbaum is concerned with the ideological and cultural fodder that Tolstoy digested and transformed and the process by which Tolstoy was himself touched and changed by that digestion. The study is fructified by a theory of considerable importance, which gives shape and coherence to what might otherwise seem arbitrary and disparate. Eikhenbaum's thesis—following Russian formalist assumptions—is that one's writing is already written for one, at least in part. What authors imagine to be immediate and personal is already shaped for them, because writers do not "create" as much as they modify. And what they modify is also modifying them. They are not free spirits, but feel the weight of the writing that has gone on before them, and it is this weight that moves their pens and shapes their imaginations. In the English-speaking world Northrop Frye and in the Gallic world Roland Barthes have said something of the same thing, but the Russian Formalists said it first and they said it better, or at least more theoretically and coherently.

Russian Formalism is often confused with "close reading," or with any procedure that concerns itself with the linguistic structure of the work. In general, to be formalistic for most people means to concern oneself with the "inside" of the work. This is true, but there is nothing more central to a formalist view of a literary work than its concern with the "outside" of a work. For a Formalist there is no "inside" without an "outside," and the central process of literary making—and consequently the central concern of the Formalists—was the study of how this "outside" became the "inside." The process was primarily dialectic, that is, it proceeded not by modification or inheritance as much as by revolt and differentiation; but every revolt included what it revolted against, so that the "inside" of a literary work was the "outside" and its negation. This was so if the work was successful. If it was not successful, it was because the "inside" was all "outside," that is, a repetition of what had already been created (imitation), or because there was no "outside" in the "inside," that is, because it was eccentric and outlandish.

The formalist contribution to Tolstoyan criticism—and not Eikhenbaum alone—was to show us how much of this massively original writer came from somewhere else, how much of his invention was continuation, and how much of what Tolstoy felt to be personal, agonizing, and individual was itself literary process and not personal experience. Russian Formalists point out what is obvious yet sometimes forgotten or ignored: that literature is literary and not experience; or, if experience, it is literary experience. Experiential situations are literary situations; personal problems are literary problems. Eikhenbaum shows, for example, with considerable ingenuity in *The Young Tolstoy* how Tolstoy's early spiritual and psychological gropings and torments are really an exploration of literary styles. Tolstoy may think he is undergoing a spiritual and moral crisis, but Eikhenbaum insists that he is trying out different modes of expression.[2]

There is no doubt that Eikhenbaum is right, at least in part. But only in part. The written work is freighted with the forms of the past, and we are formed in the forming. And probably by more than Eikhenbaum and the Formalists would have us believe. There is no reason to believe that the language that shapes us carries only literary forms and attitudes; it carries political, social, and cultural forms and predispositions also. But if all this is true—if there is impersonality at the core of every effort of personality—still we must acknowledge that there is also personality. Tradition shapes but it doesn't complete; it pressures but it doesn't dominate. If there is an experience we all share in the reading of literature, it is surely the sense of the sharpness, distinctness, and comprehensiveness of personality. Great writers are great presences, and their presence permeates everything they touch and everything that touches them. Still, strong as Tolstoy's presence is, it is not strong enough to withstand the pressure of what has gone on before him, and if Eikhenbaum exaggerates the purely verbal content of Tolstoy's moral torments, he draws our attention to how much of Tolstoy is not Tolstoy.

No one can study Russian nineteenth-century thought and literature for very long without seeing how much Tolstoy was part of his cultural and literary milieu. The West has tended to see him abstracted from the tradition from which he proceeded and to which he added, and some of his views have appeared outlandish and weird because our norms and coherences are different. In Russian literary history they may be commonplace. Tolstoy's theory of art, for example, was received by most in the West as bizarre and for many as the ravings of a demented genius. The history of its reception in the West, with a few exceptions, oscillated between outrage and dismissal. Yet Tolstoy was repeating much of what Pisarev and Chernyshevsky had said before him. The utilitarian element in his views of art has never received enough emphasis, and yet this is his major grief against the art theories and the practice and production of art in the West: that art was a pastime for the idle and the rich and that it did not serve serious and important ends for all the people. Pisarev cried out against art because Russians were hungry and art squandered the nation's resources, but Tolstoy cried out for an art that would feed the souls and emotions of all the people. If we rage against him for calling Shakespeare and Beethoven charlatans, we have not noted sufficiently that Tolstoy put forth a view of art of dignity and seriousness; for nothing could have more dignity than a conception of art that would exceed the spaces of academies, opera houses, and publishing firms and that would be as necessary as food and drink.

Both his view of culture as contrivance and his revolt against everything that was refined and sophisticated came from a belief that the past was empty and useless. Chaadaev had cried out that there was nothing but air under the feet of Russians and that Russians had to invent their reality every day.[3] Chaadaev, to be sure, longed for the fixities of Europe; Tolstoy had contempt for them, but they both proceeded from the same perception of Russian reality. Nineteenth-century Russian writers tended to recognize, between despair and arrogance, that the Russian past was empty and because it was empty, they wanted to make the future full. This was both an occasion for self-castigation and arrogance. Tolstoy chose arrogance, but he was not the only one. Chaadaev himself, though declared officially to be insane for his uncomplimentary remarks about Russian reality and put under house arrest, came from contempt for Russian reality to something of arrogance about its superiority. He argued in his later writings, as the Slavophiles later did, that the empty past was also a lack of encumbrance. Khomyakov, Kireevsky, and other Slavophiles arrogantly turned emptiness into virtues by arguing that Russia was not burdened with the accumulation of falsities, as was Europe. And if one wanted to reach past the arrogance of anything Tolstoy wrote, one need only sample pages of Danilevsky's *Russia and Europe*.[4]

It was because the past was empty that the Russians believed with such a passion in the future. There is hardly a Russian thinker or writer who did not hold his candle before the darkness of the future. There is nothing more insistent in Russian thought and in Russian literature, too, than the belief that the future will be good, that the golden gates will someday open to the holy city. The Westernizers and the Slavophiles disagreed on the shape of the city, but they agreed with a passion that a glorious future lay before Russia. For the Slavophiles the Russians had remained untouched by the civilization of the West and its spiritual principles. The basic principles of the Russian people, which guaranteed its identity and its role in history, remained uncorrupted and intact, ready to sprout with unique efflorescence. Whether for Khomyakov, Vladimir Solovyov, or Danilevsky, the future beckoned with a transformed and transfigured Russia. The Westernizers, while accepting the premises and accomplishments of the rationalistic West, carried reason toward hope and desire. The phenomenal popularity of Chernyshevsky's *What Is To Be Done?* lay, I am sure, in its promise of a purified and utopistic Russia, which consisted in more than the visions of Vera. The promise lay in the belief that a science of behavior, following on the science of minerals and chemicals, would find a special and perfect adjustment among the temperaments of people and between people and their surroundings. Chernyshevsky was persuaded, as were other utilitarians, that disharmony, stress, and disagreement were not in the order of things, and he was absolutely persuaded that the law of perfect order would be found.[5] Men were by nature destined for perfection and beauty.

Wherever one turns in the Russian intellectual and literary landscape, whether to the works of Westerner or Slavophile, believer or atheist, one finds some variant of belief that history is going somewhere for the Russians, that it is moving ineluctably toward some golden city. Dostoevsky believed in the *zolotoy vek* (the golden century) and the kingdom of God on earth; Belinsky and Chernyshevsky believed in a socialist rationalistic paradise. Chekhov's characters moan their way through the pages of the plays and lives but they also dream of beautiful futures. Tolstoy towered above the Russia about him, but his feet were firmly planted in its soil, and none of the roots he shared was deeper and more tenacious and more important than his belief that he too would open the gates to the golden city. His golden city lay in no other world, but firmly and solidly in the sensuous data of this world. It lay in the way in which one would and could seize experience and find that special relationship to the world and to others. It was inconceivable to him, as it has been to most Russians, that phenomena, circumstances, data were just there in some existential jumble. Phenomena for Russians, and for Soviets too, are normative, governed by laws which are discernible and formulatable. If the golden experience has not been discerned in the past and is not discernible in the way men lead their lives, this means only that men have to be taught to see and seize it.

From the very beginning of his creative career Tolstoy was propelled by the unshakable conviction that there was a "right" relationship in the world, a special experience in which life would beat full and before which the tensions, stresses, and disharmonies of life would melt away. He projected this conviction into the actions and beliefs of his characters, and the most profound shaping force in his works is his heroes' quest of this "right" experience. People do what they do, think as they do, have the kind of moral character they do, are good or bad, foolish or wise, beautiful or ugly, and their lives beat full or are empty because they touch or do not touch, come close to or fade distantly from the point in which experience is right, good, beautiful and full. Most of us, whatever our views of this most magnificent of Russian writers, would admit that one of the chief characteristics of Tolstoy's work is the clarity of its contours: there is no play on ambiguities, no chiaroscuro, no penumbra of indefiniteness. We know where we are in Tolstoy's world, and we know the size, weight, and value of everything we meet. Critics may disagree on a number of things in Tolstoy, but we all know that Natasha and Pierre are good in *War and Peace* and Anatole Kuragin and Princess Ellen are not. We know what is foolish, what is wise, what is good, and what is evil. There is no obfuscation, no intentional ambiguities, and no withheld information. Tolstoy does not play games with the reader and does not indulge in intellectual puzzles. Yet because Tolstoy's world spins on axes different from those we are accustomed to, there are mysteries and behavioral and value tiltings different from ours. The works of great writers accumulate a store of true but banal generalities about them and Tolstoy's have not been spared: everyone knows that the country is better than the city for Tolstoy, that great men are less important than little men, that sophistication is evil and simplicity is good. But it may not be clear why the high point of *War and Peace* and the special vessel of experience should be a sixteen-year-old girl, distinguished by no special qualities and lacking in many; as it may not be clear why Kutuzov—fat, lecherous, and asleep throughout most of the important military briefings—should be our link to the special movements of history. It may not be obvious, too, why the death of a tree is better than the death of a Christian, why grief for a dead mother is a sign of the sterility of life, that fidelity (such as Sonya's) and keeping one's word (as for Nikolay) are elements of the desiccating force of life, but not keeping one's word (as the fickleness of Natasha) is sacramental, as is indifference to the dying and the dead. Masha in *Family Happiness* goes wrong because she moves to the city and enjoys its sophisticizing corruptions and because she neglects motherhood, but she goes wrong, too, and more essentially, because she regrets her youth, grieves for her mother, and wants to hold on to the excitement of love and is sorry for the mistakes she has made. Olenin touches truth when he lies in an old stag's lair and invites the mosquitoes to devour him, and touches falsity when he worships Maryanka and wants to devote his life to her.

There is a center in Tolstoy's work to which one is attracted and from which one is deflected, and it is in this center that life beats full. The deflecting force is found in everyone, not only in negative characters. That which deflects Ellen and Anatole from the core deflects Andrey. Andrey is closer to the center and the Kuragins farther from it, but the force is the same. This means that there is a continuity between so-called "good" characters and "evil" characters. It also means that the most disparate phenomena and actions can be related along a line of distancing from the center, where real life beats. The foolishness of Napoleon, the chatter of the social salons, the scratchings on the blackboards of the arrogant and blind Teutonic generals, the sterilities of Marya's Christian faith, the tortured relations between the old Bolkonsky and his daughter Marya, and the fidelity of Sonya all have something in common. What is more, what desiccates life in *War and Peace* is similar to what dries it up in *Childhood, Family Happiness, The Cossacks* and *Anna Karenina*, and what fills it and makes it rich and meaningful is the same.

But the center changes and the axis tilts differently at different parts of Tolstoy's creative life. In *Childhood*, there is more quest than there is resolution, as there is generally in the early works. Tolstoy proceeds in his quest with courage and uncompromising realism. He is not frightened or intimidated by a world that has already been sorted out for him. If the world tells him to grieve at the death of a loved one, and he finds that such grieving narrows life and empties it of vitality and joy, then there is something wrong with the grieving; if the world tells him that one must die like a Christian, and those attending on the dying should act like Christians, and he finds in his fictive experiments that such action poisons life, then he does not hesitate to arraign the Christianity. In some respects the situations he gives us have little to do with what he pursues. The chemistry of happiness and plenitude is everywhere the same, and the deflecting and attracting forces may be operative in the most disparate situations. Hate is a manifestation of the deflecting force, but love can be too, as can be forgiveness, respect, honor, and grief. When Andrey shows his father respect by asking Natasha to wait a year before they are married, he kills life; when Marya tells us that her father is the best of men and that she wishes for nothing more than to honor and respect and serve him during his life, she is killing life; when Pierre makes a round of his estates, flushed with his new-found faith in Masonry, and practices the benevolence toward his serfs that his faith enjoins, he too kills life. Yet, when Nikolay sees the rolling belly of the old gray wolf and his throat tightens with excitement, he blesses life and nourishes it, and when Natasha thinks only of herself and her fears and hopes at the ball, she too blesses life by her immersion in self.

The development of Tolstoy's work may be compared to the pealing off of the leaves of an onion. The onion is the world, and the leaves are the deceptions of civilization that have obscured the precious center. Tolstoy is convinced that the last leaf will reveal the beauty and goodness of life. In *War and Peace* he touches what he has so patiently pursued. He peals off the last leaf and finds the golden nugget of experience. Yet no sooner has he found this golden nugget than he questions its value and what it hides inside, and *Anna Karenina*, and especially the works that follow after a ten-year hiatus, seem to signal a profound change in his beliefs and faiths. It is not the treasure but the monster that his heroes seem to have found at the end of the labyrinth. *Anna Karenina* is already the harbinger of that obsession with sex, death, and the weight of evil that so presses on his later works, all of which seem to deny and obscure the light plane on which the happy quest of the early works take place. Yet even in the later works the center remains; no existential voids open up which Tolstoy cannot conquer; life retains its coherences, and it is understandable. The deflecting and attracting forces continue to operate, if modified in nature and definition. All of which is to say that the thread that runs from the earliest quest in *Childhood* runs not only to *War and Peace* but also to *Anna Karenina* and the later works. It runs, too, from fictive to nonfictive works. Tolstoy's creative and ideational worlds are of one cloth.

This study is animated by the conviction that the immense diversity of Tolstoy's works, both fictive and nonfictive, are of one piece. Isaiah Berlin said that Tolstoy was a fox who wanted to be a hedgehog, implying by that clever and provocative imagery that there is a conflict between the two, that is, a conflict between the diversity of experience and the unity of that experience.[6] Perhaps for Isaiah Berlin, but not for Tolstoy. Merezhkovsky characterized Tolstoy—the man and his work—as torn by a conflict between pagan impulses and Christian or ascetic impulses.[7] Perhaps for Merezhkovsky the conflict exists, but it does not exist for Tolstoy. The first curiosities of Nicholas in *Childhood* and the perplexities of the dying Ivan Ilych cohere, as do the sensuous immediacies of *The Cossacks* and *War and Peace*, and the asceticisms of the nineties. The coherence is in the tilt of the axis, and it is the tilt of the axis that this study attempts to catch. The "right relationship" is not a choice between diversity and unity, paganism and Christianity, sense and asceticism, but a reconciliation of these antinomies. Tolstoy was too broad for exclusions.

Too broad, too, for one axis or one interpretation. This study is also animated by the conviction that the coherences of Tolstoy are multiple. I do not mean by this that one cannot write different books on different aspects of Tolstoy and his work. That has been done and probably will never stop being done. There are biographies to be written, source studies to be made, intellectual and cultural milieus to place him in, audience reactions to be noted, and structural analyses to be made. I mean multiple perspectives of the same aspect. I have tried in the work that follows to discern the special logic that seems to inform why characters act, think, feel, and react as they do. The study is a close reading, but not in the sense of finding image patterns unless they bear on the coherences that have been pursued; or of tracing out grammatical patterns for their own sake, as in Jakobson's and Lévi-Strauss's analysis of Baudelaire's "Les Chats"; or of the kind of statistical analysis that Andrey Bely did at the beginning of the century. Close reading is a kind of incantatory term that tells us very little, except that the user wants the protection of what everyone approves.

Nor do I mean in speaking of multiple perspectives that what I have to say is only relatively true. I am persuaded, for example, that what I have to say about *Anna Karenina* is true and illuminating. But I am less than ever persuaded that it will clear up the mystery of Anna's motives. I found that the longer I worked on the novel, the more mysterious, enigmatic, and rich the woman and the novel became. I believe that the explanation I offer of Anna's motives is consistent with Tolstoy's view of her actions and his view of what makes life rich and what makes it poor. But I am also convinced that Tolstoy's view of the world and Tolstoy's reading of the novel is not the only possible reading. I have read Tolstoy's fiction as I believe he wanted it read, and I have looked at the works as reflections of his view of the world. His world, as it is reflected in his fiction, is largely a way of coping with desire and threat. Whatever else there is of value in Freud's view of art, he was surely right that art was in some way a fictive analogue of dream work. There is nothing, for example, that characterizes Tolstoy the man more than the dogmatic, inflexible, and uncompromising way in which he attacked matters and men. Tolstoy pushes, tugs, leans, cajoles, and coerces life. Yet there is nothing more insistent about the "logic" of his world than that it is a dream of things that *take place by themselves*, that is, without coercion. The best moments always have a quality of lack of pressure, like petals falling and yet kept aloft by some force in the falling itself. Tolstoy seems fascinated with the concept of a morality that makes itself, and his dream is one of "will-less" adjustment and harmonizing of the individual and the objective state of things. In short, he believed that men could be beautiful, fulfilled, and happy without effort, without, in fact, the agonizing self-analysis (a form of mental self-coercion), effort, and struggle that so characterized his own life. He wanted a morality that took place automatically and one that could not go wrong. The scientism of the century, which he abjured and condemned, found its way in his dream of a morality that would operate in the automatic way that physical laws do. He believed, in short, in a moral, psychological, and spiritual metabolism. If this all sounds like a view of life without freedom, he did dismiss a certain kind of freedom. He did not look upon freedom as an "effort" of the will, and freedom of willed acts was a special kind of slavery for him. Freedom for him was a state in which most of the individual was engaged, not a state in which the most force was used. Freedom was the flowering of the individual, and that flowering occurred according to fixed laws.

I have developed in this study one projection of the inner man and his consciousness and fantasy, close to and not in conflict with what we know of the biographical man. But there are other prints to be developed, some of which I note in passing and many I do not note, and even more that I am not aware of. No one can read Tolstoy's works, for example, without noticing that there are no sexual relations in them in any healthy sense. In the early works, including *War and*

Peace, the sex is highly sublimated; the relations between men and women are childlike. They are either official and matrimonial, or they are pure and ideal. Natasha is not a "sexual" creature: she is a child, and when she falls in love with Andrey, there is not a hint of physical attraction in their relationship: There is awe, pity, and sympathy, but no quickening of the veins. There are, to be sure, Princess Ellen and Anatole Kuragin, and dark sexual crimes are hinted about them, but that is precisely the point: sexuality is a dark sexual crime and Princess Ellen is a "dirty" woman. Beginning with *Anna Karenina* and especially after the conversion, sex appears more and more threatening to Tolstoy, and he is more and more at pains to keep it at bay with imprecations and castigations. It would not be far wrong to summarize the sexual cartography of his works by saying that all his women are pure in the early period and all of them are dirty in the later works. *Resurrection* appears in some respects to be an advance into sexual maturity for Tolstoy because Katusha Maslova goes from clean to dirty to clean. But even that is deceptive, because she becomes clean by giving up sex and "spiritualizing" herself. Tolstoy cannot conceive of clean and sexual at the same time.

We have to confront the fact that Tolstoy was a genius who had an unhealthy view of sex. This would make very little difference if those attitudes were confined to the man and were kept out of the work, but the fact is that he has projected them into his works. With his immense talent he has insinuated them into his concepts of good and bad and made what is unhealthy appear to be plausible and even attractive. Mikhaylovsky may not have been right that great talents are dangerous, but he was surely right that great authors could go wrong and that some of their views could be unhealthy.[8] Beauty and truth, despite Keats, do not necessarily go together, and there are more times than one would like when beauty and disease go together. We have begun to perceive this in *Anna Karenina*, where no matter how refined our analysis, we cannot escape the conclusion that Tolstoy takes this beautiful and life-loving woman from plenitude and happiness to barrenness and destruction because of his own distorted sexual views and his own inadequate conception of love and sex. Kenneth Burke has told us that authors tend to use their works to work out their own problems,[9] but if by "work out" he meant "cure," then this was not always so. Authors can use a work to give their problems to others, a form of self-justification of a particularly unoriginal sort, since on a lesser scale we are all engaged in some form of such projection.

The relationship of the man to his work still remains to be worked out. Fifty years of excluding the old-type documentary biographism in American criticism (which was the right thing to do) and fifty years of insistence that the man was not in the work (which was outrageously wrong) have not settled the matter. Neither has the deeper intentionalism of more recent critics, a view that has admitted that the author is in the work and has attempted to read the work according to the total "in-work" intention of the author. Authors are, in fact, *in* and *not in* their works. It is naive to believe that they keep themselves out of their work, as many of them and many of us would like to believe. Tolstoy is massively in his works, which is not the same thing as saying that Tolstoy the man is reflected in some documentary way in his works. The relationship between the man and his work is various, and about the only thing that one can say is that it is not a one-to-one biographical relationship. Elements of compensation, displacement, self-healing, and considerable concealment are at work. There are discernible overt elements of the author's personality in a work of literature, elements that repeat some of the publicly known facts about him. There are also elements that have no public documentation; indeed, the work itself is the documentation. And in between is probably any degree of deflection from the biographical man, the lever of deflection being the amount of confession that we have in the work. In Tolstoy's case, there is surely an attempt to "spread out" his views of the world, in keeping with his pedagogical bent. But no matter how various one conceives of the author in the work, the work escapes the author and must escape him.

If one asks how a novel can contain novels that the author did not intend, if by "intent" we mean the whole pressure and force of the author's being, both his conscious and his unconscious being, the answer can be only that there are more variables than the author's being and his time implicated in the work. And if we ask how this is possible, then it must be that the concepts and objects that are dramatized hide patterns that escape the author's intention, the shape and significance of which come into being with other intentions and perceptions. The author in a sense does not use everything he brings into the work. Words carry histories and contain futures. This is mysterious and yet clear, complex and simple. Although the "psychological dramas" that we find in works preceding Freud, for example, were not put there by the author, they are still there, in the work, and were in the work when the author wrote them and before we could read them.

The study that follows is conservative in that, for the most part, it traces coherences that are not so distant from those that we can discern in the man; yet I am not so sure that Tolstoy himself was aware of the special thread that I have pursued throughout his creative life. It is enough that it is there, and by being there, I do not mean that it can be wholly authenticated by data and document. Such authentication is a special perspective, legitimate and interesting in its own light, but only one perspective. It is not mine. Creative works do not "explain" reality, and critical works do not "explain" creative works, at least not once and for all. They make the creative works more mysterious, complex, many-sided or attempt to do so. It is mystery—rich and inexhaustible—that Tolstoy offers us, and it is mystery that I have pursued.

Note

The Garnett translations are used for quotations from *War and Peace* and *Anna Karenina*; the Maude translation for quotations from all other fictional works of Tolstoy; translations from the letters and diaries, as well as from Russian critics on Tolstoy are mine.

2 Childhood and Three Deaths

In a famous work on Dostoevsky and Tolstoy, Merezh-kovsky propounded a thesis about the essential Tolstoy, in life and in his art, which has had an extraordinary durability in the critical lexicon with which we speak of Tolstoy. The thesis is in short: there were two Tolstoys, the Tolstoy of the flesh and the Tolstoy of the spirit, the pagan and the saint. Merezhkovsky said: "But Tolstoy's attitude towards Nature is twofold. To his consciousness, which would fain be Christian, Nature is something dark, evil, even fiendish. It is that which the Christian should overcome in himself and transfigure into the kingdom of God. On the other hand, to Tolstoy's unreasoning pagan side man is made one with Nature, and disappears in her like a drop in the ocean."[1] When Merezhkovsky asks himself which of the two Tolstoys is the real one, he answers it in the following way: "Is it the one that loves, or the one that hates himself? He who begins all his thoughts, feelings, and aspirations in a devout Christian way, or he who weakly gives them up to finish his days like a heathen? Or is it perhaps—and this would be for him the more terrible conclusion—that both alike are real, both sincere, and both to last as long as the breath in his body?"[2] Both Tolstoys are real for Merezhkovsky, but it is the pagan that dominates his early works (up to his *Confession*) and the saint that dominates his later works.

We find variations of this thesis in dozens of works on Tolstoy, and some variation of it can be seen even in Isaiah Berlin's provocative *The Hedgehog and the Fox*, where he reconceives the conflict as not one between the pagan and the saint, but one between the pluralist (the fox) and the monist (the hedgehog), that is, between the impulse to think and the impulse to perceive, between the impulse to catch in all fullness the sensuous world and the impulse to reduce the fullness to a single truth. Merezhkovsky's thesis has endured because it points to one of the essential traits of the man and his work: Tolstoy had a sensuous hunger for life and an intellectual and moral hunger for reducing the infinity of sensual data to the finite limits of his mind.

Merezhkovsky's thesis is brilliant and true, and it is also an oversimplification. There are more than two Tolstoys, and there is no pagan in the early work and no saint in the later work, although there are pagan and saint in both early and late works. There are many Tolstoys, or rather there is a Tolstoy who distances himself from any belief and conviction, not only from those of others but also from his own. Eikhenbaum was probably closer to the truth than was Merezhkovsky when he likened Tolstoy's mind to a corrosive fluid that decomposed any truth it came in contact with and when he attributed both cynicism and nihilism to Tolstoy. It is easy to see why he would do so. There is little that Tolstoy turned his attention to that did not earn his opprobrium and his scorn: art, religion, civil institutions, economic and social orders, governments, and civilizations were all wrong, and more than wrong—wasteful, harmful, shameful, and distortive of life. He thundered against the manner in which children were educated, the way young girls were married, and the way men tilled the land and made their bread. He was against social life, sophistication, military conscription, capitalism, the sexual standards of his day, taxes, and organized religion. Nothing for long was spared his damnation. One is reminded of Marx's fulminations against the human degradations he attributed to the English economic system. But Marx's anger was fueled by real injustices, or at least what many today would acknowledge to be injustices. Tolstoy's fulminations were against not only what was ugly and unjust but also against much that we have considered and still consider to be good and beautiful in Western civilization: art, science, education, Shakespeare, Beethoven. His anger was gargantuan, but so was his belief, and it is the belief that Eikhenbaum and those who charge him with cynicism and nihilism do not see. Isaiah Berlin saw something of it; he was more right than Eikhenbaum when he said: "Direct vision often tends to be disturbing: Tolstoy used this gift to the full to destroy both his own peace and that of his readers. It was this habit of asking exaggeratedly simple but fundamental questions, to which he did not himself—at any rate in the sixties and seventies—claim to possess the answers, that gave Tolstoy the reputation of being a 'nihilist.' Yet he certainly had no wish to destroy for the sake of destruction. He only wanted, more than anything else in the world, to know the truth."[3]

No one has read Tolstoy aright who has missed the profound passion for truth that runs through his efforts and beliefs. He held and rejected many truths, but there was one that he never rejected: his belief—profound and unalterable—that there was *a* truth to be discovered. He believed, furthermore, that such a truth would bring men to plenitude and happiness. In the final analysis, this corrosive intellect and cynical destroyer of so many truths held by others was a profound optimist about human nature and human fate. The forms in which he searched for truth were to change in the course of his development, but the essential nature of the truths was to remain unaltered. What does not change is a conception of truth that is beyond the subjective tampering of man, something that man can come to participate in but cannot change, something eternally beyond his wishes, manipulations, and supplications, and yet something he can identify with. It is this objective character of the truth that has led many—and perhaps rightfully so—to see Tolstoy's world as cold and distant; for it is not a world, as is Dostoevsky's, consumed in the passion and will of man.

No understanding of Tolstoy's work is possible without gauging the effect of his belief in an objective truth that underlies the shift of circumstance and the play of will, passion, hope, and joy. The belief in an objective truth provides him with a measure of action and motive and thus contributes to the special clarity of contour that we experience in the presence of Tolstoy's work. It is also what distinguishes his work so profoundly from the work of his contemporaries and our contemporaries. One knows from the earliest to the latest works what is true and what is false, when characters are hypocritical and when they are genuine, what is illusion and what is reality. There are no blurring of outlines and no play of ambiguities. Nicholas in *Childhood* knows what is good and what is bad and he knows when he is in the presence of something genuine and something false. We know that the old Hussar is better than the new Hussar, that the death of the tree is better than the death of the noblewoman, what is true domestic happiness and false domestic happiness. In *War and Peace* everyone knows that Berg is insufferable, that Boris is a self-seeker, that Prince Andrey is a sincere pursuer of the truth and an unalterable enemy of what is false and dishonorable, that Natasha is better than Sonya. What animates Tolstoy's work is the conviction—something that was never to leave him—that there is a truth to be seized at the core of the vast mesh of human relations, that this truth is good, and that if formulated and expressed it will resolve the antinomies that so plagued him and mankind. His creative works are a series of fictive attempts to dramatize the operations of such truthful laws.

Merezhkovsky saw something of this in his theory of two Tolstoys: a Tolstoy torn between wanting to be a pagan and wanting to be a saint.

But the antinomy that Merezhkovsky concerned himself with and which he saw as central to the understanding of the man and his work was only one among many; though important, it was perhaps not the most important. It can stand, however, as an example of how one can misunderstand the antinomy. Merezhkovsky's view that Tolstoy subordinated the saint to the pagan in the early work, and the pagan to the saint in the later work, is an oversimplification. The evidence for considering Tolstoy a pagan in the early half of his career is taken largely from the words and character of Eroshka in *The Cossacks*, who says: "God has made everything for the joy of man. *There is no sin in anything*. Take the example of animals. They live alike in Tartar thickets and in ours. What God bestows, that they eat. But our people say that instead of enjoying this freedom we are to lick hot plates in hell for that. I think that everything is a cheat. . . . You die, and the grass grows: that is all that's real."[4] But Merezhkovsky gives us no evidence that Tolstoy felt similarly, and, as a matter of fact, the biographical materials give us a very different Tolstoy. There is very little of the pagan in the diaries of the late 1840s and the 1850s. These diaries are a dreary recital of moralistic impositions upon himself and lamentations on his inability to meet these impositions; hardly a day passes without expressions of disgust at having failed to meet his goals. The following excerpts from his diaries are representative: "During this whole time I did not conduct myself as I wanted to conduct myself" (April 1847).[5] "I suddenly wrote down many rules and wanted to follow them all; but I was too weak to do so" (April 18, 1847).[6] "I am so weak! I must fear idleness and disorderliness as I fear gambling" (November 2 and 3, 1853).[7] "I shall destroy myself unless I improve myself" (September 21, 1855).[8] Although he mentions drinking and whoring, the sins of the flesh are less in prominence in the diaries than the sins of will and mind. What he castigates himself for most repeatedly is laziness and vanity. What he strives most for is to achieve some sort of self-effacement before his fellow man. He is convinced in a fairly conventional way that good is living for others and evil is living for oneself.

There is considerable evidence in the early biographical materials that for Tolstoy the senses and consciousness were in conflict, but no evidence that Tolstoy pursued a life of sensuous fulfillment and ruthlessly suppressed the spirit and the mind. What is daily, or almost daily, in evidence is an agonizing and unremitting struggle against the weight of the flesh, and analysis after analysis as to how will and clear consciousness may repair the failures of the past. The neatness of

Merezhkovsky's thesis obscures a much more refined relationship between the saint and the sinner, the intellect and the senses, the affirmation of the self and the denial of the self.

What we find in the early creative works is a Tolstoy attempting to find some bridge between the flesh and the spirit and between life and the consciousness of life. It is not the conflict between these two sides of his character but a persistent attempt to overcome the conflict that characterizes the man and the work of the early years. Tolstoy's deepest and most unrelenting search is to find some right relationship between the flesh and the spirit so that the conflict will disappear, not by suppression of one by the other, but by some harmonizing principle. One may look at his early works as a series of creative experiments to see what is wrong and right with the affirmation of instinct and what is wrong and right with the denial of instinct, and most of all to see how one can exist, and possibly enrich, the other. The form of the conflict in the creative works is often different and more complex than any set of opposites can make it, and the formulations are far more refined than the blunt and conventional formulations we find in the early biographical materials. Tolstoy's consciousness was bruised daily by the constrictions of reality, but in the freedom of fantasy he was able to explore and embody, without the constraint of actual circumstances, the mesh of possible relationships that might dissolve the conflict and bring life to harmony, plenitude, and happiness. In his diaries and letters the conflict is stark, simple, and repetitious. In his creative works the conflict is dynamic, multifaceted, and refined. Merezhkovsky assumes that the man and the artist are one, and he is right, but not in the literal manner in which he puts it. They are one, but there is more of Tolstoy in the art than in the commentaries; what he discovers in the diaries and letters about himself and about the conflict has already been examined in his creative works. The man lags behind the artist, and the artistic consciousness precedes the philosophical and discursive consciousness.

The search for the right relationship was to be long and arduous. Merezhkovsky may be partly right that the man tried to make himself whole by subordinating one part of himself and then another part, but the artist was bent on suppressing nothing but permitting both parts to express themselves. He did not want to give up one or the other but to find a whole in which each would enrich the other. He was able to do so in his art, but not with any finality. Every artistic resolution raised difficulties he had not seen, and the difficulties were to be a spur to reconceiving the relationship between the conflicting parts.

His conceptions of the right relationship were to change with the development of his art. The right relationship was never fully to be seized but always doggedly pursued and always firmly believed in. The "second" real Tolstoy of the postconfessional years was as firmly convinced as was the first that such a right relationship exists.

CHILDHOOD

The search for a common truth is already in evidence in *Childhood*. Tolstoy himself, in the first draft of *Childhood* (cast in the form of a series of notes sent by the writer to a friend), explains his purpose: "most important I wanted to find in the imprint of my life only some principle or purpose to guide me."[9] That imprint, if it is in the tale, has not been discerned in the sketch by critics and commentators, and most have taken the scenes as a random collection of impressions of a young man as he is introduced to various aspects of life.

Boris Eikhenbaum in *The Young Tolstoy* spends considerable time trying to justify the order of the scenes, and finds such justification in the novel's orientation towards "minuteness" (*melochnost'*).[10] By this technique, according to him, Tolstoy breaks the hold of traditional formal properties of plot, intrigue, and drama. Eikhenbaum admits that such an explanation is concerned with external connections, and he is troubled by the lack of "inner connections." I take inner connection to mean ties between these specific scenes, situations, emotions, observations even though the specificities might be of various kinds. Eikhenbaum's fussing about inner connections brings him only to the theme of "mother," which he insists runs like a leitmotiv throughout the sketch. This is a rather fatuous conclusion to be drawn from such elaborate theorizing. Furthermore, it is not true. Many of the important scenes have little or nothing to do with the mother: the hunt scene, the Seryozha scene, and the Grisha scene are examples. When Eikhenbaum takes up the analysis of the tale in his multivolumed critical work on Tolstoy in 1928, he omits this point about the mother and seems resigned to characterizing the sketch as somewhat random in structure, justified still as reorientation of the traditional autobiographical sketch toward microscopic observation. He says: "In essence the structure of *Childhood* consists of a juxtaposition of separate scenes linked by generalizations and lyrical commentary."[11] Christian makes almost the identical point: "*Childhood* as we know it in its published form is a collection of scenes and portraits from the reminiscences of Nicholas Irtenev, told in the first person and bound together by commentary and generalization."[12] He attempts, too, to link these portraits and reminiscences by the theme of happiness and death. The focal point of the story is that "childhood is an unforgettably happy, innocent, and unique period of life, but that lurking behind its happiness is the inescapable and incomprehensible reality of death."[13] This is more helpful and true than the theme of the mother, but the theme of time pressing happiness toward death is something broad enough to include a considerable part of Western European literature. Still, the thematic attempts of Eikhenbaum and Christian to get at the structure are more helpful than the repetition of many critics that the point of *Childhood* is to reproduce for us the inexpressible joys of childhood. Tolstoy himself may have given an impetus to such statements by his remark, long after the writing and publication of the novel: "When I wrote *Childhood* it seemed that no one before me had so felt and depicted all the charms and poetry of childhood." Simmons, for example, sees the story as "simply the story of a child's life up to the age of about fourteen," the point of which is the recall of impressions that are "infallibly true and altogether delightful."[14]

But we have also Tolstoy's remark that he wanted to discern in the experiences pictured some guiding principle to his life, and the cast of his mind and his moral passion would lead us to look for more than a picture of innocent childhood delights and for something more specific than thematic linkages of death and mother. Tolstoy was never the indifferent observer and painter. There is little likelihood that the story is simply a random collection of scenes celebrating the initiation of a young boy into the important experiences of love, death, society, nature, and friendship. Nicholas has already a definite point of view and more than a modicum of moral and psychological passion. I am persuaded that Tolstoy the monist is already spying on the pluralist, and that Nicholas learns if not a common truth, at least a common problem and one important enough for Tolstoy to take up again and again in the works that follow.

Nicholas learns, first of all, that the world of nature and things is different from the world of people. Tolstoy's descriptions of nature in the sketch have been praised almost without qualification by most critics, especially for the vivid, specific, and sensuous immediacy of the details. The praise is justified. There is no generalizing of images in the descriptions. Everything is individual, sharp, and clear. The little roan Nicholas's father rides has a "playful step," and his thick tail busies itself brushing off the gadflies and gnats that settle on him. The peasants are individualized, such as the woman grasping the stalks and swinging the ears of the stalks. Sound, smell, and sight assail the senses: ''The peasants' voices, the tramp of horses, and creaking carts, the merry whistle of quail, the hum of insects hovering in the air in steady swarms, the odour of wormwood, straw, and horses' sweat, the thousands of different colours and shadows with which the burning sun flooded the light yellow stubble, the dark blue of the distant forest, the light lilac clouds and the white cobwebs that floated in the air or stretched across the stubble—all this I saw, heard, and felt.'' Tolstoy is, however, intent upon more than description for its own sake. He is no Turgenev creating atmospheres, nor a Bunin patiently accumulating sensuous detail. He has the Parnassian skill, but not the Parnassian indifference to moral and intellectual meaning. He is closer to Hemingway than to these in the way he uses the detail as an analogue of right perception and right feeling. The details are there as contrast to what is going on inside the boy and as a measure of right feeling and right perception. No ambiguity or doubt blurs the outlines of the natural descriptions. They are given and they are certain, and the quest for something just as clear, given, and unambiguous is part of the quest of the young boy. Tolstoy is looking for something as firm and immediate inside the boy as the natural details outside the boy. Nature is already for Tolstoy a kind of touchstone for what is good in the sense of something given and something definite. He is already looking and will continue to look for an *inner nature* that has the same harmony and the same absence of subjective distortion and the same unity of being as does *outer nature*.

This is Tolstoy's intention and this is what the analytic narrator understands, but it is not what the young boy perceives. He has some intimation of the harmony between what he feels and what he sees in physical nature, but when he turns to the world of people about him, he feels no such harmony. He is told one thing and he feels another; he is expected to act in a certain way and he finds he can act only in another way. He is confused by what the world about him demands and what he can give, what adults see and what he sees. He looks for truth and he finds lies. The world of people about him presents him with one reality, and he comes to learn gradually that there is another reality. He learns something about these two realities and something about himself, for example, when he joins a group of children to spy on the praying of the holy fool Grisha. The scene begins with the laughter and antics of the group, but when the voices of the group are silent and Nicholas is alone with his own perception and understanding, he discovers something about Grisha and about himself. It is the group that leads him to raillery and amusement, but it is his own intuitive feeling that leads him unexpectedly to compassion. In the Grisha episode Nicholas learns that his own feelings may be true and real and the feelings the group gives him may be false. In the manor house and in the presence of the family, Grisha's words are disjointed and his face is inane, but alone, with the artificial light extinguished and his face illuminated by the natural light of the moon, he becomes dignified. Both the boy and the beggar have to be set apart from the relationships and perceptions of the group before the beggar becomes a human being and the boy sees him as a human being. Group opinion is set against individual conscience and the public voice against the private voice.

The same opposition of group and individual can be seen in the Seryozha episode. Nicholas is playing a variation of cops and robbers with the Ivins. During the game Seryozha bruises his leg but refuses to cry out in pain. Nicholas, however, is so disturbed by the fall that he forgets to arrest Seryozha as the game requires. Seryozha holds on to the illusion of the game, but Nicholas does not. Once again, as in the Grisha episode, the private truth opposes itself to the public "illusion." The game requires the boys to obey certain rules, no matter what. For Seryozha the pain does not exist because the rules of the game say that it does not exist. For a moment, at least, something real inside Nicholas leads him to disregard the rules of the illusion. He learns that in playing at life he "misses" life. He learns, too, with increasing perception and no little measure of agony that the adult world which appears so formidable and mysterious is also a "playing at life," but playing with consequences more harmful than those of children's games.

The games that the children play are analogous to the "forms" that the adults live by. Each has its rules. Each has sorted out reality and commanded feelings and reactions. Each leaves little room for individual reactions and feelings, and each is, from Tolstoy's point of view, a collective illusion. The adult games, the forms of social convention, are more fixed and held to more undeviatingly. The games of the children are temporary, dropped at a moment's whim and dissolved by boredom, indifference, and at moments by compassion. Nicholas knows that he is playing a game in a way that Nicholas's father or grandmother do not know that they are playing a game. Something of another world—something inside him—interrupts the games, as his compassion for Seryozha and his compassion for Grisha had interrupted the games. Nicholas can see the games for what they are because he is still a boy, and his perception has not yet, as it has for adults, hardened into collective and distorted seeing.

Nothing is more in evidence in the story than the pressure of the adult world about the boy to learn and to conform. Eikhenbaum and Aksakov have spoken of Tolstoy's microscopic observation, but one could also add to this that the observation—the orientation toward minutiae—is there as a response of a sensitive boy to the complex, sometimes subtle, but always irrepressible pressure of adult forms and conventions waiting to receive, channel, and shape the freshness and immediacy of the child's feelings. If there is some of the unforgettable charm of childhood that Tolstoy spoke of, there is something of Wordsworth's prison house, too. It is childhood slipping into adulthood, and there is some strain and resistance on the part of the child toward the ready-made grooves that have been set for him, and considerably more strain on the part of the mature narrator to see alternatives to this process. What is communicated to us, and in a different way to the boy, is the power of adult forms to catch, form, shape, impersonalize, and corrupt a given feeling; there is also a fascination with how this is done and how one might escape from it. I have difficulty understanding all the paeans that have been sung to the thoughtless and careless scenes of childhood that Tolstoy is supposed to have evoked; it is not charm that is evoked in these scenes as much as anxiety.

The poem that Nicholas writes for his grandmother may appear to have little to do with the Seryozha and Grisha episodes, but it is another "playing at" feelings and another distortion of them by group expectations. The young boy is expected to give his grandmother a gift for her name day, and he decides to write a poem as his gift. For help in writing the poem he turns first to models like Dmitriev and Derzhavin, but he is intimidated by their talent. He turns then for help to the banal verse of his tutor. The effort to express his feeling by way of art turns him first to imitation and then to banality. In the end it turns him to lies. He has much difficulty in making the last two lines of his poem rhyme, and he succeeds only by stating that he loves his grandmother as much as his mother. He knows that the thought is false, but it is only by making the thought false that he can make the lines rhyme. What Tolstoy is showing—in his first work as he will do in one of his last, *What Is Art*—is that art by its nature leads one to imitation and deception. It is the formal element that manipulates the boy's thoughts and leads him to falseness.

The little boy is still young enough and unformed enough to feel uncomfortable with the artificiality and falseness of his poetic attempt. When he presents the poem to his grandmother, he is convinced that everyone will notice the lie that the poem expresses, and he expects his father to slap him and call him a horrid boy for forgetting his mother. To his astonishment the adults find the verse charming. The adults are no longer able to distinguish between feigned feeling and real feeling, and the small boy has received his first lesson in the deception and distortion of feeling by art. When in the late 1890s Tolstoy outraged critical opinion by maintaining that art is not only artificial but pernicious, he was doing nothing more than express more baldly what he had stated and believed in his first published work. In the scene describing the writing and presenting of the poem, as in the Grisha and Ivins scenes, a private, personal feeling and perception is set against the collective voice, here expressed by the convention of art. In the first two scenes the relatively unformed and intuitive perception of the child is set against the nascent abstractions and false feelings of children at play; in the scene about the poem, a child's intuitive feelings are set against the false feelings of adults.

Tolstoy uses the game and the convention to emphasize the manipulation of the individual by the group. But if we were to characterize the structure of events in terms of a conflict between the public and the private voice, the formulation would break down, because, in some of the scenes, what mars the good experience and distorts reality is not something outside the child but something inside him, not the group but the individual himself. In the hunt scene, for example, the conflict is not one of inside and outside, but of inside and inside. In this scene the little boy is assigned to wait at a particular spot with the dog Zhiran. He makes the mistake of releasing the dog at the wrong time, and the hare escapes. If we ask what went wrong, we must say that the young boy failed to "catch" the hare because he was inattentive, and the inattentiveness came about because he permitted his mind to drift off into revery and make-believe. After waiting for a while he had become bored, and began to play with oak leaves, dry bare twigs, and a swarm of ants. His attention was first diverted by the ants and then by the actions of a butterfly. His construction of another reality, a substitute reality, in fancy and revery is the cause of his inability to seize the here and now of reality. Make-believe is to be found not only in children's games and adult conventions but also in his own mind. Not only the group but also the individual can distort reality. In his search for what is real, the boy will have to be attentive not only to the false voices outside him but also the false voices within him.

The same conflict between the facts and his imagination is present in the scene about the death of his mother. The young narrator sees his mother twice, once when she is apparently dying and once when she is dead. On each occasion he registers disbelief, shock, and horror. Tolstoy makes no effort to mitigate the reality. The horror of death is recorded with unflinching realism: the sunken eyes, the dreadful pallor, the pale lips, the dark spot under one of the cheeks. All the gruesome details of death are clinically and naturalistically recorded; and as if to confirm that the narrator is capable of recording the facts as they are, Tolstoy has him describe the objects in the room in detail and register the sights, smells, and sounds of the objects. Despite this, the young narrator cannot help remembering the mother as alive, vital, and blooming with happiness and joy. He imagines her as she was, and then he sees her as she is: pale, lifeless, and ugly. Dreams of the past and perception of present reality struggle: the mind's pictures and the eye's perception contend, but each time "a consciousness of the reality destroyed the dreams. At last my imagination was tired out; it ceased to deceive me." The mind itself from desire, comfort, and a craving for security can recoil from pain and ugliness, deny reality, and substitute cheating forms. Even when the mind remembers reality as it was—for the boy remembers the mother as she actually was—the mind distorts the present by clinging to the past. The past itself becomes a cheating form and, as such, similar to fantasies and imaginings. Nicholas's relentless attention to what is real and his instinct for discerning what is false have led him to find the impulse of distortion in the very faculty of seeing. Yet no skepticism assails Tolstoy. He is convinced that though the mind can trick us into taking wishes for reality, it can also be disciplined to reject imagined reality.

What is it then that links the scenes that show a conflict between the private voice and the collective voice (the Grisha and the Seryozha episodes) and the scenes that show a conflict between what the mind sees and the mind imagines (the hunt and death scenes)? Is it not that both are in different ways a kind of make-believe and, as such, a distortion of reality? This is obvious in the hunt scene and in the scene describing the death of the mother, where a substitute and imagined reality struggles with the reality that one sees. But the collective reality, structured according to the rules of convention, is also a "make-believe" in the sense that a collective imagination has been imposed on reality. A convention is an abstraction from reality and in this sense a simplification and distortion of reality. It is as much a substitute reality, though more stable and permanent, as are the imaginings of individuals.

There is a scene fairly early in the sketch that highlights the dilemma that the young narrator finds in attempting to understand what is true and false, real and illusory. This is the scene, after the hunt, when Volodya refuses to play Swiss Family Robinson with the other children because the chairs and sticks they imagine to be horse and guns are not real. The young narrator is forced to admit that Volodya is right, that sticks cannot be guns and chairs cannot be horses. But then he adds wistfully: "If one goes by reality, there can be no games, but if there are no games, what will be left?" What is left is, of course, reality. And it is "reality" that the young boy, and Tolstoy through him, are intent on finding. If one asks what this reality is, the young narrator and Tolstoy can tell us largely what it is not: it is not the make-believe games that children play, nor the make-believe games that adults play. It is not something learned because it is prior to and contradicts such learned things as social forms and art. It is not the past, nor what the mind imagines, nor what the group commands. Real feeling and perception seem to be something given rather than learned, something present in the individual before they are distorted by the collective forms of perception and feeling. What is left after the games and what is there before the games is a kind of moral and sensory elementalness.

In a remarkable essay written as a review of *Childhood*, Chernyshevsky was the first to point to this quality of moral elementalness. The essay has gained wide prominence in the Soviet Union because of Chernyshevsky's use of the term "inner monologue" (*vnutrennii monolog*) to characterize Tolstoy's narrative point of view.[15] No discussion of Tolstoy's works, especially of *Anna Karenina* and *War and Peace*, is complete today without some reference to the term. But to my knowledge no one—American or Soviet—has pointed out Chernyshevsky's equally important perception that Tolstoy's early genius lay largely in his expression of moral elementalness. Chernyshevsky calls this trait "the purity of moral feeling" (*chistota nravstvennogo chuvstva*). The term has nothing to do with moral feeling in the ethical and conventional religious sense, and Chernyshevsky explicitly distinguishes his meaning from the conventional meaning.[16] The feeling is pure because it is unsullied by the accumulated distortions, prejudices, and weight of the past. It is feeling which has not yet ossified in the ready-made forms of society. It is pure because it has not yet been defiled.

Tolstoy was able to catch and express this purity of moral feeling by his analysis of experience into the particles of sensation and thought at the point at which those particles took form in human experience. Chernyshevsky saw that Tolstoy was intent at seizing experience, perception, sensation, and thought at the point at which they exist before human manipulation. Chernyshevsky surely, and Tolstoy probably, were not interested in extolling some kind of Lockean sensationalism or Wordsworthian primitiveness. Chernyshevsky saw such expression as experience before it is sullied by political and social convention. Tolstoy's interest was broader than this, but not in conflict with Chernyshevsky's understanding. He wanted to know what the sensations and thoughts were before they were caught in the public forms of perception. Tolstoy was convinced that there was something pure behind or before the impure forms that the child is introduced to. He was able to sketch with some precision already what some of these impure forms are, but the pure forms or the real reality remained something of an unknown x for him. The boy is right more in quest than in fulfillment. If we ask for an embodiment of right experience in the novel, the closest we come to is to be found in the character and actions of the house servant Natalya.

Natalya's right relationship is contrasted with the grandmother's wrong relationship in the matter of grief for Nicholas's mother. The grandmother's grief is loud and deep; she does not speak to anyone; she refuses to take food; doctors fear for her life, and she does not sleep. Natalya, on the other hand, seems hardly to grieve at all. She seems almost callously indifferent to the mother's passing. At one point she is pictured as assuring the young narrator that his mother has gone off to heaven, when she is interrupted by another house servant who has come for some provisions. The last traces of sorrow occasioned by their conversation vanishes when Natalya sets herself to the task of dispensing the sugar, raisins, and rice. Yet it is clear, and the narrator states, that the sorrow of Natalya is greater than the grandmother's. The narrator does not explain why this is so, but it is consistent with what has been dramatized in the novel. Natalya's reactions are characterized by acceptance of what has happened, the grandmother's by protest. The death of her daughter is taken almost as a personal insult, and the personal hurt expresses itself in vengeance upon those about her and against the universe. Her protest is a command to the universe to be different from the way it is, and as such it is an act of vanity. Natalya does not demand anything from the universe and therefore does not grieve, at least not in the conventional way that the grandmother does. She understands, at least unconsciously, that grief is a subtle command that the universe be different from what it is, and

she is Tolstoy's heroine because she has understood that the universe is
not hers to command. Tolstoy has perceived already in this first sketch
a germ of that momentous wisdom that consists in a certain kind of
acceptance of reality. We may ask how such an acceptance of reality is
consonant with what I have said about the right experience being a
kind of elemental perception and feeling undistorted by the mechanisms of conventions and the mind's tendency to substitute a pleasant
and imaginary reality for a real and unpleasant one. The grandmother's grief is a desire for reality to be different from what it is. The
small boy's temptation to substitute the pleasant past for the ugly
present is a different mode of the same thing, as are the adult social
forms and the conventions of art. All are manipulations of reality for
certain ends, even though that manipulation may be unconscious.

Childhood is not merely a depiction of "all the charm and poetry of
childhood," or of a child's initiation into adult life, or a nostalgic
memory of how it felt to be a child. It is also a subtle artistic and
psychological exploration of the springs of true and false feeling. The
diversity of experiences is matched by a diversity of false forms, which,
no matter how different they appear, have some central rudder that
sets them adrift of right feeling and right perception. The central
thrust of his perception seems to be that the spring of false reality
comes from the mind's freedom to imagine and construct another
reality. Grief, imagination, convention, art, and society are all in
diverse ways "substitute realities."

What Tolstoy perceives in *Childhood* raises as many questions and
problems as it settles. One wants to know at this point whether
substitute realities are wrong in themselves or whether it is these
specific substitute realities that are wrong. If the former, then it would
seem that the very function of the mind is being called into question,
since consciousness is in its nature a distillation of reality, an
abstraction and hence a simplification and a distortion. There is no
answer to be found in *Childhood* or in Tolstoy's biographical materials
to such an epistemological problem, although it is perhaps significant
that he said the following in an early diary entry: "I shall always say
that consciousness is the greatest moral evil that can afflict man."[17] If
consciousness is an evil because of its innate tendency to substitute a
subjective reality for an objective reality, what is the alternative?
Surely not, as far as we can tell, the lack of consciousness, but a
consciousness that in some way reflects what is actually there in its
plenitude, a consciousness that in some way reflects the whole rather
than a part.

Still this leaves the character of the whole to be determined, and although there is no way of determining what the whole means for Tolstoy at this point, one can be sure of certain things it does *not* mean. It is surely not some undifferentiated sensuous congeries, some relapse of consciousness into animal sensuousness. Although some of Tolstoy's subsequent admiration for the passivity of peasants and for animal and vegetable life would almost seem to indicate this, his aim will always be to discover how life can be more human, not less human; and if he speaks in *Three Deaths* of the death of a tree as being more beautiful than the death of a Christian, this is so because there is something in the death of the tree that a human being might embody without ceasing to be human. Tolstoy was, despite his apparent antagonism, a product of his times, and his primitiveness was a response to the sophisticizing and rationalizing of reality. He must have sensed that man was rapidly creating a reality that answered to his needs and conceptions and was progressively tearing himself away from his natural and organic roots. Lenin sensed something of this kind when he paid tribute, in perhaps the most influential essay ever written on Tolstoy, to his revolutionary conservatism.[18] He saw in Tolstoy's dogged and massive negative response to many of the features of modern life—to its science, industrialism, government bureaucracy, army, and mass education—a conscious embodiment of the unconscious feelings and sentiments of the great mass of Russians. What was positive for Lenin, the representative of the most systematic organization of the forces that Tolstoy opposed, was a resistance to the false organization of human consciousness. There is no indication in Lenin's writings on Tolstoy that he was aware that Tolstoy was opposed to all false (because partial) organizations of human consciousness, nor any hint that Tolstoy would have opposed even more vigorously the socialist organization of human consciousness.

Marx, and Engels, and Lenin following them understood that man was progressively conquering nature, and that a second, man-made nature was being constructed, composed of the objects that man was producing at an astonishing rate. They saw also that this second, artificial nature was becoming man's new sensuous environment and, in consequence, affecting and forming his subjective self. For them this was no disaster but was, on the contrary, a welcome phenomenon; they looked forward to the day when man would stand triumphant in a world that was entirely man-made. Tolstoy understood that this was happening and that, in the most sophisticated circles, it had largely happened already, but he knew, or believed, also that man was inevitably and eternally part of an incomprehensible, eternal, and infinite nature. Marx and Engels believed that the new nature man was creating was supplanting and would supplant the old, and that the artificial world was of preponderant importance in determining the quality and value of human life. Tolstoy believed that man's attempt to create his own world inevitably struck his life with sterility and meaninglessness. What this immeasurable and incomprehensible nature consisted of was precisely the unknown x, which was the object of his search in the creative experiments of his early works. It was, to use Merezhkovsky's image, the unknown core of the onion. Tolstoy had begun pealing off the leaves of the onion in *Childhood*, and he remained persuaded that if he pealed off enough leaves, he would find the x. Eroshka may say that all there is is death and grass on one's grave; Prince Andrey may see life on the eve of the battle of Borodino as a procession of cheating and illusory forms, and Anna Karenina may see the world as dirty and ugly during her last days before suicide, but Tolstoy will not see the world this way. He will create and confront his Eroshkas, Prince Andreys, and Anna Kareninas. The creation of these magnificent characters may dramatize his own fears that the core of the onion is empty, but he will persist in his belief that their questions are great and their answers wrong. And he will create his Natashas, Pierres, and Karataevs to justify this conviction. He will, in short, find his unknown x.

THREE DEATHS

In *Childhood* Tolstoy contrasts the way Natalya grieves for Nicholas's deceased mother and the way that the grandmother grieves. He prefers, as does Nicholas, Natalya's grief, even though it is matter-of-fact and unemotional. The contrast must have intrigued him, for he takes up a similar contrast in *Three Deaths* and explores it further. A. A. Tolstoy, a relative of his, did not like what he wrote and took exception to the unfavorable contrast between the death of a Christian and that of a brute peasant. In a letter dated 1 May 1858 Tolstoy replied to her in this manner:

> You have looked in vain for the Christian point of view.
> My thought was the following: three beings died—a noblewoman, a peasant, and a tree. The noblewoman is pathetic and disgusting, because she has lied all her life and is still lying at the point of dying. Christianity, as she understands it, has not solved the question of life and death for her. Why die when you want to live? She believes in the promise of future life only with her imagination

and mind, but her whole being rears up against it and she has
no other consolation (other than the pseudo-Christian one). She is
disgusting and pathetic. The peasant dies peacefully, just because
he is not a Christian. His religion is different, although he fulfills
the Christian rites by habit; his religion comes from the nature he
has lived with. He has himself cut down trees, sowed rye, cut it,
slaughtered sheep; and sheep have been born for him and children
also; old men have died. He knew the law well and always followed
it; he faced it squarely, but the noblewoman had not. *Une brute*,
you say, and what's so bad about being *une brute*? *Une brute*
means happiness and beauty, harmony with the whole world, and
not the disharmony the noblewoman experiences. The tree dies
peacefully, honestly, and beautifully. Beautifully—because it
doesn't act up, doesn't fear, and doesn't pity. That is my thought,
with which you, understandably, do not agree, but which you
can't argue with.[19]

Tolstoy makes it quite clear in this letter, as does the story, that the
deaths of the peasant and the tree are good and the death of the
noblewoman is bad. His cousin had expressed astonishment at the
unfavorable contrast for a Christian, and Tolstoy answers her by telling
her that Christianity has little if anything to do with what he is
expressing: "You have looked in vain for the Christian point of
view." Both the noblewoman and the peasant are Christians, but they
die well and badly for other reasons. It is these other reasons that are
important.

Christianity is only one of the obstacles that the overt content of the
story presents to a correct understanding. The class contrast has been
seized on as the point of the story by the Soviets and, indeed, by some
Western critics. The dying woman is after all a noblewoman, and
Tolstoy makes a great deal of the luxury and attentions that are paid to
her. But one does not die well or badly because one is a peasant any
more than because one is or is not a Christian. Such details as
Christianity and class differences are what Lévi-Strauss would call
Tolstoy's *bricolage*—the matter at hand which he uses to make other
distinctions.[20]

One might suspect that Tolstoy is pursuing a moral contrast,
perhaps one of hypocrisy and genuineness or of false compassion and
true compassion. It is true, of course, that the noblewoman is
hypocritical, self-pitying, and egotistical. She is incurably sick and
incurably dishonest, and she provokes the same kind of dishonesty in
others. No one dares speak the truth to her, and she does not dare
speak the truth to herself. She makes others feel her sickness and she

exacts emotional tribute from all who will pay it. The concern and pity
that her husband, doctor, and friends show her are false and
dishonest. If Tolstoy were pursuing a contrast of emotional honesty
and dishonesty, then one would expect him to show that those who
surround the peasant in his dying are genuinely concerned, pitying,
and compassionate. But he does not. The old man goes to his grave
unmourned and unmissed. Even worse, the whole interest of others in
his dying lies in the nuisance he has created while living and the
advantage he leaves in dying. The cook needs the space he has been
occupying and the coachman needs the boots he is wearing. If there is
a contrast in compassion to be formulated, it would have to lie in its
expression for the noblewoman and in the lack of it for the peasant.
Yet we are being asked to disapprove of the compassion shown for the
noblewoman and to approve of the lack of compassion shown for the
peasant.

What makes the approval even more difficult is that the attitudes of
those who surround the peasant are described in terms we would
ordinarily consider callous. The cook profits from the death of the
peasant by regaining the space she had grudgingly given to him,
and the coachman profits by obtaining a pair of boots. Neither shows
any grief or compassion for his dying. There is no mistaking Tolstoy's
pursuit of this point, since he makes the same point with the tree, and
the death of the tree is there to underscore what he has to say about
the death of the peasant. The death of the tree is the most beautiful
death, but it provokes no grief—only joy, song, and advantage for
others. The birds sing all the more merrily, the remaining trees show
themselves even more beautifully in the space left by the fallen tree,
and the sun floods the trees and the dew with its light. Only twice in
the scenes describing the noblewoman do we meet with attitudes
similar to those of the cook's and the coachman's: once when the
peasant girls peer into the carriage to see the noblewoman out of
curiosity, and again when the children play noisily and self-absorbedly
in the halls, while relatives, doctors, and clergy crowd about the sick
woman in her last hours. It is clear that Tolstoy approves of both. The
children and the peasant girls are as cheerfully indifferent to the dying
woman as is the robin, which hops to another branch, to the dying of
the tree. The conclusion seems inescapable and outrageous: Tolstoy
believes that indifference and joy, rather than grief and compassion,
should attend the death of a fellow being. The living thrive on the
death of others.

It is not, of course, callousness and self-profit that Tolstoy is recommending, although this is how we would normally call what he represents. What he is showing and recommending is something more subtle and more in keeping with the "right" attitude toward the reality he had begun to discern in *Childhood*. We can get some clue to the meaning of the deaths by observing how thoroughly subjectivized the world is in which the noblewoman's death occurs. She is a flurry of motion and noise. She protests, complains, hopes, regrets; we meet her on her way to Europe where she is convinced, with no grounds whatsoever, that she will be cured. Her life is not as she would have it. There is the external turmoil of the moving carriage and the inner turmoil of her emotions. Nothing is right: the weather is not right, the journey is not right; her husband is not right. The peasant, on the other hand, is humble, uncomplaining, and accepting. He knows that he is going to die, and he suffers without making others suffer. He waits for his death silently; the noblewoman never stops talking, demanding, cajoling. The peasant occupies a small corner of a stove, a space emblematic of his moral posture; he knows his place and he does not intefere with what goes on about him. The noblewoman impinges on the space of others: her hat dangles in front of the maidservant's nose, her dog rests on the maidservant's lap, and her boxes on the floor force the maidservant to raise her legs. She is reluctant to grant the doctor and her husband the right to move off and eat when they stop at a station; and even the motion of the carriage is emblematic of the space consumed and the lives affected in her insistence on her right to live.

The room in which the peasant dies is "stuffy and dark"; there is an "oppressive smell of baking bread, cabbage, sheepskin garments, and humanity" in it; and none of these details has anything to do with his sickness and dying. The objects have their own being as do the people who surround him. They go on with their duties with only occasional reference to him. The coach of the noblewoman is stuffy with the smell of eau de cologne, with her bags, with her maid. The world exists for her as an appendage to her desires, fears, and longings. It is her voice that we hear or the voices of those responding to her complaints. But it is the carriage driver's voice and not the peasant's we hear; the cook's complaints and not his. It is not his death but a pair of boots that is the center of interest and discussion. The voices, concerns, expectations of others are what rise into prominence. As we go from the scenes portraying the dying of the noblewoman to those portraying the death of the peasant, and especially to those portraying the death of the tree, the objective world rises into substance, solidity, and density. The context in which the dying occurs widens and the importance of the dying becomes smaller and more proportionate to the objective state of things. The descriptive detail in the scenes of the dying noblewoman are almost exclusively connected with her; the details describing the death of the peasant are only incidentally about him, and the death of the tree is only a small incident in the luxuriance, fullness, and indifferent joy of the life that surrounds its dying.

Clearly Tolstoy is showing that one kind of dying contracts life, narrows it, and interferes with the lives of others; and that another kind of dying permits the world to continue unaffected and undisturbed and perhaps even improved by the dying. We have no trouble in disapproving the way that the noblewoman dies, but it is troubling and upsetting to have the right kind of dying portrayed as advantage to others, who are, moreover, indifferent to the dying person. It does no good to blink at this or to translate it into our familiar scale of values by which sacrifice is good and selfishness is bad. R. F. Christian does this when he says: "The dying peasant who gives his new boots away, instinctively acts for the good of others."[21] This is just not true, much as we would like it to be true. Fyodor asks for the boots repeatedly, and his requests are met with silence on the part of the dying man, a fact that must be interpreted as at least reflective disinclination. It is only when the cook (who is his creditor) scolds him and reminds him that he has no longer any use for them that he grudgingly agrees. Even then, he does so only by requesting something in return. This is hardly the instinctive generosity which Christian speaks of. Yet Christian's attempt to ennoble the dying peasant is understandable, for Tolstoy gives us very little to assimilate into our normal scale of values. If the noblewoman is concerned only with herself, so too are Fyodor and the cook, and perhaps even the peasant himself. We are asked more or less by Tolstoy to choose not between selfishness and generosity or traditional self-interest and disinterest but between two kinds of self-interest. That said, one must not in any way identify morally the noblewoman and the peasant and those surrounding each. Tolstoy is insisting on a contrast, but a contrast different from what we would ordinarily expect from a Christian. The difference seems to lie in the kinds of self-interest that are portrayed. The noblewoman's self-interest preys upon the world about her. She is concerned that the world wait upon her, that others serve her, grieve for her, give her their time, emotions, prayers, that doctors cure her and priests pray for her. The cook, the coachman, and the peasant are absorbed in their immediate self-interest, but the self-interest is not at the expense of others. Their indifference is also an absence of claim upon others.

We can explain the self-absorption of the cook and the coachman as healthy by labeling it "natural" or "pagan," but the labels will not explain anything. The clue to the explanation lies in that pattern of progressive rising of the world into solidity, density, and independent existence that attends on the peasant's dying, and that pattern of subjectivizing and dependence that attends the noblewoman's death. Tolstoy seems to be groping in this early and complicated story toward the perception that self-absorption, if it is truly that and not the absorption of others for self, permits others an existence undistorted and unmanipulated by the persons absorbed. The peasant can go on with his dying, and the cook with her cooking, but the doctor, husband, and relatives of the dying noblewoman cannot go on with their living—only with their grieving.

Tolstoy is beginning to perceive that grief, longing, fear, compassion are all claims on the world, and as such distortive of the world and manipulative of other people. Grief is a claim on the past and beings of others. The lives of those who surround the noblewoman are, for the time of her dying, suspended and fixated; they belong to her and to her dying. The lives of those who surround the peasant are undistorted by the dying and continue unrestricted in their independence and spontaneity. It is not a matter of true or false grief. The excoriation of the hypocrisy that attends the noblewoman's dying is an invitation to misinterpret the story, as are the themes of true and false Christianity and the class differences of peasant and noblewoman. For Tolstoy the noblewoman's death would be no different if she were another kind of woman, less captious, petty, demanding, and hypocritical. The falseness of her death does not lie in her character anymore than it does in her Christianity or class. Even if the compassion she provoked were true compassion and the pity genuine, the crying would be wrong and the attitudes of those who surround her would be wrong. It is the compassion, not its falseness, that is wrong. Tolstoy says almost the same thing in the letter to his cousin, when he calls the death of the tree beautiful "because it doesn't act up, doesn't fear, and doesn't pity." The implication of the story that compassion, grief, and pity are false is a provocative and outrageous flouting not only of Christian but of humane attitudes. Tolstoy is determined to confront the conventions men live by and to expose their falseness, not, however, in some spirit of nihilism, but in the search for some principle of plenitude and happiness. He begins *Family Happiness* with a scene in which a family and a young girl have impoverished their lives by their grieving, and he goes on to examine another emotion, love and domestic happiness, so as to peel off what is false and to find what is real.

3 Polikushka and Family Happiness

The Soviet critic Bychkov finds the quality of Tolstoy's *Family Happiness* to be severely diminished because Tolstoy's theme is remote from the social reality of the time.[1] Yet Tolstoy was responding as much and as little to the contemporary scene in *Family Happiness* as he would be in *Polikushka*, a tale that Bychkov and others point to as revealing Tolstoy's renewed interest in the questions of the day. *Polikushka* was published in 1861, the year of the liberation of the serfs, and general interest in the conditions of peasant life may have moved Tolstoy to take up the theme. But in *Family Happiness*, too, one can argue that he was responding in a similar way to a contemporary issue: the woman question was one of the insistent problems pursued by the radicals of the late fifties and the sixties, and the cause of women's rights was to be aggressively put forward a few years later in Chernyshevsky's *What Is To Be Done?* Tolstoy seems in the tales of the fifties and early sixties to be removed, as Bychkov claims, from contemporary issues, except perhaps for the Sevastopol sketches, but closer examination shows that almost all his works respond to some social or artistic issue of the day.

The Two Hussars seems at first to be an exercise in nostalgia for a bygone time and type, yet the short novel is after all a generational contrast, in basic theme not so different from Turgenev's *Fathers and Sons*, a novel that everyone rightfully takes to be addressing itself to an issue of the day. The autobiographical sketch was very much in the air in the late forties and early fifties, when Tolstoy wrote *Childhood*, *Boyhood*, and *Youth*—as Eikhenbaum has copiously documented[2]— and in attempting *The Cossacks* Tolstoy was clearly responding to the Russian reading public's fatigue with the unreal romanticisms of a previous generation and a hunger for ethnographic data about the unknown region of the empire. Tolstoy tended, however, to distance himself from the enthusiasms and popular attitudes of the time. He praises the father and not the son in *The Two Hussars*, and he puts forth as the right role for women marriage and motherhood and not occupational and sexual liberation. He also tended to dissolve and decompose topical questions into timeless concerns, so that it did not matter very much whether the issue was radical or conservative.

POLIKUSHKA

Polikushka looks like a topical theme, but here as elsewhere Tolstoy deflects our interest from social motivation and carries it toward areas of permanent concern. R. F. Christian is much more sensitive than Bychkov to the complexity of the story and the different ways that it can be read.

> The story may be read in different ways, for it is neither moralistic nor overly didactic like the stories of the later 1850s. Those who regard it as a salutary illustration of the theme that money is the root of all evil are rebuked by Tolstoy's former secretary, Gusev, who declares categorically that the basic theme is "the moral oppression of serfdom." But this contention ignores the universal applicability of the mental anguish of a man who feels he has let down a person who has helped and trusted him. A Soviet Poli-kushka might have done the same thing if his "benefactor" had been his factory manager. The ownership of one person by another, disgraceful as it is, is not the real cause of human misery—not but what a reading of *Polikushka* strengthens one's antipathy to the evils of serfdom, the squalid lives of its victims and the iniquities of the recruiting system. But here the emphasis is surely on the moral dilemma of trust seemingly betrayed and this is enhanced by the detachment with which Tolstoy writes without betraying his own sympathies and without apportioning vices and virtues, praise and blame in a schematic and preordained manner. The tragedy is not the inevitable outcome of serfdom (Rebecca West once some-what flippantly observed that it could have been avoided if there had been a reliable postal service) but it is enacted against an un-lovely background where the peasant Dutlov is, if anything, a more unattractive character than the mistress of the village.[3]

Christian is sensitive to the universal concerns that underlie the topical theme of peasant life and the oppressions of serfdom, and his tentative conclusion that the story is about the dilemma of moral trust is a more suggestive reading than is Gusev's or Bychkov's. Yet he may have universalized the story too much, because if the tale cannot be limited to the topicalities of serfdom, it cannot be divorced entirely from such topicalities. The betrayal of moral trust is too general, and the ownership of one person by another, which Christian rejects as the

real cause of misery, is too narrowly construed by him. Tolstoy has not
chosen his overt subject matter indifferently; he sees in the ownership
of one person by another more than Christian assigns to it. Serfdom
was a political, historical, and economical manifestation of a principle
that is universal in people and does not cease because serfdom is
abolished. Nor is it an impulse that is present only in economic and
political situations. I am leaping far ahead, but Tolstoy was to
see—and in part was already seeing—the principle of coercion as an
impulse that took many forms and could be found not only in
institutions but also in personal relations of every imaginable sort and,
indeed, in one's relations with oneself. The tracing of the principle of
coercion (because every act of coercion, whether physical, psychological, or moral, is a form of owning someone else) led Tolstoy to
believe eventually that noninterference in the life of others was the
greatest virtue. The principle of noninterference led him on a political
level to champion a position of political anarchism, on the economic
level to belief in the evils of exploitation, and on the religious level to
his belief in nonresistance to evil.

   Polikushka can probably best be read as a series of "ownerships"
and hence as a series of "coercions." The masters own the serfs and
the state owns at least a portion of the able-bodied men for military
service. The institutionalized exploitation of bodies and work has
established itself among the peasants themselves, as Dutlov's influence and actions make clear. The noblewoman comes off better
morally than does Dutlov, but her "moral" feelings are perhaps the
most subtle and most complete form of "coercion" and "ownership."
Though Polikushka has many burdens to bear, the hardest and
cruelest is the trust that the landlady places in him. Tolstoy has
already begun to discern, as he did in *The Landowner's Morning*, that
faith and trust as a desire to reform can be destructive and coercive.
The noblewoman has no right to experiment with another's soul and
sensitivities—whatever her charming motives; the burden is too great
for the sensitive Polikushka. Too great, too, for the material and
psychological conditions. It is a cruel irony that Polikushka is true to
his trust, and it is only by virtue of an accident that he "betrays" that
trust. Yet moral intensities and intentions take place in a real world,
where accidents do occur. Nor is the accident as much so as it appears.
The rotten hat into which the money is stuffed and through which it is
lost is a fact of his miserable material condition; and the moral
intensity and care with which he checks and stuffs the money in the

hat is a consequence of his sensitivity to past failures. The novel, one of the most important among Tolstoy's early works, touches on the harm that good can bring when it is abstracted from the complexity of real circumstances. Tolstoy doubtless had something of this kind in mind in the overt social issue that is found in the story; he also probably had some criticism in mind of the "abstract" social issues that were in the air. But he took most social and contemporary issues as reflections of more essential concerns, which for him were always moral, psychological, and universal.

FAMILY HAPPINESS

Tolstoy seemed to have more than one end in writing *Family Happiness*, but the treatment of the woman question was very much in keeping with his reflex of lifting topicalities to universalities. He was in part addressing himself to the romantic commonplaces with which love had been treated in European and Russian literature and which continued to be admired in the works of George Sand and in some of the works of Turgenev. The novel, too, was biographically topical, since it reads in part as a transcription of the letters he had written to Valery Arsenieva, to whom he had been engaged and with whom he had carried on an intensive and—for her—exhausting analysis of their relationship and the nature of married love.[4] The novel permits him to finish the lecture that Valery finally and understandably could not stand. It seems at some distance from the peasant-landowner themes of *Polikushka* and *The Landowner's Morning*, but it is concerned, as they are, with tracing out subtleties of coercion. In very great measure a good domestic love for Tolstoy is one that is free, and a poor domestic love is one that is constrained. But free means for Tolstoy a love that is natural, and a natural love is one that is free of social conventions. Such conventions include the commonplaces of romantic love as well as the artificialities of salon flirtation. A natural love is free, too, of the constraints that desire imposes on love by fixing it in time and special moments.

It is this level of subtlety that a critic of such sensitivity as Troyat misses when he criticizes Tolstoy for a lack of originality in treating domestic love: "Tolstoy was not able either to dominate or to say anything really new about the relatively trite theme of the transmutation of conjugal love into maternal love, and the story, a novella rather than a novel, was uneven, clumsily constructed and lacking in originality.''⁵ This is a harsh and unfair statement. Too many readers have fallen under the charm of his picture of young love, its trials, and its growth into a mature domestic love. The following evaluation by Noyes, even though in its uncritical acceptance it is hardly more accurate than Troyat's, is more characteristic of readers' reaction to the novel.

The tale has a wonderful freshness and poetic charm. The portrait of the man is delightful, with his clumsy kindliness, his sincere friendship for the girl whom he has watched develop from childhood, and his joy when he perceives that after all she may sometime be able to love him otherwise than as an affectionate old friend. The girl, with her genuine sweetness and faithfulness, combined with an eagerness for admiration that arouses her husband's jealousy, is even more appealing. This is a true love story, that of a courtship that does not cease with marriage.⁶

Troyat charges Tolstoy with not saying anything new about a trite theme, but he misses the point that Tolstoy was deliberately courting triteness and banality and bringing the everyday and the typical into the province of art.

Both the critic and the admirer miss the tough vein in the story that raises banalities to art. The point of the tale is not that romantic love is false, or that the city is artificial and filled with snares, or that there are inevitable problems in a May-December marriage, or that the reason for marriage is children and sitting on a veranda holding hands with one's partner; nor is the point, Noyes notwithstanding, that courtship "does not cease with marriage." These things may be true, but they are truths that deflect one from the more complex and penetrating things that Tolstoy is communicating. Masha's grief for her mother, her courtship by Sergey, the early happiness of her married love, the sterile years of sophisticated courtship in the city, and the return to her husband are all situations and states by which Tolstoy attempts to penetrate to the core of what constitutes marital happiness and marital unhappiness; and by way of that analysis to attempt another understanding of that unknown x that he had begun to discern and to pursue in *Childhood*. Tolstoy is looking for a common substratum for the relationships that bring one closer to that "right harmony," whatever the area of life; and also for that principle that deflects and repels one from it. He was concerned for it in the stages of a child's initiation into adulthood in *Childhood*; in the deaths of a noblewoman, peasant, and tree in *Three Deaths*, and in how one falls in love and out of love in *Family Happiness*. To take the overt content as the message is to institutionalize and essentialize what is meant to be in part sign. Much of *Family Happiness*, for example, is about nature and sophistication, but it is a mistake to deduce from this—as has been done repeatedly—that Tolstoy is communicating merely the vacuous truth that the country is good and the city bad. The nature is there to communicate something about human beings and how they touch—in this instance—truth and how they miss touching it.

In *Family Happiness* Tolstoy uses the natural seasons as an analogue to the movement of emotions. The analogue is not original, but Tolstoy's particular use is revealing of some aspects of his search for the magic x of experience. When the story begins, for example, the snow drifts have piled up higher than the windows and the windows themselves are dimmed by the frost, as the life inside has been dimmed by death and closed to the outside world. Dead nature outside reflects the dead life inside. Masha comes to life with the quickening of feeling for her neighbor and future husband and the quickening of nature outside her. She falls in love with him in spring, marries him in August when nature reaches its fruition, and begins to be estranged from him in winter, when nature dies. During the years that she spends in the city and becomes more and more estranged from her husband and even her child, almost no mention of nature is made, and it is difficult even to get a sense of time passing. When the natural feelings of wife and mother begin to die in her, her consciousness of natural time-seasons becomes remote and unreal. Masha and Sergey are reunited in the country in spring, and the renewal of their love takes place in a chorus of natural sounds and sights. The climactic healing scene brings to completion the nature analogue which Tolstoy has pursued throughout the story. By and large, Tolstoy uses the changing seasons as an analogue to the emotions that Masha feels. When things are right, her heart and emotions blossom and reach fruition as do things in nature; and when her emotions and feelings are wrong, her inner life is analogized to either dead nature (winter) or no nature (city).

Tolstoy handles a rather conventional rhetorical figure with considerable skill; and if this were the only point of the figure, one could note it and go on. Many have so noted it, leaving the analogy as merely some kind of sympathy that Tolstoy communicates between his heroine and nature. But I am persuaded that Tolstoy is attempting to do a great deal more. What he is attempting to communicate in the broadest sense is that life—and, in this specific instance, love—is right, real, and good when it is natural, that is, when what is going on inside is subject to the same laws as that which is going on outside.

That is, when the self (emotions, impulses, will) is not separated from what we ordinarily look on as impersonal processes that take place outside of ourselves and inside of ourselves, then something real and right is occurring. In the most literal sense, the use of such a word as "blossom" both for the setting in which Sergey and Masha celebrate the awareness of their love and for what is going on inside Masha is not really an analogy: the same laws push forth the flower outside Masha and inside her. One touches the x of life when inner nature and outer nature are one. Tolstoy will, of course, take up the nature figure again and again, and he will do so with even greater skill: Nikolay's hunt scene in *War and Peace* and Levin in the mowing scene in *Anna Karenina* are two consummate examples of such attempts. In both cases the union of nature and internal subjective processes are used to crown supreme "sacramental" moments when a kind of ultimate harmony exists in the participants. He is not as good in these early stories in representing artistically such union. The identity of inner and outer nature will be vastly more significant and complex in *War and Peace* and *Anna Karenina*, but the quest, in its beginnings, is the same.

In *Childhood*, Tolstoy had already recorded the attempt on the part of the child to find something as firm, unequivocable, and unambiguous within himself as are the natural forms he perceives about him. Underlying all these attempts there must have been a kind of conviction that it was possible and desirable for man to become naturelike. It is the subjective nature of man—his consciousness, feelings, perceptions, and wishes—that make him conscious of being something other than that which surrounds him: separate not only from physical nature but also from certain physical processes that go on inside him. What Tolstoy wants—though it must have been at this point only dimly perceptible to him—and what he strives for, to use the testimony of later works, is a formulation by which the self and something other than self could be resolved. But making oneself like nature implies many things. Nature changes, grows, and becomes something different with time. A self that becomes like nature would necessarily be a self that changes and one that resists the immobilization that conceptualization and consciousness bring. Such a "natural" self would be subject to impersonal and necessary forces. Tolstoy's recommendation of "natural" life conceals subtleties which will be conceived and reconceived with every work.

The narrative is in large part a fictive tracing out, one might even say a testing, of such subtleties—what happens to love when it is naturelike, that is, when it changes, grows; and what happens to it when it is unnatural, that is, fixed into something unchanged and unchanging. The novel begins with emotions that have become unnatural in the sense that they have become immobilized. Masha's mother has recently died, and for months since her death the emotions of Masha and the inhabitants of the household have been dead inside. No one goes out to visit and visitors are rare; members of the household whisper, tiptoe, moan and groan. Masha refuses to play the piano or to read, and every call to do something arouses from her the retort "to what end?" The grief, in short, has immobilized the life of the household, robbed the inhabitants of happiness and variety, and imprisoned them in a single and unvarying emotion. Masha and the inhabitants of the household do what convention and, indeed, what our normal humane and sensitive emotions have accustomed us to do, and yet it is clear that Tolstoy looks upon grief as wrong. He has taken up again what he first pictured in the contrasting reactions of Natalya Savishna and the grandmother in *Childhood* to the death of Nicholas's mother, and the contrasting reactions of those who surround the dying noblewoman and the peasant in *Three Deaths*. In each instance, Tolstoy seems to be saying that there is a distorting and life-killing principle in what we conventionally call grief. There is no doubt that he is saying the same thing in the opening scenes of *Family Happiness*, and doing so with more complexity and at greater length. The unchanging and all-encompassing grief that Masha is expected to feel and express goes against what she actually feels, and it is the actual feelings that are right, even though they may do violence to what we expect to be expressed on such occasions. What Masha actually feels is the passing of her youth, joys being missed, and new desires and experiences awaiting her. She was supposed to go to Saint Petersburg with her mother the very year her mother died. She mourns the passing of her mother, but she also mourns the passing of the delights the trip had promised. Masha feels many things, but the social convention permits her to feel only one thing, or at least to express only one emotion. There is an element of coercion in the grief, both of others and of oneself, as well as a simplifying and impoverishing of the actual inner reality of the participants.

Sergey Mikhailovich, a neighbor and good friend of the family, understands that the pall of grief in the house is wrong. Whereas everyone has lowered his voice to whispers, Sergey enters the house talking loudly. He smiles, laughs, says not a word about the dead mother. Rather he insists on bringing up the memory of the father, who had loved life very much, and he assures Masha that she would have loved him very much. On the mention of the dead father, Katya, the servant, insists on turning the reminiscence to the service of grief, pulls out her handkerchief and begins to cry. Sergey refuses to enter the prison of Katya's fixed emotion and pointedly changes the subject by asking Sonya to show him her toys. Soon, his loud voice and Sonya's delighted squeals are heard coming from the young girl's room. Sergey acts similarly with Masha: he will have nothing to do with her regrets, her lassitude, or her dejection. He tells her she has no right to be bored, and that she must do what is at hand: read, play, make plans, and live her youth now. Sergey insists on the right and even the obligation to live in the present moment. Masha does not have the right, according to Sergey and Tolstoy, to live in the past, either the past of grief or the past of regret. She has the obligation to live in the present.

Sergey and the feelings he arouses in her, as well as the advent of spring, contrive to bring Masha back to what is concrete and present in her. She plays the piano, reads, and responds to what is going in inside and outside her and not to feelings she is expected to have. She comes back to life when she touches what is real and natural within her, and what is natural and real changes with different periods of her emotional life. It was conventional expectations that killed life in her at the time of mourning for her mother, and it will be the expectations of certain desires to deny change and hold on to special moments of reality that will be the source of her marital unhappiness. She is closest to what is real within her and outside her, and closest to that "right" relationship with life, when she is falling in love. Nowhere, too, in the early works is Tolstoy's art more charming and beautiful than in those scenes when the first bloom of love graces both Masha and Sergey. One of the characteristics of the "best" moments of Tolstoy's world will be the identity a person experiences with the world about him. In this instance the difference of age that had bothered Sergey is, at least for a time, obliterated and in some magical way overcome. There is something of a regression on Sergey's part to a childhood state. He becomes a little boy, playing with Masha, scampering over fences, and enjoying what would ordinarily be called silly games. In action and sentiment love works the miracle of identification.

Nowhere is the harmony between the natural love within them and the natural process outside them more eloquently expressed than on the night when Masha realizes that they are in love, even though no words had been spoken of love. The natural light of the moon floods into the room through the open doors to supplement the artificial light of the candles while Masha plays Mozart at the piano. As natural love illuminates their hearts, they leave the artificial light and step into the moonlight outside. The moonlight floods the natural scene, illuminates to a jewellike luster the dew and re-creates the forms of the bushes and trees. Tolstoy wants to communicate that real love transforms the world and the perception of the world, and he does this by re-creating the natural forms of the garden by the moonlight. As the habitual relations with the family friend are being transformed by love, so too is the familiar garden being transformed by the natural illumination. The sense of love as something endlessly new is caught by the image of the path as ending and not ending. The path they walk on seems to end and not to end, as the bushes and trees lining the path close and open into new vistas as they approach.

The paths close and refuse to open when Masha attempts to hold on to what the love was during the courtship and to mold it to what her mind imagines it should be. A hint of her future dissatisfaction is already present on the day of the ceremony itself, when the reality of the ceremony and the matter-of-factness of the event confront her with disillusioning contrast to what she had imagined. The first months of the marriage are different, too, from what she had imagined, even though they are months of harmony, love, and satisfaction. She had expected marriage to be hard work, duty, self-sacrifice, and constant devotion to others, and she is surprised and pleased to learn that the perfect happiness she experiences consists only of the selfish feeling of love, the desire to be loved by the other, constant causeless gaiety, and oblivion to the world beyond the private world of loving and being loved. When she begins to expect marital love to be what the mind imagines and the desires crave, a distorting principle is introduced into the marriage. With the advent of winter, her desire for excitement and heroic sacrifice work to poison her happiness. She has fantasies of another kind of love: of standing on a precipice and having herself saved from falling by the strong arm of her lover. She wants excitement, intensity, and new experiences. She wants the dizzying feeling of courtship and first love to continue. Even though the calm and unvarying routine of domestic love of the first months of the marriage are, by her own admission, not inferior to the other kind of love, she clings to the desire of the unchanging excitement of first courtship, and it is this courtship that she attempts to find and hold onto in Saint Petersburg.

In a grotesque sense, this is what she experiences in Saint Petersburg;

she attends balls, listens to compliments, and is courted by the sophisticated men of society. The courtship of Sergey takes place out of doors, amid the scents of spring, and in a magical garden; the feeling of love is celebrated by moonlight and studded by dew. The courtship in the city is an artificial and false one of idle compliments and unreal emotions, tirelessly repeated in the same way. It takes place under artificial light, with studied language and gestures, unlike the silly, abandoned play of Sergey and Masha in the garden. The courtship of Masha by Sergey is characterized by the sense of newness and change at every moment, and what characterizes the unreal courtship is habit, sameness, and boredom. What had appeared to be excitement and variety to Masha, becomes, even to her at the end, habit and repetition. But it is a long time coming, and Tolstoy shows—as he will many times hereafter—how in our sophisticated environment a substitute reality of great subtlety can take possession of a person's being and give him a second nature, in which false feeling, thinking, and even will can replace what is naturally given. The city and its sophistication are analogues to certain distorting and corrupting processes in the individual, but one cannot take them literally as the corrupting processes. Masha's estrangement from real life and from her husband begins in the country, and what estranges her in the country leads her to seek the city and sophistication and not the other way around. The artificial social forms which for a time she comes to accept as reality are a consequence of certain subjective impulses in her and others, the point of which seems to be to remake life into an image that is comforting, secure, and manipulable.

There is a third courtship in the novel—the coarse and mechanical attempt at love by the Italian marquis. The fact that only ''sex'' remains when real feelings have been killed may be already an indication of Tolstoy's later identification of sex and death. The scene in Baden among the ruins is not very well done, nor is it really necessary since it makes even more obvious what Tolstoy has been saying about Masha's years of separation from Sergey and the country. Tolstoy may even have placed the seduction scene among the ''ruins'' of civilization so as to emphasize what sophistication does to natural feeling. The best one can say for it is that Masha needs some blow to move her back to the country, to Sergey, and to natural domestic love; and Tolstoy does not have the patience to wait—as James does characteristically—until the consciousness of what she has experienced in the city matures and moves her.

Once back in the country, Masha despairs of her lost happiness. Her young heart has turned from falsity but not to truth. It is a tangle of confusion, but the confusion changes to illumination in the conversation she and Sergey have on the veranda while they look upon the beauty of mixed rain and sunlight. The analogy that Tolstoy pursues between nature outside and inside men is caught here in images and words that express at the same time the physical and the spiritual. The tears that purify Masha's feelings are analogized to the gentle rain that purifies the earth about her. The same word "clear" (*yasno*) is used to express the physical scene about them and Masha's inner state. But it is not clear at first for her. Everything is beautiful about her, but everything is confused, baffling and full of vague longings inside her. She asks Sergey again and again if there is anything he wishes for, or anything he regrets. Sergey answers again and again that he doesn't wish for impossibilities or regret anything. And when she asks if he would not alter the past, he answers resolutely, "No, never. It was all for the best." The conversation at the end takes us back to the conversation or the situation at the beginning. What Sergey tells Masha in this last scene is what his actions implied in the first: that regret, wishes, hopes, and longings are wrong. They are wrong because they attempt to remake life and reject what is. Regret is after all a kind of "past imagination," and it is tied with wishes, hopes, longings, because like them it is an imposition of the mind upon what is. Wisdom for Sergey and for Tolstoy lies in acceepting what is, and what is, changes. The distilled version of what Sergey expresses and what Masha begins to understand at the end is caught beautifully in Sergey's statement, "Each time of life has its own kind of love" (*v kazhdoy pore est' svoya lyubov'*). The Russian word *pora* can mean both "time" and "season"; thus in one word Tolstoy reminds us of the natural analogy that he has pursued throughout the novel. Since each time of life has its own kind of love, happiness depends on accepting what time brings, and unhappiness consists in attempting to impose on life one's own conception of happiness.

Tolstoy is giving us an early statement of what will have implications for his mature reaction to life and experience. Something of his later acceptance of necessity is already expressed here. Man is not free to form life but only to accept it. Moreover, what is to be accepted is not an essence but something that changes without and within. The substitute realities that the mind creates are motivated by such impulses as grief, desire, regret. What is common to them is an attempt to immobilize life according to some subjective pattern. One cannot control the "necessity" of life; every attempt to do so and to live by the substitute reality separates one from the plenitude of life. Masha's tale is a particularization of these principles. What she learns is that the world and domestic love cannot be what she imagines them to be or what she wants them to be; nor can they be one unchanging thing. Domestic happiness is one thing when one is young and another when one ages. She cannot change the fact that Sergey is much older than she is, that he is a different person than she is, as indeed Sergey cannot change the fact that she is much younger than he is and consequently must learn for herself from the mistakes and errors of youth. One cannot change (to return to the natural symbolism of the novel) the course of the seasons, and one cannot change the course of the "season-times" (*pory*) of one's inner nature.

The dramas of Nicholas in *Childhood* had to do with the incongruity between what the child found within him and what he saw without him, the contrast between the private world and the public world, between the instinctive feeling within him and the ready-made feelings, perceptions, and conduct that the adult world presented him and the games of childhood prepared him to accept. The emphasis in that autobiographical sketch is on the "false" realities. The unknown *x* of reality is not stated, but in *Family Happiness* Tolstoy attempts to formulate it in one area, domestic happiness. Although the formulation is partial and not entirely clear, something of Tolstoy's later formulations is already apparent. One is right in saying that domestic happiness is peace, love, children, and hard work; that it is not the vanities and excitement of the ballroom and certainly not the crudities of the Italian marquis. But such an answer is a banality, though true. Domestic happiness is accepting what is real and seeing what is real. What is real, however, is different in every age and different at every moment and with every circumstance. What links the diverse "wrongs" such as grief, regret, romantic excitement, and social banalities is the imposition on life of some concept, habit, expectation, or command that it be this or that. Masha is disappointed in the early months of her marriage because the marriage doesn't fit her expectation of romantic sacrifice. It is her expectation that creates the disappointment, not the marriage. The implication of Tolstoy's story is that domestic happiness and real love come when one accepts what is the nature of the beloved and one's own nature, as well as the nature of changing experience; when one sees that there is a delicate and exquisite correspondence between the circumstances within and the circumstances without, between the nature within and the nature without.

One cannot in prospect and retrospect avoid seeing the novel as something of an anticipation of *Anna Karenina*. There are a number of similarities between the two works, apart from the fact that both have to do with marital happiness. In each case the girl is married to an older man; both Sergey and Karenin are very sure of what their lives are supposed to be. Masha runs back to the comfort and security of her domestic life when she is tempted by the Italian marquis; Anna, too, returns with relief to Saint Petersburg and to husband and child after she is tempted by Vronsky at the ball and on the train. Sergey's sentential wisdom on the veranda clears away the confusions of Masha's heart; but Karenin's sentential lecture to Anna on the duties and responsibilities of marriage fail to penetrate the armor of Anna's delight. The feeling of responsibility to the children is the cement that binds Sergey and Masha at the end of the novel; the child is used by Karenin to punish Anna, and Anna uses her second child to punish Vronsky.

The greatest difference between the two novels lies in the way Masha is brought back to sanity and domestic happiness from the error and destructiveness of passion and vanity. Masha seems to tempt Anna's fate: she becomes estranged from her husband; she neglects her child; she becomes coquettish, flighty, vain, as Anna does in the later period of her life with Vronsky. She even comes close to satisfying a guilty passion. Though she suffers from boredom, aimlessness, and ennui, there is none of the anguish and physical suffering that Anna goes through. Time, a calm and patient husband, and the bond of children are enough to take Masha from foolishness back to domestic peace and happiness. Masha's story has a fablelike and happy quality: Anna's is dark and demonic. Still, Anna's passion is an extension of the impulse Masha feels to wrench life after the fashion of desire. What happens in the expanse of time and art between the story of Masha and the tragic fate of Anna is apparently Tolstoy's conviction that life is not a simple problem and a simple solution. He will continue, in *Anna Karenina*, to see the distorting principle of domestic happiness as similar, but he will also see that the distorting principle is deeper, more complex, and more impervious to change and solution. *Family Happiness* is a sketch; *Anna Karenina* is a wise and deep vision of life and an agonizing admission that a beautiful nature, an intelligent spirit, and good intentions are not sufficient protection against the ravages that the desire for life may bring. In *Family Happiness* everything is clear and understandable; in *Anna Karenina* we are left with paradoxes and mysteries.

One must remember, though, that Tolstoy portrayed, too, in *Anna Karenina* the domestic happiness of Kitty and Levin, which bears perhaps a stronger resemblance to the domestic life of Sergey and Masha than does the life of Anna and Karenin. Levin, like Sergey, is older than his wife, dislikes living in the city, and dislikes the vanities of social forms. He is as insufferably sententious as is Sergey, but perhaps less sure of his opinions about marriage and life. Sergey is surprised by nothing; Levin is surprised at the course of his marriage, at the depths Kitty reveals, and surprised too at his own changing opinions about his life. Children for Levin and Kitty are a bond that keeps them in happiness, and the final scene of *Family Happiness* and that of *Anna Karenina* are similar. If Tolstoy has discovered something about the passions in Anna's fate that does not have its anticipation in Masha's fate, he nevertheless reasserts the fundamental view of domestic happiness that he puts forth in the early novel. There is no comparison in artistic quality or breadth of life between the two works, but, that said, one can read *Family Happiness* as an outline of what, at least in rational terms, lies at the core of Anna's fate.

4   *The Cossacks*

The Cossacks is regularly referred to by Western and So-
viet critics alike as the best of Tolstoy's early works and often as one of his
most beautiful works. The tradition of praise is extraordinary since the
novel has some clear deficiencies. The work does not read as something
all of one piece, and one can sense something of the construction that
took place in fits and starts and over a period of a decade. The novel has,
for example, a curiously indecisive movement: Olenin is the central
consciousness, indeed the center of interest, and it is his attempt to
purify and remake himself that provides the motive force for our
interest and, generally speaking, for the movement of the novel. But
this line of interest is constantly being diverted by what one might call
a general ethnographic description of Cossack life, where for considerable stretches one almost forgets Olenin. Nor are these details
"symbolic" or "functional" in any way; they are not there as
reflections of Olenin's spiritual state or as an indirect comment on
him. Nor do they advance the action in any way. At best they would
seem to delineate a situation or atmosphere in which Olenin attempts
to find a more authentic self. It is quite possible that these descriptions
are a kind of ethnographic residue from earlier versions of the tale and
from its long and uneven history of writing. But it is unlikely that
Tolstoy, careful writer that he was, would have left such long
descriptive passages in the novel without some connection to Olenin's
attempt to pass from the corruptions of Moscow to a better and purer
life in the Caucasus.

John Bayley and R. F. Christian have taken the ethnographic
material as evidence of Tolstoy's serious purpose to give us an objective
picture of Cossack life, an end that is at odds with the subjective
distortions that Olenin introduces. Bayley's key statement—picked up
and approved by Christian—is: "Are we to have 'The Cossacks' or
'The Cossacks as seen by Olenin'?—that is the question which Tolstoy
cannot be said to have resolved."[1] The point is, according to Bayley,
that even in those scenes where Olenin is absent, Tolstoy has so

identified his own point of view with Olenin's that he is unable to give us an objective description of the Cossacks and Cossack life. It is true that the reader is at times unsure whose point of view he is getting. This situation is, however, much less frequent than Bayley would like us to believe. Bayley insists, for example, that we see the village through Olenin's eyes even though he has not yet arrived, but it is inconceivable that the following topographical and historical description could possibly be confused with Olenin's sense of things: "To the north of it begin the sand-drifts of the Nogay or Mozdok steppes, which fetch far to the north and run, Heaven knows where, into the Trukhmen, Astrakhan, and Kirghis-Kaisatsk steppes. To the south, beyond the Terek, are the Great Chechnaya river, the Kochkalov range, the Black Mountains, yet another range, and at last the snowy mountains, which can just be seen but have never yet been scaled."

Bayley's implication that Tolstoy was unable to choose between Olenin's sense of things and some objective sense of things is a Jamesian prejudice that has been imported into Tolstoy's intentions. It is a prejudice that Lubbock had already expressed in *The Craft of Fiction* and one that English Tolstoy critics seem condemned to keep repeating. Tolstoy was not trying, and failing, to achieve a single point of view. He wanted and needed two articulated points of view. If there is some weakness in the way the points of view are handled, it does not lie in Tolstoy's inability to give us consistently either Olenin's sense of things or some general, and presumably authorial, sense of *The Cossacks*, but in Tolstoy's inability to achieve a sharper and more distinct separation of these two and a more emphatic affirmation of both. Tolstoy needs both the objective description and Olenin's sense of things. An objective sense of things permits us to measure and judge Olenin's misunderstandings and misperceptions. When Tolstoy tells of the somewhat casual and even slovenly way the Cossacks keep guard, even while an attack by the Abreks is in the offing, he is preparing us for the romantic and ennobling distortions of Olenin's perception of Cossack life. So, too, when he shows us Maryanka milking a cow, slopping through the mud, responding good-naturedly to a certain amount of ribaldry, he is giving us an "objective ground" against which we can measure Olenin's misperception of her as an ideal and unapproachable creature.

One cannot emphasize too strongly the importance of recognizing Tolstoy's efforts to articulate such an "objective ground," not only in this tale but in all his early works. Tolstoy assumes that there is an objective reality undistorted by the partial views of individuals.

Tolstoy's view of reality is very different from that of most twentieth-century writers. By and large, writers like James, Conrad, Woolf, and Joyce assume that reality is fragmentary, subjectivized, partial, relative, and in any complete sense beyond formulation; that is, that reality is how it is seen by the individual. James's special excellence lies in his ability to catch and convey with such fine complexity the impressions of his characters, but there is no reality outside these impressions. Faulkner, for example, is at pains to tell us that there is no objective history but only the history that men carry in their minds. Even that is imperiled by memory and the passions and prejudices of those who carry the past into the present. But Tolstoy believes firmly that there is a "real" world apart from our understandings of it, and he is at pains to objectivize that real world, even though his conception of it changes with his development.

It is, of course, a matter of considerable technical interest how Tolstoy manages to communicate the presence of such a world. The communication depends very much on a strong and unambiguous authorial presence, even though the authorial presence is presented in a variety of ways. Sometimes it is direct and intrusive, but it can also be fully dramatized and presented with great subtlety. We can assume that the ethnographic matter in *The Cossacks* functions as an impersonal and objective ground against which we can measure the partial and changing views of Olenin. Nature in *Childhood* is firm, clear, and specific, and is used as a backdrop for the child's perception of various subjective distortions. In *The Landowner's Morning*, *Polikushka*, and later in *Anna Karenina*, the peasants themselves are presented as a kind of recalcitrant reality against which the efforts of the well-intentioned landowners come to naught. Whatever its embodiment, the objective reality is always presented as something impervious to the manipulations of wish and desire.

Much of the drama of Tolstoy's works—early and late—has to do with the distance between subjective understanding of such objective reality and the various efforts of characters to impose partial and personal views on the reality about them or on the reality of their own beings. Nicholas's temptation to flee before the horror of his mother's death is such a struggle, as is Masha's attempt to hold on to the charm and poetry of courtship after the "reality" of her being and the conditions of her life have changed. The beginning of "wisdom" is the recognition that one cannot remake such objective reality according to one's wishes; the completion of such wisdom lies in bringing one's own subjective world into relationship with that "independent" reality. The "right relationship" which I have posited as the central quest of Tolstoy in the early works is the identification of one's subjective being with this objective ground. To be sure, the situation is complicated by the fact that Tolstoy is not sure at this point what that objective ground is, and he can seize it partially only in discrete experiences and for the most part only in what it is not. But there is never any doubt that it exists, that it is good, and that harmony, well-being, and plenitude of life follow upon bringing oneself into alignment with it. *The Cossacks* represents another attempt to seize the "truth" of this objective ground and to formulate what it means to make the inner self and the outer world one.

The paradoxical character of this "right relationship" can be seen in the fact that it is experienced and embodied in a weird and mystifying scene: Olenin touches truth when he is lying in the lair of an old stag. This is the scene in which it is most difficult to separate Tolstoy's sense of things from Olenin's. For a short time the distance between them is closed, and Tolstoy's sense of right relationship and Olenin's are one; but this endures only for a short time. The renewed separation begins when Olenin begins to think on the significance of what has happened to him.

Olenin, having been shown the old stag's lair by Daddy Eroshka, sets off alone in the woods and settles unaccountably in the lair. The day is hot and the insects swarm, and Olenin's body quickly becomes covered with mosquitoes. He is about to go home because of the pain, but he decides to bear it, and gradually the sensation of pain turns into a peculiar pleasure and into a causeless happiness. He calls upon the mosquitoes to devour him, and feels himself in some way in blissful harmony with the nature about him. Olenin knows that something important has been revealed to him, that he has touched some source of life, and in gratitude he crosses himself. There seems to be no irony here. Tolstoy does not conceal his ironies, but his mockery is quiet when Olenin feels joy, crosses himself, and calls on the mosquitoes to devour him. The experience is right and Olenin is right. But it is not right for long. Shortly after the sacramental scene, Olenin begins to reason on the event, and on the meaning of life and happiness, and he comes to the conclusion that what has been revealed to him is the necessity of sacrificing himself for others. As soon as the idea of self-sacrifice forms in his mind, the joy he has felt leaves him, the wilderness grows dark, the trees look strange, and he is filled with fear of the Abreks. He has been led to the truth, but the grooves of habits lead him away from it. Nothing in the experience in the stag's lair leads him to the necessity of self-sacrifice. The mosquitoes do not sacrifice themselves but attack and eat him. Reflection distorts what he experiences. The bleeding pheasant head, severed from its body, which remains in his belt after a day of hunting, is a fitting, if not subtle, symbol of intellection and abstraction that Olenin takes away from the truth he has experienced.

The decision to sacrifice himself is wrong, and Tolstoy shows that it is wrong by what follows upon the decision. The self-sacrifice furthers Olenin's alienation from Cossack life and from Maryanka. It leads him to further idealization of his motives, to further romantic fantasies and further self-deceptions. Lukashka looks upon the horse that Olenin gives him as a bribe of some sort and is persuaded that Olenin has evil intentions against him. Because he believes he is doing something wrong in accepting the horse, Lukashka lies about the horse to his fellow Cossacks. When the villagers learn that the horse was a gift, they become suspicious of Olenin and put themselves on guard against him. The Cossacks act as if Olenin's self-sacrifice were a selfish act intended to hurt them, and they are right in their feelings. In this respect the stag's lair scene is quintessential of the novel: it summarizes Olenin's perception and misperception of himself and of the world about him, a process that takes place throughout the novel.

The misperception has begun with the opening scene in Moscow. On the eve of Olenin's departure for the Caucasus, several friends give him a farewell party. Olenin's coachman waits outside for four hours in freezing weather while Olenin indulges himself with food, drink, and sentiment. Olenin is intoxicated with self-analysis and does not notice the yawns and drooping eyes of one friend and the indifference of the other. He is interested only in himself, and his friends are interested only in themselves, but the conventional gestures and sentiments of good will and affection screen the self-interest and express what is not felt. At the moment of separation the friends bring themselves to tears and Olenin to blubbering. But once he has left, the friends talk of Olenin only for a moment before turning to the perfunctory matter of the following night's dinner. Tolstoy does not conceal the contrast between the sentiments poured out and the actual feelings experienced, nor the ironic contrast between Olenin's understanding of the situation and the understanding the reader is intended to have. Tolstoy says of Olenin, for example, after he has set off on his journey: "He remembered all the words of friendship heartily, bashfully, spontaneously (as he believed) addressed to him on his departure." The authorial presence is direct and unqualified. That

Olenin is deceiving himself, Tolstoy does not hesitate to point out by commenting parenthetically on what Olenin has just thought or expressed. Immediately after the opening scene Tolstoy gives us a summary analysis of Olenin's past and character—not the kind of analysis that Olenin would have made of himself. It is dry, objective, detached, and laconic. For the most part Olenin is painted as a young man whose heart and beliefs are at variance with his actions. We are told for example: "He had come to the conclusion that there is no such thing as love, yet his heart always overflowed in the presence of any young and attractive woman. He had long been aware that honours and position were nonsense, yet involuntarily he felt pleased when at a ball Prince Sergius came up and spoke to him affably."

Olenin is a superfluous man: he believes in nothing; he has no relatives, fatherland, religion; he has accomplished nothing even though he has experimented with social life, the civil service, farming, and music. He shares too the typical preconceptions and clichés about the Caucasus. The Caucasus for him is a region of beautiful and mysterious women, precipices, perils, and rushing torrents. It is a place of pristine purity where one may become as pure as the snow-capped mountains. Olenin's sweetest vision is a tritely romantic one of a Circassian woman utterly devoted to him, living in a lonely mountain hut, waiting on the threshold for his return, her eyes deeply submissive. He would return covered with dust, blood, and fame from vanquishing innumerable enemies. His Circassian beauty would be enchanting, wild, uneducated, but in the long winter months he would patiently teach her French and introduce her to the master-pieces of French literature. The vision is banal and fantastic enough to jolt even Olenin into exclaiming "Oh, what nonsense!" but it is attractive and real enough for him to slip back into a contemplation of the vision.

Olenin's journey from Moscow to the Caucasus to find a new life and to make himself into a new man has its mythic resonances in the body of Russian literature. Olenin, as a superfluous man in search of a more authentic self, reenacts a rite that is essential to much nineteenth-century Russian literature. The "holy temple" is never far from the minds and visions of fictive and real life heroes of Russian literature and life. Tolstoy actualizes the form by changing it from the traditional political utopianism and topographical primitivism to a psychological and spiritual quest. He also deals with the quest ironically. There is nothing very pristine and elemental about Caucasian life; it is shown to be dirty, humdrum, tedious, artificial in parts (witness the Cornet's speech and actions) and very unromantic, all obvious qualities that Olenin fails to see. But all is not irony. There is something new, wild, and elemental in man, and it is something that Olenin touches briefly in the stag lair scene. Olenin looks for a new and authentic self in his imitation of Cossack life, but he does not find it, although he never realizes this.

When we meet him three months after the opening scene, he is in some respects a changed man. His sallow complexion has become red with a healthy sunburn, and he breathes of health, joy and contentment. Yet Tolstoy is careful to point out that his Cossack dress and mannerisms are awkward and imitative and that any Cossack would easily recognize him as a Russian and not as a Tartar brave. He has become a Cossack in dress but not in feeling. The form and the gesture have changed more than have the substance and the spirit. The Cossacks, sensing the unnaturalness, instinctively dislike him. He inspires constraint, distrust, and suspicion. He is very much the outsider looking in. Beletsky, in contrast, the typical nobleman, has no trouble becoming part of Cossack life in a few weeks. He is liked and accepted, as Olenin is not. The difference is that Beletsky accepts unthinkingly what he is and how he is regarded by the Cossacks: a Russian nobleman in the Caucasus who does not attempt to play a different role. Olenin sees a Caucasus that exists in his mind; Beletsky sees the Circassian town as a provincial hole, where a Russian nobleman accustomed to pleasure must find what amusement he can in any way he can. It may seem perverse that Tolstoy should put forth the superficial, pleasure-loving rake Beletsky as in some way more admirable than the ideal-seeking, self-denying Olenin. Yet there is no doubt that he is doing so. Good intentions and even good deeds are no defense against unnaturalness and falsity. If reality lies beyond the manipulations by individuals and moves in its own course regardless of the wishes, hopes, and fears of the individual, so too does inner reality. One cannot make oneself what one wants; no matter how beautiful the self one imagines, the wages are always some form of falsity and separation from one's inner reality.

Olenin's misunderstanding and misperception of himself and of the reality about him is played out repeatedly and even with some obviousness, yet the tradition of critical commentary on the novel has by and large taken Olenin's sense of things as the real sense of things. Olenin maintains—and most critics concur—that he changes in the course of the novel: that he begins as a spoiled, self-deceived, and generally useless person, but that he is somehow stronger in self-

knowledge and action by the end of the novel. Except for moments of
perception and consciousness, this is not true. At the end of the tale
we meet an Olenin who is essentially the same: he is still romanticizing
himself and his desires; he is essentially useless to the village life about
him as he was useless in the capital. At the beginning of the tale he is
pleased with his garrulous self-analysis; and at the end of the tale he is
loquaciously absorbed in detailing his life in self-flattering terms in
diary and letters. He is the superfluous man in Moscow, and he is the
superfluous man in the Cossack village. When the life and death trial
of the battle occurs in the struggle between the Cossacks and the
Abreks, Olenin is not only useless at the scene but a positive obstacle.
As always he is an observer of life and not a participant. Before the
novel begins, he has played at being a farmer, civil servant, musician,
and lover. And at the end of the novel, he is playing at being a
Cossack, and, though he doesn't know it, he plays at being in love
with Maryanka and in sacrificing himself for others. At the core of
his idealizations, romanticizations, self-sacrifice is a certain self-
indulgence, which Tolstoy expresses again and again. He goes to the
battle between the Cossacks and the Abreks because he feels it would
not look right if he did not go. After the battle he returns to Maryanka
to take up where he left off, as if nothing had happened and nothing
mattered but his feelings. When he returns and sees Maryanka's back
turned to him, he concludes unaccountably and egotistically that she
is shy, that is, that she is reacting to him. She is, of course, not
thinking of Olenin but is consumed by grief. When she tells him to
leave her alone, he asks obtusely why she is crying. Maryanka answers,
"Cossacks have been killed, that's why." He can think only of grief in
personal terms, and asks, "Lukashka?"

Olenin seldom sees a thing for what it is. He never sees the Cossack
village for what it is: the environment of real people living in real
conditions; and he never sees Maryanka for what she is: a practical,
average, village girl, who is capable of grieving for the death of fellow
Cossacks and who loves Lukashka with simplicity and dignity. Near
the very end of the novel he is still writing of Maryanka in the
following terms: "Every day I have before me the distant snowy
mountains and this majestic happy woman." He seldom sees others
for what they are because he seldom sees himself for what he is. He
sees only what his mind wants and he and others are functions of this
seeing. But there is the scene in the stag's lair: weird, mysterious and
puzzling; yet with the unmistakable stamp of truth and reality on it.
The causeless happiness that Olenin feels is a sign of that right,

unreflective confrontation with truth, as much so as the leap of joy that Nikolay will feel at the sign of the old wolf in *War and Peace*. In trying to seize the truth that lies at the core of this scene, we are led inevitably to Daddy Eroshka, because it is he who has led Olenin to the stag's lair and it is he who propounds a view of life that is increasingly attractive to Olenin. Eroshka represents an elemental sensuousness as opposed to Olenin's intellectualizings, unrestraint against restraint, indulgence against self-denial. The purpose of life as it is exposited and exemplified by Daddy Eroshka is not morality nor the manifold disciplines that man has invented for himself, but the pursuit of immediate sensuous pleasure. Eroshka drinks, hunts, and lives with his senses; when he was younger, he had killed, stolen, and enjoyed the favors of women. Moral and religious prohibitions, for him, are the fantasies of the Mullah. The real law is the fire in one's blood and the appetites one feels, which one rightly asks to be satisfied. About the enjoyment of women, he says, "Is it a sin to love her? No, my dear fellow, it's not a sin, it's salvation. God made you and God made the girl too." Tolstoy summarizes his view of experience with the generalization that justifies the life Eroshka has apparently come to accept: "When you die, the grass will grow on your grave and that's all." It would seem, given the contrast that Tolstoy pursues between the two men, that Olenin has for a time in the stag's lair accepted Eroshka's view of life. The happiness he feels there seems to be the sign that Tolstoy and Olenin are siding with Eroshka.

Olenin's decision to devote his life to self-sacrifice represents a reversion to that view of life he had held prior to Eroshka's influence. Since Olenin's program of self-sacrifice is represented by Tolstoy as self-deception, then it would seem that Tolstoy is recommending Eroshka's program of simple, natural, and elemental enjoyment of life. This is essentially the way that Merezhkovsky understands the conflict in Tolstoy's attitude, using Eroshka's world view as decisive evidence that the Tolstoy of the early period resolved the conflict between satisfaction of instinct and the denial of instinct by subordinating one to the other. Eroshka is the model, for Merezkovsky, of Tolstoy's early views and the clearest embodiment of what Tolstoy believed in and lived by.[2]

But neither the biographical data nor the evidence of the novel itself will permit us to identify Tolstoy's views with Eroshka without serious qualification, or to accept Eroshka as the philosophical hero of the novel. If Olenin is mocked and satirized because of his romanticizations, idealizations, self-deceptions, and unconscious hypocrisies, Eroshka is similarly mocked, though more subtly. In other words the characterization and representation of Eroshka and Olenin are so made that the reader is asked to distance himself from both and to reject the beliefs of each. What happens in the stag's lair to Olenin is neither an affirmation of Eroshka's philosophy nor an affirmation of self-sacrifice as the goal of life. Neither Christian nor pagan impulses, neither love of the flesh nor hatred of the flesh, neither indulgence nor denial are affirmed in the scene. What Olenin misunderstands is something different and new, something Tolstoy has pursued since he wrote *Childhood* and something that is clear enough for him at this point to dramatize, if not to explain.

Both Eroshka's indulgence of self and Olenin's self-denial are wrong, and the common "untruth" is revealed by the similarity that hides beneath the contrast between the two men. On the surface they could not be more different; Olenin is the sophisticated nobleman from Moscow, reflective, dreamy and sensitive; and Eroshka is the down-to-earth woodsman and the man of action. Yet they get along well. Indeed, Olenin feels at home only with Eroshka; he makes the other Cossacks uncomfortable, but he is at ease with Eroshka and Eroshka with him. What binds the men is a common distance from the real business of life. Tolstoy makes it abundantly clear that Daddy Eroshka is not representative of Cossack life, and that he is not fully part of Cossack life any longer. In the village he is a useless old man, an object of indifference and occasional mockery, someone given to drunkenness, slovenliness, and long stories. Eroshka romanticizes his past and Olenin romanticizes his present and future. But there are two Eroshkas; the Eroshka of the village, where he is something of a pathetic figure, and the Eroshka of the woods. Tolstoy mocks Eroshka in the village, but he does not mock Eroshka of the woods, suggesting that the elemental sensuousness, which has taken perverted forms in his drunkenness, carousing, and sensuality, has its pure and true form in the woods and away from its civilized forms. This conclusion would seem to be strengthened by the manner in which Tolstoy narrates Eroshka's introduction of Olenin to the woods and to the stag's lair.

The Eroshka who takes Olenin hunting in the woods and initiates him into the elemental life of the forest is not the Eroshka who brags about his exploits, reminisces about the past, drinks, and recommends an unrestrained sensual love. In the forest he is the wise old man leading the sophisticate to the elemental conditions of life. The scene reminds us of the initiating scenes that are so common in the works of Hemingway and Faulkner. In the woods Eroshka and Olenin leave behind the sounds and forms of the village, as well as the garrulity of Eroshka and the introspection of Olenin. Eroshka is serious and ritualistic as he leads Olenin to the lair of the old stag. The next day, like Faulkner's Ike McCaslin who must brave the woods on his own, Olenin goes off by himself. There he has his sacramental moment. He finds the lair and settles himself into it, feeling by some process of decivilization that "he was not a Russian nobleman, member of Moscow society, the friend and relation to so-and-so, and so-and-so, but just such a mosquito, or pheasant, or deer." The layers fall away, and the superficies are erased, and for a moment the essential Olenin is revealed. We seem to be confronted for a moment with that core of the onion that Tolstoy seems intent on finding. The experience seems to embody some form of depersonalization, for everything that had constituted Olenin's personality and identity drop away: his social position, name, family, and friends. Such depersonalization would support Merezhkovsky's view that Olenin experiences an immersion in the general life of sense and instinct, as would Olenin's explicit identification with the stag, the mosquitoes, and the creatures of the forest. He says of the mosquitoes: "Each one of them is separate from all else and is just a separate Dmitry Olenin as I am myself." Yet this consciousness of the separate identity of the individual mosquitoes expresses not an immersion in some general life, but intense consciousness of different centers of existence and of his own center. Tolstoy believed intensely in the uniqueness of the individual. An immersion in some general impersonal life was always abhorrent to him. The scene would seem then to present us with a dilemma: it makes clear that Olenin's identity drops away and at the same time that Olenin has an intense consciousness of identity. We can extricate ourselves from the dilemma by noticing that what drops away is Olenin's general and abstract personality, something as general as the sensuous life he is presumably experiencing.

What falls away is a personality composed of such general qualities as position, name, social status, and interpersonal relationships. What falls away, too, is Olenin's conception of himself and his conception of the world about him: what he thinks he is and what society thinks he is; what society has imposed on him and what he has imposed on himself. What remains is an Olenin purified for an instant of the encrustations of the past and the future, of social and personal expectations, of thought and desire. At the height of the experience he does not think of anything or desire anything. What remains is an intense present moment, and an intense consciousness of himself and of the world about him. The "normal" Olenin has kept life at a remove by the abstractions that constitute his specious and willed perception of the world. His own conceptions, thoughts, desires keep him out of touch with reality as much as do social expectations. He touches some immediate source of life when he is emptied of past and future Olenins, and when thought (though not consciousness) and desire are quiet. The purified Olenin is not some undifferentiated and impersonal part of nature; rather, he is intensely conscious of a new identity, the condition of which is the consciousness of the unique identities of other creatures of the world. In this respect the experience is not so much different from those moments of consciousness in *Childhood*, when Nicholas perceives something about himself and the world about him that is different from his own expectations and the expectations of others. Nicholas is in touch with reality and some mysterious source of being when he can separate himself from the expectations of the group.

What Tolstoy is groping for is some definition that escapes the dichotomous oppositions of sense and consciousness, of civilization and primitiveness, and even that of pleasure and pain. Olenin recognizes that the experience would not have had its special happiness if he had not come to experience and accept the pain of the mosquitoes. He even admits that the pain, which almost drove him back to the village, turns into a peculiar pleasure. There is no doubt that Tolstoy has a deep-seated sense of the artificiality and sterility of social forms, but his opposition to such forms does not place him automatically on the side of what is ordinarily opposed to such forms: primitiveness, sensation, and lack of form. Just as his rejection of an abstract intellectual view of the world does not place him automatically on what we ordinarily oppose to intellection: sense. Merezhkovsky's failure to see that there was something other than a choice between sensuous self-fulfillment and self-denial is characteristic of critical opinion on Tolstoy, and explains why we have critics calling Tolstoy the champion of the rational and critics who see him as the champion of the irrational. The thrust of Tolstoy's thinking is to show that some common element underlies such oppositions.

There is a general consciousness and there is a general sensuousness. What Tolstoy is trying to express here and what he is groping for is the conditions under which the world is neither sense nor consciousness but both: something new, thoroughly individualized in sense and consciousness, and something full and good. He seems to have come upon the paradox that the intense, full, and joyful consciousness of oneself is necessarily tied to the recognition that the world about one is just as distinct and unique as one is. One becomes oneself when one permits the world to become itself. In the experience of the stag's lair, life, for Olenin, is no longer at the remove of intellection and dream. Olenin accepts himself and he accepts what is around him. What exists does not exist as a condition of what his idea of existence should be. He permits himself to be and he permits the mosquitoes to be, and no idea, desire, or wish is a condition of what should be. Olenin experiences all this, but he does not understand it.

While he is conscious of what is happening to him, he sees the world about him in sharp and individualized contours; he sees the old and the new trees, one of which is entwined with wild vines; he feels the flutter of pheasants about him and senses that they may be conscious of their slain brothers; and he perceives that the mosquitoes have as much right to exist as he has. But as soon as he begins to reason, the experience becomes confused, and when he reaches the conclusion—to sacrifice himself for others—the joy turns to foreboding, fear, and darkness in his soul. He asks himself presumably the right question: "How then must I live to be happy, and why was I not happy before?" But the very fact that he asks the question puts his present life at the remove of reflection. The experience has shown that Olenin touches deep sources of a new and vital personality when he gives up his special knowledge about what the world is and what he ought to be. Sacrifice is the very opposite of what the experience has shown him. It is a form of imposition on others as aspects of thought and desire are an imposition on one's own life. Tolstoy had already shown the egotistical and self-serving character underlying sacrifice and its baleful consequences in a number of early works, notably in the actions of Masha in regard to the poor peasant Simon in *Family Happiness* and the noblewoman in regard to *Polikushka*.

What is insistent in the three novels that have been considered is the conviction that something good, true, and real exists before it is spoiled by human manipulation, the forms of which, however, seem endless in complexity and subtlety. What the good, true, and real is eludes Tolstoy, at least in clear and full explanation. Whatever he examines turns out to be false. If sophistication is false, so too is simplicity and elementalness. Self-indulgence is as deceptive as is self-sacrifice. If the mind cannot be trusted, neither can the senses. Nothing, except for a few intimations, seems to resist the corrosive and destructive power of Tolstoy's analysis. Yet Tolstoy holds fast to a conviction that there is beneath all the cheating forms some core of reality and truth. The child narrator in *Childhood* knows what is false because he feels what is right; Masha learns what is wrong because she glimpses what is true; and Olenin experiences for a moment what is right even though he misunderstands it.

By the time *The Cossacks* is published Tolstoy has begun to live the golden years of life and art. He is newly and happily married, comfortably settled on his estate in Yasnaya Polyana, and hard at work on *War and Peace*, his most massive attempt to seize the hare. He will be successful beyond his most cherished dreams. In *War and Peace* he will have taken off the final leaves of the onion and will gaze on the firm core of reality. It will seem, after *War and Peace*, that no more need be done or can be done in art and in psychological and philosophical perception. The quest would seem to have ended, and in a sense it is. But not for Tolstoy. He will look at the core of the onion, and he will wonder if it is really the core and whether there is something inside it. A new search and a new start—less light and less happy—will begin with *Anna Karenina*.

5 *War and Peace*

No work in English on Tolstoy has shown such sensitive understanding of important issues concerning *War and Peace* as has Isaiah Berlin's *The Hedgehog and the Fox*. The book is our only extensive and informed study in English of Tolstoy's theory of history. Ostensibly a specialized study, it touches on problems of general import, and none of the problems is more important or has been more widely debated than that of the unity of the novel.

Isaiah Berlin has restated the issue of unity in a new and provocative way. He senses that at the base of all the movement, agitations, searchings, and decisions lies some common truth toward which the "good" characters tend and *from* which the unsympathetic characters have departed. He is persuaded that the acts, quests, agonies, and triumphs of Tolstoy's characters have not been rendered indifferently by Tolstoy but hide meaning and significance. He is persuaded that a center exists, but the center eludes him, and in vexation he cries out, "What is it that Pierre has learnt, of which Princess Marie's marriage is an acceptance, that Prince Andrey all his life pursued with such agony? Like Augustine, Tolstoy can only say what it is not. His genius is devastatingly destructive. He can only attempt to point towards his goal by exposing the false signposts to it; to isolate the truth by annihilating that which it is not—namely all that can be said in the clear, analytical language that corresponds to the all too clear, but necessarily limited vision of the foxes."[1]

If there is a common truth underlying the various experiences of the novel, and the novel has a well-constructed unity, then that truth must in one way or another run through all the experiences. It must be visible in the smallest details and in the major incidents, must embrace the sympathetic and the unsympathetic characters, and must be an important element in the agonized decisions and in the trivial and random decisions. The chatter of the salons must have something

An earlier version of the last section of this chapter (pp. 112–28) appeared in *Midway* 9, no. 2, pp. 117–35. © 1968 by The University of Chicago.

to do with the chatter of the briefing rooms of the Teutonic generals; the truth Andrey searches for with so much agony must have something to do with the truth that Natasha embodies on the night of the ball; what Platon symbolizes, what Pierre discovers in prison, and what Andrey never quite understands must have something in common. Such a common truth must explain for us why some characters founder and why some find meaning and happiness, why some are detestable and why others are loved and admired.

In Berlin's exasperation there is the implication that there may be no center, that magnificent as the novel is, it suffers from a fatal structural flaw. In that attitude there remains a residue of the tradition of English criticism that has looked upon *War and Peace* as something beyond structure and form. Early criticism on the novel was exclamatory in its praise and insistence that the work was in some way more than "art." Matthew Arnold saw Tolstoy's works as "life" and not "art";[2] Havelock Ellis saw Tolstoy as holding up "life up to light" and saying simply, "This is what it is!"[3] Edward Garnett said that "the field of human life explored in *War and Peace* is alike vaster and more detailed than in the Greek epic."[4] For Fausset, *War and Peace* was "less a work of art than a great natural growth";[5] and even such an intelligent critic as Edwin Muir could see "life" as the only point of general reference.[6] Such recent works as Logan Speirs's *Tolstoy and Chekov* and Elizabeth Gunn's *A Daring Coiffeur: Reflections on Tolstoy's "War and Peace" and "Anna Karenina"* have continued this tradition. Logan Speirs says, "His characters are not illustrations of elements in experience, rather they are faithful reproductions of experience itself,"[7] and Elizabeth Gunn says, "We feel we can take it as read, that we have nothing to learn from it. We do not pause to reflect that our reaction, our boredom even, is itself a tribute to Tolstoy's art, the lifelike effect he achieves."[8]

The James-Lubbock attack on the novel owes something to this tradition. Like his English predecessors, James granted Tolstoy "all of life," but what was for them—and continues to be—a term of admiration was for him a term of rebuke. In the preface to the revised version of *The Tragic Muse*, James said of Dumas and Tolstoy, "What do such large loose baggy monsters, with their queer elements of the accidental and the arbitrary, artistically *mean*? We have heard it maintained, we will remember, that such things are 'superior to art'; but we understand least of all what *that* may mean, and we look in vain for the artist, the divine explanatory genius, who will come to our aid and tell us. There is life and life, and as waste is only life sacrificed and thereby prevented from 'counting,' I delight in a deep-breathing economy and organic form."[9] James was right that a novel is never life and is always art. But he was never more wrong and more blind when he denied art to *War and Peace*. Tolstoy's art was not Jamesian art, and James seemed unable to forgive him that.

What James asserted, his disciple Percy Lubbock attempted to explain. Lubbock's Jamesian study of *War and Peace* in *The Craft of Fiction* summarizes both the enthusiasm of the exclamatory tradition and the criticism of Henry James. Lubbock acknowledges generously the first and restates forcibly the second. He grants Tolstoy everything but "design." He finds life, wealth, variety, scope, and the themes of youth and age. But he can find no way of linking the various strands: "It is a mighty antinomy indeed, on a scale adapted to Tolstoy's giant imagination. With one hand he takes up the largest subject in the world, the story to which all other human stories are subordinate; and not content with this, in the other hand he produces the drama of a great historic collision, for which a scene is set with no less prodigious a gesture. And there is not a sign in the book to show that he knew what he was doing; apparently he was quite unconscious that he was writing two novels at once."[10] Several thousand manuscript pages of plans and reflection on the execution of the novel are, among other things, evidence that Tolstoy was very much aware of what he was doing.

Tolstoy has not wanted for defenders against James and Lubbock. Albert Cook has discovered the unity of *War and Peace* in the fact that war and peace are repeated in variation: "The Fifteen Books and the Epilogue are orchestrated into an almost contrapuntal order, war and peace being not as Lubbock thought, disorganized strands, but the basic alternation, each defining the other, of the plot's form. War is repeated with variation; so is peace."[11] R. F. Christian makes the same unhelpful point more abstractly: "In the early parts of the novel the principle of juxtaposing and contrasting peace and war scenes is very obvious. Volume I is divided into three parts. The first is exclusively peace; the second war; the third begins with peace and ends with war. Volume II covers the biggest span of years (1806-12), and except for some brief chapters in the second part it is all peace. Volumes III and IV describe a continuous period of war. But the threads of 'war' and 'peace' are no longer separate and parallel. They are very closely interwoven."[12] John Hagen has given us a "metaphorical" unity. He has told us, for example, that "Anatole's attempted seduction of Natasha is a brilliant anticipation of the rape of Russia by the French in the book which immediately follows, Natasha having been virtually identified with the spirit of the Fatherland in the famous description of her dancing at Uncle's"; and "Anatole's misplaced assurance of success in his proposal to Mary indirectly mocks what is only a little later shown to be the misplaced confidence of the Russians in their victory at Austerlitz."[13] In this interpretation, one may note that Anatole is supposed to be France, Natasha, Russia; and Marya, the battle of Austerlitz. More recent articles—and there has been a perceptible increase in number and quality—seem to be giving up the search for a unifying principle, while not giving in to James and Lubbock. If James and Lubbock implied that the novel was in-coherent, Jerome Thale has boldly put forth incoherence as the virtue of *War and Peace* in a provocative article entitled *"War and Peace*: the Art of Incoherence";[14] and Bert O. States has done something similar by denying that there is any overall unity and insisting that there are "centers" in the novel but no "center."[15] But the defense of *War and Peace* on the grounds of variety and dispersity is an evasion; the definition of unity as a quantitative alternation of chapters of war and peace is a mechanical and external view of unity.

The most tenacious critical tradition on *War and Peace* has been the use of binary critical and evaluative terms. We have been told again and again—both in Western and in Soviet criticism—that the novel is about "illusion" and "reality," or the "city" and the "country," or "primitivism" and "sophistication," or the "rational" and the "irrational" and many other pairs of terms. "City" and "sophistica-tion" are supposed to be bad, and "country" and "primitivism" good. Yet the high point of the novel—Natasha at the ball—takes place in the most sophisticated of settings, and many of the ugly scenes—such as Anatole's attempted seduction of Mlle Bourienne—take place in the country. The "rationality" of the German generals may be bad, but the irrationality of Nikolay's "We must conquer or die" is silly. The following is an example of such frequent binary criticism: "Tolstoy celebrates the intuition over the logic, the heart over the head, the wisdom of experience over the pretensions of theory."[16] But Tolstoy does not always celebrate the heart over the head; sometimes he has contempt for the heart: when it regrets, sentimentalizes, mourns; and sometimes he champions the head over the heart: Prince Andrey's "head" is seldom clouded by the heart, and yet few characters have Tolstoy's approval as often as does Prince Andrey.

People are good and bad for Tolstoy in both city and country; irrationality is pilloried (as in Masonic mysticism) and extolled (as in Platon's simple faith); Natasha's feelings are almost always good; Sonya's often are not. The conventional sets of antithetical terms do not tell us why Andrey's head is sometimes right and sometimes wrong, why Natasha is right at the ball and wrong at the opera, why Sonya says all the right things but inspires constraint and even distrust. Most of all, they do not tell us what the Prussian and Austrian generals, the opera, Anna Pavlovna's salon, and Anatole Kuragin have in common, since it is clear that Tolstoy disapproves of each; or what Natasha, Pierre, Andrey, Platon, and Nikolay have in common, since it is clear that by and large he approves of each.

The design Isaiah Berlin asks for in vexation is something more than the abstractions of city and country, heart and head, naturalness and primitivism; and it is surely more than knowing that war and peace alternate in the chapters of the fifteen books; and he is not content to excuse Tolstoy by granting him "centers" but no "center." He knows that Tolstoy was hedgehog enough to seek a center, and he sees that what happens in *War and Peace* is measured against some standard which eludes him but of which Tolstoy seems sure. Tolstoy himself invited such a search by the unambiguous way in which he sets off his admirable and unadmirable characters, by the indications in situation and detail that there is some measure by which to discern when certain vital principles of life are touched and when they are not. It is this measure that Berlin charges Tolstoy with failing to make clear.

But the center is there, and without a clear conception of it we will have no adequate conception of the unity of the novel. My conviction in the existence of such a center stems not only from the extraordinary genius of Tolstoy and the firmness and wholeness with which he views the artistic task he understakes, but also from the distinctness with which value situations are communicated. There is no ambiguity or uncertainty about who is good and who is evil, who is wise or foolish, cunning or ingenuous, and what is vain, false, and hypocritical. We know whom to admire and whom to contemn. We know that Princess Ellen is a coarse and stupid woman, that Anatole is vicious and predatory, and that Prince Vassily is a consummately fashioned social creature, just as we know that Ilya Rostov is a delightfully foolish but well-intentioned person, that Prince Andrey is strong-willed, austere, and honorable, and that Natasha is a lovely and beautiful creature. What is more, we not only recognize these distinctions easily but we accept them as probable. We accept without demur a thousand value distinctions that have been silently integrated into the dramatic structure of the novel. We would not respond to such distinctions if they were not there, and we would not accept them as probable if they were based only on authorial decree. We accept them because Tolstoy has so presented his world that the nexus of circumstances and the movement of events operates without violating our sense of fitness, logic, and probability. In other words, we accept some principle by which we instinctively measure what is right and wrong. That measure is our center. Unless we can discover that measure, we will fail to grasp the wholeness of the structure and the principle of its life and movement, and our interpretation of various characters and actions will be based on other "wholes" drawn from the works of other authors or from our own experience.

The core is there even though Isaiah Berlin failed to find it. Tolstoy constructs *War and Peace* on a gradation of deflections from that magic core where life is full and the truth is lived. Such deflections do not coincide with any neatness with the particular characters. It is obvious that Pierre is better than Prince Vassily, that Natasha is better than Ellen, that Andrey is better than Anatole. But Pierre and Andrey are not always right, and when they are wrong, they are wrong for reasons that are grossly manifested in Prince Vassily and Anatole Kuragin. If one were to use an image to explain the deflection of life from the truth, it would consist of a center with concentric circles of increasing size and distance from the center. The distance of each concentric circle from the center would be the measure of deflection from the truth. Some characters like Prince Vassily, Boris, Julie, Ellen would be condemned to some outer circle, there to revolve without change and life throughout the novel. Others, like Nikolay and Princess Marya, would revolve in nearer circles without change until a decisive moment in their lives propelled them for a time into the inner core. Pierre would stumble in and out of it. Natasha, for a while, and Platon Karataev would stand in the very center. Most important, the distorting or deflecting principle that keeps one from the magic center would be the same, though more forceful and tenacious for some than for others. It is not the "right" character and the "false" character that will lead us to an explanation of Tolstoy's truth, but the right force and the wrong force that draws some *at some moments* to the inner core and keeps some by a counter force revolving lifelessly on the edges. Andrey, whose fate we follow with so much attention and care, will have traveled throughout most of the circles and touched on occasion the center, without ever fully making it his own. His is the most agonizing search.

Andrey

No one searches for the truth with more agony and persistence than does Prince Andrey, and no one is better equipped to find it than he. Tolstoy has given him almost everything: character, keen insight, intelligence, independence, high birth, wealth, courage. Andrey hates what is stupid and corrupt and admires what is true and good. It is he who sees that Napoleon is a strutting peacock, vain with the imaginings that he moves history; that war is not glorious but a dirty business, filled with illusion and deceptions; that Speransky and the world of politics, like war, are deceptive and trivial. He sees the inanities of the generals, the foolishness of Nikolay's romanticism; he is able to understand what is wrong with his father's life, and he is even able to understand that Princess Marya's faith is abstract, rigid, and unreal. Yet he is not able to understand what he is looking for, even when on occasions he experiences it. He almost understands; he touches the right relationship, but something within him keeps him from the truth.

In his quest for the truth he is deflected again and again from the center of truth and happiness. It is almost as if the very force of his intellect is the deflection that keeps him from entering the radiant center. He gives his beliefs repeatedly to what he thinks is true, and repeatedly his beliefs fail him. Each time this happens, he withdraws into the carapace of cynicism and skepticism. He has lived for love and marriage and they have failed him; for glory and Napoleon and they have failed him, for Natasha and reborn love, and she has betrayed him. Whenever faith has filled his heart, life has poisoned it. Even the last sanctuary of faith in family ties is held on to by form alone, as he goes off to join in the battle to save Russia. As the invasion of Russia draws near to his beloved Bleak Hills, he cannot feel a shred of affection for his son; he cannot follow his sister into her unreasoning faith; and he can only pity a father who has outlived his wits and who is victimizing his daughter. He has seen life for what it is, and what fools and hypocrites accept he refuses to accept. When on the eve of the battle of Borodino he goes over his life, the summing-up is terrifying. For him the deceptive light of life is like the light of a magic lantern, which throws over reality the false and cheating colors of glory, of the good society, of love for a woman, and of love for the fatherland. His sharp intelligence and perception have brought him to see life free of illusion and deception, but what is left without the cheating colors is the cold light of annihilation and meaninglessness. On the eve of the battle the green and yellow leaves and the white bark of the birch trees, the clouds, and the fires—false and cheating colors—become weird and menacing to him. There remain only death and annihilation, and Andrey on the eve of the battle goes willingly to embrace them.

Andrey is right about almost everything. He is right that war is romantic nonsense, that Napoleon is pompous and vainglorious, that the salons of Saint Petersburg are beneath contempt, that his father has outlived his wits, and that Princess Marya is deceiving herself with a false faith. He is right about everything, except the biggest thing. In Andrey's own words: "There was something in this life that I didn't understand and don't understand." He almost understands—on the battlefield of Austerlitz when he gazes at the sky, when he looks at the old oak and carries on his strange and meaningful dialogue with it, when he stands on the ferry with Pierre and looks once again at the sky, when he falls in love with Natasha, and when he looks at the face of his dead wife. Tolstoy calls these his "best moments." In each of them he comes close to important things that he does not understand, but each time something deflects him from the truth.

We meet him first at Anna Pavlovna's soiree, in the atmosphere of falseness where the impresario Anna Pavlovna has arranged her spinning shuttles so that everything and everyone will fit into the atmosphere of graciousness and propriety. Andrey has already come to regard this kind of life with barely disguised contempt. The image of the half-closed eyes that Tolstoy gives him is a sign of the distaste he has for society, a physical reflex that half shuts out the repugnant world he must take part in. He is sick to tears with the salon chatter, the innane forms and hypocrisies of social life; and he is sickest of all of his wife and their marriage. Whereas Andrey does not fit into the social setting, Andrey's wife is the perfect product of that climate. She is a butterfly sprung from the social larva and kept alive by the chatter, the warmth of the room, and the glitter of the jewels. She flutters from guest to guest and from flowery compliment to flowery compliment. Only Pierre stirs the life of warmth and friendship in Andrey. Like him, Pierre does not fit into the social mechanism. He does everything to upset it; he bumps into people, interrupts conversations, raises his voice, defends the wrong causes, and argues too long and too heatedly. But Andrey knows he doesn't fit and Pierre doesn't know it. Pierre doesn't fit because he doesn't see; Andrey doesn't fit because he sees too much. Pierre violates all the forms and doesn't know that he is violating them; Andrey obeys most of them but does so perfunctorily, tiredly, and with scarcely disguised contempt. He tells Pierre, "I am a man whose day is done."

But it is not done, because the possibility of living for glory revives his faith, and he goes off to war to find his "Toulon" as did Napoleon. The same corrosive intellect that has led him to see the triviality and falseness of society leads him to see the deceptions and illusions of war and glory. Tolstoy measures Andrey's development toward disillusion by contrasting it in the Austrian campaign with Nikolay's reaffirmation of illusion. Both men go off to war with faith in the rightness of war and the personal significance of glory. Both men meet situations that are at variance with what they believe, and one accepts what he encounters and alters his beliefs, and the other disregards what contradicts his beliefs. At Ems and Schongraben Nikolay learns that war is confusion, that situations and not men command, and that he can fear for his personal safety and even commit a cowardly act. Yet he comes out of his baptism of fire with his illusions of glory and personal bravery intact. His initiation into the hypocrisies and illusions of war is crowned by his acceptance of a lie as truth, when he is forced to give up personal honor in order to save regimental honor and affirm—against the grain of his personal experience—that there cannot be thieves in a hussar regiment.

Andrey sees that war is confusion; encounters the imbecilities and indifference of the Austrian court; perceives that it is Tushin and not Bagration who saves the day at Schongraben; experiences the dirt, cruelties, and hypocrisies of war—but accepts them and is changed by them. He is still romantic enough at Austerlitz to pick up the standard and to charge the enemy; but as he lies near death on the battlefield and gazes at the sky, a decisive change takes place in him. What Andrey perceives as he gazes at the limitless and infinite sky and listens to the vainglory of Napoleon is a contrast between the limitless expanse of life, both within and outside him, and the narrowness of man's conception of it. Napoleon is the embodiment of the early glory; his voice is specifically contrasted to the vast silence of the infinite sky, as the scudding clouds (a metaphor for the temporary and constantly changing circumstances) are contrasted to the unchanging and immovable blue. Andrey feels that he has perceived something important but misinterprets the experience, as he will misinterpret all his "best moments."

What moves in Andrey's soul at Austerlitz is similar to what moves in Natasha's soul and what Platon Karataev believes in and what is one of the elements of the magic core: that life is incomprehensible. Andrey takes this to mean that there is nothing to know, and as a consequence lapses into skepticism after Austerlitz. But the perception and belief that life is incomprehensible does not mean for Tolstoy that there is nothing to be known, but only that the mind cannot know it. Andrey turns incomprehensibility into comprehensibility. Andrey Bolkonsky knows what life is: a mean and dirty business, where only the values of family and one's immediate interest are of any account. Part of the deflecting force for Andrey is the control he exercises over experience. The universe is never an "unknown" to him; it is always known, and this "known" judgment oscillates between positive and negative poles. When one set of beliefs fails, Andrey reasserts another set, and by such reassertion reaffirms his control of what life is and what it should be. In this respect, as in others, he is the son of his father, lacking only the single rigid and unvarying code by which his father lives. It is only when he is caught off guard, when his intellect and judging faculties are relaxed, that he glimpses truth and comes close to the center. This happens on a number of occasions, but each time only for a short while before his mind stops the flow within him and reduces its complexity and joy to the measure of his own conceptions. It is a weakened, wounded, and half-conscious Andrey that touches a truth on the battlefield of Austerlitz, a weary and depressed Andrey who looks at the sky again with Pierre on the ferry, and a day-dreaming, half-dozing Andrey who catches sight of something significant when he sees the slender black-eyed girl in a yellow gown at Otradnoe. In each case the truth comes to him when he has stopped trying to reach it, when his thinking and judging faculties and acute self-attention have been relaxed, either by sickness, exhaustion, or a kind of absent-mindedness.

We get our first impression of Andrey after the battle of Austerlitz, when Pierre, flushed with his new-found faith in Freemansonry and with his plans to regenerate the human race, visits him at Bogutcharovo. Andrey is happy to see Pierre, but Pierre sees an Andrey whose face is dead; his eyes are lusterless, and no gleam of happiness lightens his face. Andrey's life has grown small, and he has withdrawn into himself and to what is close to him. His view of life, to Pierre's consternation, is resigned and cynical: he does not believe in God, reforms, love of one's neighbor, self-sacrifice, and living for others. He believes only in himself and in those closest to him, his son and his family. Only what is private and personal have meaning for him, and he tells Pierre that the only evils in the world are remorse and sickness. With this doublet we think of his father's insistence that the two evils of the world are idleness and ignorance. Whenever Andrey feels bitter about the world, he resembles his father in word and gesture. Pierre has just returned from a tour of his estates, where he has worked to bring about needed reforms: to lighten the load of the peasants, liberate pregnant women from hard work, reduce taxes, and encourage education. Andrey does not believe in the usefulness of any of this. He is convinced that schools destroy the peasant's animal happiness and teach him to toss in bed thinking about problems he doesn't need; and that medicine stretches out the life of an invalid when it would be a kindness to let him die.

Pierre's goals by every conventional touchstone are admirable and Andrey's are reprehensible. Yet Pierre's aims and efforts come to nothing, and Andrey's to fruition. Pierre is duped and deceived by the peasants: the chapel he thinks he is having built was built many years ago by wealthy peasants; he believes that he has lightened the lot of the peasants, but nothing really is changed, and nine-tenths of them continue to live in destitution; he orders nursing mothers to be relieved of working on the master's lands, but they are forced to work harder on their own plots; he orders the rent on the land to be lowered, but his steward raises the labor so as to more than compensate for the lowered rent. Although Pierre glows with a sense of accomplishment, his actual effect on the life of the people is nil, and in a few cases he has hardened their lot. Andrey, on the other hand, has quietly liberated three hundred serfs, changed the lot of others from forced labor to payment of rent, engaged a trained midwife at his expense to assist the peasant women in childbirth and a priest at a fixed salary to teach children to read and write. Andrey insists that he is not contradicting himself in stating that he believes only in himself and his family and then doing acts of seeming benevolence for others. He insists that his acts, though seeming to be benevolent, are practical acts, the consequences of which accrue to his favor.

The ironic disapproval of Pierre's conscious benevolence is not unexpected since Tolstoy had expressed disapproval of such conscious goodness in many of his early stories—explicitly in the aunt's letter to Nekhludov in *The Landowner's Morning* and in the disastrous consequences of the lady's faith and trust in *Polikushka*. Tolstoy knew and showed repeatedly that conscious goodness and benevolence were self-serving and abstract, almost always an application of principle without regard to the actual circumstances at hand and consequently almost always ineffective and often harmful. In this respect, then, Andrey is speaking with Tolstoy's words, as he surely is, despite the seeming callousness of the pronouncements, when he speaks of the harm of education and medicine. Yet despite the fact that Andrey expresses some of Tolstoy's basic beliefs and is surprisingly effective in his practical reforms, he does not embody Tolstoy's right relationship to life. The true sign of the right relationship to life, as will be so clearly evident in the instance of Natasha at the ball, will be the fullness of life. Andrey is not happy and his life is emotionally barren. Yet Andrey, in his insistence on living for himself, touches on what will be one of the elements of Tolstoy's right relationship to life, as is the element of incomprehensibility. But just as Andrey minunderstands the "incomprehensibility" of the infinite sky at Austerlitz, so too he misunderstands and misapplies the true meaning of living for oneself.

In the beautiful and eloquent scene on the ferry when Pierre and Andrey, believer and skeptic, share a moment of deep friendship, Andrey himself perceives for an instant how barren his life is. Pierre has just waxed eloquent about his view of God: "We must live, we must love, we must believe that we are not only living today on this clod of earth, but have lived and will live forever there in everything (he pointed to the sky)." Andrey, his eyes fixed appropriately not on the sky that Pierre had pointed to, but on the reflection of the dying sun on the bluish stretch of water—that is, not on the symbol of truth but only on its temporary reflection—sighs and turns away with the words, "If it were only so." He is skeptical and weary and unbelieving, but as he turns to leave, he glances at the sky, and "something that had been asleep in him, something better in him, suddenly awoke in his soul with a young joyous feeling." As at Austerlitz, the sky awakens something within him more full and lifegiving than the narrow confines that cynicism and skepticism have made of his life.

Both Pierre and Andrey, at the Bogutcharovo meeting, are convinced that life will not change the faith of one and the skepticism of the other. But a short time later life has worked changes that neither had thought possible. Pierre's faith is eroded by circumstances and time, and Andrey's skepticism is dissipated by reentry into political and social life of the capital and by his love for Natasha. Tolstoy will show again and again that every belief, principle, ideal, and value and every intention, judgment, and understanding of others and of oneself will be modified by time and circumstance and in ways that are impossible to foresee. When, after betraying Andrey, Natasha sobs out her conviction to Pierre that her life is at an end, the tears she sheds in Pierre's presence water the tendrils of his heart. As the death of Petya brings Natasha back to life, so the misfortune of imprisonment brings the good fortune of inner peace and happiness to Pierre. Events are not always what they seem to be, and people are not always what they seem to be to others and to themselves. Nikolay Rostov, a slavish adherent of the hussar code, is naive and incompetent in money affairs. Yet after his father dies and the Rostov fortunes disappear in a mire of debts, he reveals suddenly an unexpected reserve of character and stoically repairs the Rostov fortunes. Princess Marya cannot guess at the fund of will and determination she discovers in herself after her father's death; Andrey cannot know when he talks to Pierre on the ferry and tells him that life holds nothing for him that he will soon be madly in love with Natasha. Pierre cannot know after he leaves his wife Ellen, and when life appears to him to be without logic and meaning, that he will soon be a devout believer in Masonic truths and that later he will find them to be foolish and hypocritical. Time and the incomprehensible flow of events that it carries within itself are always beyond the will and understanding of individuals. This is something Andrey never understands.

One is always conscious of the gnawings of time in *War and Peace*. Edwin Muir has spoken of an astronomical clock that hovers over the world of Tolstoy and against which human events are measured with a deadly regularity and a celestial indifference to the hopes and wishes of individuals.[17] He is only partly right, because the clock ticks away in the phenomena themselves; any rampart thrown across the underground channels of time collapses in the end, and nothing can contain its force except that which moves with it. This is true of Nikolay's "forever" vow of love and fidelity to Sonya, Bolkonsky's fortress against time and contingency at Bleak Hills, Marya's dedication to the other world, the inexhaustible coffers of the Rostov's culinary munificence, and the form and texture of Russian life before Napoleon's invasion. Andrey can say after Austerlitz that he will never serve in the army again, even if the war should come to Bleak Hills itself. But his "never" is an idle straw in a gale; Napoleon does come to Bleak Hills and Andrey discovers feeling he had never believed possible within him. No ideal, no matter how noble, can withstand the grain of time that seems to wear all things away or, more accurately, never ceases to change them, into outlines that no one can anticipate. What changes is good, and what does not is bad. By virtue of such an axis, what we ordinarily consider to be good can be bad, and what we ordinarily consider to be bad can be good. Sonya's fidelity to Nikolay strikes her own life with sterility and for a time strikes Nikolay's life with constraint, uneasiness, and some deception. If it does not change, the most disparate phenomena meet or turn on the axis of lifelessness and sterility, as do love, the inanities of military strategy, and faith in God. But to acknowledge that the ends toward which one travels are incomprehensible is to acknowledge that one can be different and that those about you can be different—all of which Andrey cannot do.

Yet Andrey does change in part as he is confronted with new circumstances and always in ways that he did not anticipate; yet in the end he misunderstands the new life that wells up within him and by that misunderstanding dries up its springs. After Austerlitz and the conversation with Pierre, Andrey rediscovers life even though he believes that there is no life to discover. Tolstoy expresses this renewal by a natural symbol. In the spring of 1807, Andrey makes a trip to check on his son's estates in Ryazan. The weather is soft and the dormant forces of nature are stirring with the promise of wild profusion. In a forest covered with the sticky sprays of green birch leaves, Andrey comes across an old oak ten times the thickness of the tallest birch, double a man's span. Spring has not touched the old oak; dressed in its bare and broken branches and gnarled arms, it appears like an aged, angry, scornful monster among the smiling birches. To Andrey the oak seems to say, "Spring and love and happiness! Are you not sick of that eversame, stupid and meaningless chatter?" To Andrey it seems that the oak by virtue of its age and experience has lost its faith in life and by virtue of its wisdom is refusing to give it back again. It seems to say what is in Andrey's soul: "Others, young creatures, may be caught anew by that deception, but we know life—our life is over."

But the sap of life runs in Andrey also and the desire for life springs out unexpectedly, even while the mind denies it. When he rides down the avenue leading to the Rostov house in Otradnoe (on his trip to see the marshal of the district, the old Count Rostov), and sees the slender, black-eyed girl in the yellow gown, playing and laughing, in her happiness completely unaware of his existence, something stirs deep within him far beyond the control of his mind and will. That night, he cannot sleep. In a scene reminiscent of the night in which Masha and Sergey fall in love in *Family Happiness*, the trees Andrey looks at from his window are black on one side and silver on the other; drops of dew sparkle on a roof not far away, and below his window a moist profusion of vegetation stirs. Looking out over this almost magical setting, Andrey overhears a restless Natasha, filled with impossible spring joy, exclaim to Sonya that she cannot sleep. Nature, moonlight, and the young girls's voice stream through the open window. For the second time that day something Andrey does not understand stirs within him. Her voice calls forth in him forgotten youthful hopes and desires. On his way back he looks for the old gnarled oak. He has a hard time finding it, and when he does, he cannot see it, for it has changed radically. Life has panoplied it with a tent of sappy green leaves, and nothing of its old aged mistrust can be seen. Life has conquered it, as it is beginning to reconquer Andrey.

The stirring of new life within Andrey, as a result of the experience with Pierre, and with the oak and of his meeting with Natasha, moves Andrey to seek new activity and to take part in life in some way. But again Andrey misunderstands what moves within him and seeks life in the wrong place. His admiration for Speransky is like his admiration for Napoleon—an admiration of worldly power. He understands the stirring of life within him in terms of power, will, and control. He gains the favor of Speransky, sits on councils, ponders the political fate of Russia, and wishes with all his heart that he had the thoroughly rational control of life that Speransky possesses. What had stirred the renewal of life within him was a thoughtless young girl wholly absorbed in her own being and the circumstances of the moment, and the sight of an old oak, which abandoned its mistrust to the wild profusion of life. Yet Andrey seeks to confirm and realize these stirrings of new life within him by the practice of rational control of life. It will take the meeting with Natasha at the ball to renew what had stirred within him and to bring it to reality.

After the ball, Natasha's first effect upon him is to provoke his disillusionment with Speransky. He had been for Andrey the cleverest, the most perceptive, and the most rational of men; after the ball he becomes suddenly something of a fool. Everything that had charmed Andrey—the same characteristics, the repartee, the clever remarks—all produce exactly the opposite effect. Andrey marvels, too, how he could have spent four months occupied with things so trivial as the translation of the Roman and French legal codes into Russian, his project for army reform, and the sittings of various committees. Just as he had lost his faith in marriage and in glory, so now he loses his faith in political astuteness and in liberal reform. The force of life that had been revealed to him when he lay on his back at Austerlitz now reveals itself for him in his love for Natasha. The love for Natasha that fills his heart is the same immeasurable and illimitable force of life that had stirred in him for a moment at Austerlitz and on the ferry with Pierre. Yet he is unable to keep Natasha. Once again the golden apple has only dust at its core for Andrey. His great love ends in a great betrayal and in what seems to him to be a foolish, tawdry escapade. Once again Andrey is hurt and disappointed by life and once again he withdraws into a carapace of cynicism and skepticism. The pattern is clear: faith and betrayals and withdrawal from life for Andrey, with increasing disillusionment, increasing reluctance to trust life, and increasing skepticism about love and values in general. The love he feels for Natasha will be his last great faith. It had taken Natasha's extraordinary vitality and love of life to overcome his distrust of life. After the loss of that love he will have nothing but doubt and cynicism to give to the world.

When Pierre sees Andrey on the morning after he returns to Moscow, after he has learned of Natasha's betrayal, he meets a cruel, hard, and pitiless man. The love that had filled Andrey's life is now presented as an interruption in his public career. Pierre enters to find Andrey engaged in a conversation about Speransky's dismissal. What had occupied him before his love for Natasha continues to occupy him after the love is dead. Once again, though with qualification, he is defending Speransky. His pride, too, has swallowed up all his other emotions, and he seems to want to obliterate every trace of what he had felt for Natasha. Neither the love he had borne her, nor pity for her suffering, nor understanding, compassion, or memory touch him. Pierre's look of compassion for him angers Andrey. He answers Pierre's repeated attempts to stir his pity for Natasha's suffering and sickness only by cold and formal politeness, punctuated by a laugh that resembles his father's. Natasha is no longer a particular person but "the countess." When Pierre says, "She is very sick," Andrey answers, "Oh, she's still here"; when Pierre says that she has been near death, Andrey retorts with the formal, "I am very sorry to hear about her sickness." He wants to show that the betrayal was expected (as he tells his sister), that it was a paltry thing (his unruffled concern with the events of the day), and that it has made no difference (he tells Pierre this). What had been personal and concrete becomes public and impersonal. Andrey is no longer living for what he feels but for what society has decreed. Though he has only contempt for society, he reaffirms its hold on him by his bitter concern for his honor. It is Andrey's ugliest moment, ugly because he is concerned with abstractions and not with the living person.

With the failure of love, Andrey falls into the deepest skepticism yet. The disorder and destruction the war brings to Russia answers to the mood of Andrey. As he goes off to fight, life appears to him to be a series of senseless phenomena following one another without connection. His hopes, talent, intelligence, and lofty feeling have come to shoal on the rocks of indifference and despair. But when he realizes that his beloved Bleak Hills is in danger and his family threatened, he makes a sentimental journey back to the estate. The threat of the approaching French has emptied the place. Only a house servant has been left behind, who, sunk in reading the lives of the saints, seems dreamily indifferent to the events swirling about him. As Andrey is leaving, he sees two little girls who have just stolen some green plums and, on seeing him, scamper off squealing. For an instant he sees and becomes aware of human interests, lives, and feelings utterly remote from but just as legitimate as his own. He has had such a perception and sensation before, at Ryazan, when he first saw Natasha. The charm and nascent love he had felt then had come from the mysterious awareness of a being other than himself. Something for an instant moves inside of him when he sees the little girls with the stolen plums, so that for a moment he seems to understand the one big thing he has not understood. But the feeling passes away, and Andrey goes off to war and the decisive moment of Russia's destiny. He goes off with a mind understanding less and less and a heart sick with unmeaning and chaos.

What he has not understood he seems to understand when he is moved in the presence of death to forgive his enemy Anatole Kuragin: that the truth resides in the Christian love and the forgiveness of one's enemies. He forgives his enemy Anatole and the woman who betrayed him, Natasha. He seems to speak with Tolstoy's words when he says, "Love hinders death. Love is life. Everything, everything that I understand, I understand because I love. Everything that is, everything exists only because I love. Everything is connected with this. Love is God, and to die means that I, as a particle of love will return to the universal and eternal source." Yet there are troublesome parts to Andrey's meditations: "The more he thought about the essence of eternal love, which had been recently revealed to him during the hours of lonely suffering and half-delirium, the more he renounced unconsciously earthly life. To love everything and everyone, to sacrifice oneself always for love meant to love no one, meant not to live this earthly life. And the more he penetrated into the essence of love, the more he renounced life and the more completely he annihilated that fearful barrier between life and death. During that early period when he remembered that he had to die, he said to himself: 'Well, so much the better.' " Love that leads one to renounce earthly life and to love no one seems like a caricature of love. Indeed, Tolstoy seems to insist on the opposition of life and divine love by showing that Andrey departs from divine love to the extent that he becomes reattached to Natasha. When hope and desire arise, divine love wanes and the fear of death grows.

These scenes have been taken almost without exception as evidence of Andrey's "rebirth" and illumination before death. The forgiveness of Anatole, the words "God is Love," fit comfortably into beliefs Tolstoy is known to have espoused as a man most of his life but especially after his conversion. But they do not fit in with the "truths" that Tolstoy dramatizes in the novel itself: there is little talk of God in the novel, and the sacramental scenes—those in which we know that something true and real have been touched—have more to do with an immersion in the sensuous life of this world than with Christian beliefs. Nikolay's sacred moments at the wolf hunt, Natasha's at the ball, are affirmations and not denials of sensuous life. Pierre's revelations in prison have little to do with God and divine love and much to do with giving up his preconceptions of what the world and his life should be and an acceptance of what life brings. Even "Christian" Karataev talks very little about God and acts out a passive and unquestioning acceptance of the moment and the reality at hand. God, if he is present in the novel, is never a litany of conventional Christian beliefs, but an incomprehensible force which is identified with a flow of phenomena beyond the conceptions, plans, and designs of any particular individual. Kutuzov acts on such a belief, and invokes God's name only in ritualistic and conventional religious scenes. Princess Marya is the only sympathetic character who seems devoutly to be a believer in Christian concepts. Tolstoy undercuts her beliefs, however; he points out that they are something of a compensation for a narrow and constricted actual life by revealing to us her secret dreams for the earthly joys of marriage and children.

We can make Andrey's "conversion" a revelation and attainment of the truth he has sought only by ignoring much of what Tolstoy has said in the novel, and by substituting the "conventionalities" of Christian belief that Andrey espouses on his death bed for the vital truths that Tolstoy has dramatized. The words about God and divine love are not Andrey's; they contradict the kind of character that has been painted for us in hundreds of pages; they are a set of beliefs that a dying man has accepted intellectually and under stress. Tolstoy himself seems to support this interpretation by characterizing Andrey's words of universal love as too intellectual: "These thoughts seemed to him comforting. But they were only thoughts. Something was wanting in them; there was something one-sided and personal, something intellectual, they were not self-evident." Andrey goes to his death without finding the truth he has searched for so long. His words when he is taken off the battlefield of Borodino best characterize his life at its end: "There is something in this life that I didn't understand, and don't understand." His religious faith on his deathbed is like all his other faiths, something abstract, intellectual, and removed from experience.

Although Andrey dies without understanding that "something," he has almost understood it in what Tolstoy calls his four "best" moments: when he sees the old oak panoplied in green, "all the best moments of his life rose to his memory at once: Austerlitz, with that lofty sky, and the dead reproachful face of his wife, and Pierre on the ferry, and the girl thrilled by the beauty of the night." To understand why they are the best, one has to find out what they have in common. Three of them involve the sky: Austerlitz, the black night when he first meets Natasha, and the sky when he talks to Pierre and something youthful and joyful moves in him. The sky is that infinite and incomprehensible world in which the individual lives and which answers to the incomprehensible being in himself. The Andrey who judges, analyzes, reasons, and thinks is limited by the will and conceptions of Andrey, but the sky is there as a reminder that there are other Andreys and that life within him is infinite. In each of the moments he catches a glimpse of something that is not circumscribed by his understanding. It may be difficult to think of the reproachful face of his wife as a "best moment"; yet in that moment Andrey understands, for the first time, that he has violated by his judgment the sacredness of her being. She has always been for him an object of scorn and disapproval, and what he understands is that her life was not his to circumscribe and delimit.

Andrey's "best" moments are related to other best moments in the novel: Pierre in prison and Pierre's friendship for Platon Karataev; Nikolay at the hunt; and most of all Natasha at the ball. If we can seize what is common to these moments—what it is that animates Natasha at the ball, what happens when Nikolay gallops across the field to kill the old wolf, and what it is that Platon Karataev represents and what Pierre learns from him—we will have seized the core of Tolstoy's onion and will have understood what Berlin asked for and concluded in vexation was not there.

Whatever that core is, Andrey does not seize it. The one big thing he fails to understand is that the universe is not his, that life is independent of his beliefs, wishes, and expectations. In regard to people this means that other people need not be what Andrey expects, wishes, wants, and demands that they be, and Andrey need not be what he expects and demands that he is. The world is not Andrey's alone; it has millions of centers, and one begins to see reality when one acknowledges centers of interest, feelings, wholly different and yet just as legitimate as one's own, as Andrey does for a time when he is in love with Natasha, and as he does for an instant when he sees the frightened squealing little girls who had stolen the plums. To see the center of another is at the same time to acknowledge the uniqueness of that person. But to acknowledge the uniqueness of another person and to acknowledge the uniqueness of oneself is to permit life to be what it is: that is something incomprehensible in its movement and change. It is to permit life to be beyond one's knowing, beyond the categories of thought and the impulses of emotion to limit it; it is to refuse to enclose it in static thought or emotions or to imprison it by judgment.

Pierre

If Prince Andrey never finds that "something," Pierre does. Andrey touches the rim of the inner circle, but the force of his judgment and his inability to permit life—his own and others'—to be different from what he can conceive and what his subjective nature demands deflect him from the core. Pierre steps into the center, at least for a while, and touches the magic point as Andrey does not. Tolstoy gives to the life of both something of the same pattern, so as to throw into relief the difference. Pierre, like Andrey, alternates between faith and dis-illusionment and trust and skepticism. Pierre is trapped into a stupid marriage, as Andrey felt he was trapped into a trivial marriage, but we cannot conceive of Andrey being manipulated, as Pierre was, into a marriage with someone as stupid and coarse as Ellen. Pierre, who gives his faith with less discernment, arrives at his disillusionment more slowly and clumsily than does Andrey. We cannot imagine Andrey believing in the foolishness of Masonry or in a destiny of saving one's country by killing Napoleon. In comparison with Andrey, Pierre is foolish, unattractive, naive, and at times stupid. Yet it will be Pierre, and not Andrey, who discovers for a time that right relationship with reality that Andrey has sought with so much strength and discern-ment, and it will be Pierre who marries the girl who is the best embodiment of that right principle of life.

What is involved here is more than an impulse on Tolstoy's part to defeat expectations, although this undoubtedly plays some part. Our normal expectations as readers would be to have the best of men, Andrey, fall in love and marry the best of women. Tolstoy almost permits this to happen, but only, I think, to raise and defeat our romantic anticipations. Still, Pierre is more than a factor in a process of deromanticization. The qualities he embodies are elements of the right relationship to life. His clumsiness, naiveté, inattentiveness to social detail, blundering idealism are all necessary conditions to lead him to the truth; they are not the truth but they permit him to receive the truth. By and large what distinguishes Pierre from Andrey is a looser hold on experience, a less rigid judgment of what is right and wrong. Like all the characters who glimpse and embody the truth, he does so for a short time. When he believes in Napoleon or Masonry or in his appointed role to save Russia by killing Napoleon, he is deflected from the center. But when, in prison, on hearing of the execution of prisoners, he confesses to the incomprehensibility of life and the ways of men, he is on the threshold of truth. Although despair on this occasion is the condition of truth, it can be also the deflecting force, as it was on former occasions when Pierre lapsed into despair after the duel with Dolokhov and after he became disillusioned with Masonry. Neither belief in Masonry nor disillusionment with it brings him to the truth. Neither a belief in human perfectibility nor a belief in human viciousness take him to the circle. Tolstoy's world spins on another axis.

It would appear that Tolstoy approves of Pierre; that Pierre is a carrier of some truth value for Tolstoy because of his antisocial or asocial stance. Pierre does not fit into the sophisticated, polished society of Saint Petersburg, and no contrast could be greater than the consummate product of that society—a Prince Vassily, for example—and Pierre. Tolstoy likes to emphasize the self-regulating power of such a society, in which everything fits and everything has its place, and everything is anticipated. He shows the effect of this upon its participants in the opening words of *War and Peace* in the conversations between Prince Vassily and Anna Pavlovna, by emphasizing not only the marionette quality of the behavior but also by underlining the automatic quality of the speech. Each anticipates what the other is going to say; each completes what the other starts. The opening conversations set the tone to the rest of the evening, in which human relations are shown to be arranged, planned, predictable (even spontaneity and unpredictability have been prearranged) and consequently inhuman and dead. Neither Pierre nor Andrey are part of Anna Pavlovna's spinning shuttles, and it is clear that Tolstoy marks that as a sign of spiritual health. Pierre breaks in on conversations, talks too long and too heatedly; he is absent-minded (while saying good-bye he pulls out the feathers from a general's hat), and he is a constant threat to Anna Pavlovna's arrangements. He is moved by some force inside him, not something outside him.

It is this "unfinished" quality in Pierre that is subsequently brought into the machinery of the sophisticated social life, first by Anna Mikhaylovna—a kind of desperate and poor female Prince Vassily—then by Prince Vassily, and finally by Pierre's marriage to Princess Ellen. There is no doubt that Tolstoy looks upon this process of "socialization" as a process of "corruption"; still, it would be a mistake to localize, as has been so often done, the spiritually deflecting or corrupting principle in "society" and the spiritually attracting or purifying principle by some antisocial or antisophisticated principle. The truth is not that crude, and there is too much in the novel to deny it. One need only point to Prince Andrey, who is so carefully compared to Pierre and embodies much of the same rhythm of belief and despair that Pierre does, to deny this relationship between society and corruption. There are, of course, even more blatant exceptions to such localization: Natasha, who will be our fullest embodiment of the right relationship, lives in a sophisticated setting, and her highest moment takes place in the most sophisticated setting, the kings's ball. The old Prince Bolkonsky will have nothing to do with salon life or the corrupted life of the cities and the courts; yet, whatever his rough charm, he is stuck whirling on some concentric circle at mid-distance between the center and the peripheries. The best one can do is to take note that the "corrupting" principle is at work in sophisticated circles (but is not to be identified with it topographically or socially). It is without doubt at work in all members of the Kuragin family and in Boris's mother and indeed—except for a few lapses—in Boris himself. With these qualifications firmly established, we can go on to trace the progressive, though temporary, corruption of Pierre at the hands of Boris's mother and the Kuragins. The efficiency and speed of their corruption of someone as basically good as Pierre are testimony to what Tolstoy, in *Anna Karenina*, will call "this crude power."

When the novel begins, Pierre is on the fringes of society in habits and position. He is brought back to the realm of the socially respectable by the power of the wealth he inherits from his father and the ministrations of Anna Mikhaylovna. He is the supremely manipulable person, and Anna Mikhaylovna is the supremely manipulating person. Vicious and desperate, she will do anything to assure her son's future. Pierre is her pawn. By helping to establish him as the rightful heir, she hopes that he will be more easily persuaded to help

Boris. She embodies the predatory reality of the society she lives in, without being veiled by its usual good manners and propriety. She cannot afford the good manners. In the world of the Anna Mikhaylovnas and Prince Vassilys, Pierre is stupid and helpless. As Anna Mikhaylovna guides him up the back stairs to his dying father, Pierre feels that everything that is happening to him is inevitable and that he is taking part in a mysterious and secret ritual, the signs of which he cannot interpret. The point of this journey to the dead is to take him from the shores of unrespectability as a bastard to social respectability as the legitimate son of one of the richest and most powerful men in Russia. He is being reborn and invested with a new identity. The priest and priestess of this rite are Prince Vassily and Anna Mikhaylovna. Tolstoy likes to convey the power of the "socialization" of the soul as the spiritual "remaking" of a person, so that the qualities we find in a person spiritually alive are duplicated in a mechanical and dead way in the sophisticated setting. A kind of compassion, love, kindness, and friendship continue to take place in a ghostly and ghastly imitation. Prince Vassily, for example, actually feels pity for Pierre's dying father, and tears flow from his eyes. The second life has so established itself in his body that the tension of hypocrisy or the consciousness of imitation are no longer there.

Nowhere does Tolstoy show the operation and nature of such "imitated" spiritual life better than in his description and narration of Pierre's love affair with Princess Ellen. The love affair and marriage are the completion of what Anna Mikhaylovna had initiated in taking him to his dying father and legitimacy. With his father's death, Pierre becomes one of the richest men in Russia. Just as suddenly he also becomes, in the eyes of those who surround him, a new and different Pierre—no longer awkward, fumbling, absent-minded, but attractive, interesting, and good. Pierre's courtship of Ellen is a grotesque parody of natural love, as society itself is a grotesque distortion of natural life. During the courtship Pierre listens to two voices—the small voice within him and the louder voice of society, which is embodied in the insistent hum of Prince Vassily's suggestions. When Pierre listens to the voice within him, he sees things as they are and he is ashamed of what is occurring. His inner voice tells him that Ellen is stupid, coarse; that he cannot possibly fall in love with her. But the voice of society tells him that Ellen is beautiful, gracious, and clever. Pierre never courts Ellen, never falls in love with her, and never proposes to her. It is all done for him. Society creates the courtship and the love, as it has created Pierre as a clever, interesting, and attractive creature. He is

expected to court Ellen. Anna Pavlovna brings them together; Prince
Vassily leaves them together, and everyone expects them to remain
together. They are bound together not by feeling but by the glances of
Anna Pavlovna, the remarks of Prince Vassily, and the attitude of the
guests. What Pierre is expected to feel is assumed by everyone about
him, and he is too weak to defeat their expectations. After six weeks of
courtship Prince Vassily is ready to consummate what he helped
create. The guests at Ellen's named-day party laugh, jest, talk, drink
their Rhine wines eat their ices, and studiously ignore Ellen and Pierre.
By ignoring them everyone implies that they are very much in love and
cannot possibly be interested in the trivial banter of dinner talk. The
choices are made for Pierre and even the actual proposal is made for
him. Prince Vassily makes it for him by assuming that it has been
made, and Ellen, not Pierre, seals it with a brutal kiss. It is no accident
that she takes off his spectacles—as a final sign of his inability to
see—before she kisses him. Pierre is taken from courtship to marriage
without desiring, acting, or feeling.

The separation I have endeavored to make between society as such
and the corrupting or deflecting force may be seen in the process of
corrupting Pierre temporarily. It may be formulated in this way: Pierre
is manipulated into the marriage by the expectations of Vassily, Ellen,
and others of the society. The society preempts his choice, gives him
feelings (or attempts to give them to him), and generally assumes in
advance what it wants to see. Pierre's actions and feelings do not
follow upon the movement of his heart but upon what is assumed.
The sexual feeling he experiences when he leans over Ellen to see the
snuff box is not, for Tolstoy, some upsurge of a natural instinct but is
itself part of the repertoire of socially-conditioned feelings and actions.
What corrupts Pierre is present in the sophisticated salon society of the
life of people like the Kuragins. The corrupting force, however,
has its roots in something more basic and something more widespread
than in a specific social class. Though salon society may do the
corrupting, the social relations that obtain there have been themselves
corrupted by something broader and deeper and less easily extirpable.
Indeed, what I have called the deflecting force is not coextensive with
class, or specific beliefs, or indeed with religious attitudes. The
corrupting force of the Kuragins—as they trap the hapless Pierre into a
marriage he does not want—may be a particularly blatant form of the
principle, but it is in kind no different from the deflecting force in
Pierre's idealism and his despairs. Nor is it different from Andrey's
truthful analyses of the world on the ferry with Pierre, or from the
deflecting force that is lodged in Princess Marya's religious faith. Yet

that said, one must admit that at times Tolstoy seems to charge salon society with a personal invective more intense than it would merit in the structure of his world.

Pierre's openness to experience makes him susceptible to the kind of manipulation that the Kuragins habitually exercise. But only for a time. After the duel with Dolokhov and his estrangement from his wife, Pierre falls into a skepticism about the value of life as deep as Andrey's. Yet it takes only an hour's chance conversation with a Masonic leader to rekindle his faith in mankind. Pierre accepts the juvenile formulations of the Masons with studious seriousness. He accepts the hypocrisy, muddledness, and childish play as true coin. That Pierre gives his faith willingly is both his undoing and his salvation. What is empty ritual, he take to be the embodiment of the highest aspirations and the model for moral rejuvenation. His foolish willingness to believe will set him apart from Andrey. Pierre is always ready to believe; Andrey, to disbelieve. The pattern of his life is to be repeatedly duped, then, recognizing how he has been duped, to yield to skepticism. Duped into the marriage with Ellen, he falls into a state of hopelessness; duped into believing in Freemasonry, he then retires into the mire of the English club in Moscow. As the novel progresses, he loses his faith in society, marriage, Freemasonry, and in his ability to work for the improvement of the human race.

No experience shows the difference between Pierre and Andrey more graphically than does the battle of Borodino. Borodino and the war seal Andrey in his despair; for Pierre too they lead to despair but also to a new life. Throughout their lives both have swung between belief and disbelief, but with the war Andrey's pendulum grinds to a halt and Pierre's swings more frantically. Borodino has the function of bringing the various fates of other individuals too and the nation itself to a climax and resolution. Tolstoy pursues an analogy between domestic affairs and the war. As Russia's fate reaches its crisis, so too do the fates of his principal characters. As the war overwhelms Russia, so too does it overwhelm and demolish the princedom and life of old Bolkonsky; it disorders and reorders the life of Princess Marya, destroys the love for her father, brings her a love for Nikolay Rostov; the war brings to Natasha the love of Andrey and its loss, then the new love for Pierre; it is before and at Borodino that Andrey confronts the confusion of his beliefs, seizes and misses something true in his last visit to Bleak Hills when he saw the girls stealing plums. It is also the time when the various strands of Pierre's life come together, in a way of course, that neither he nor we could have anticipated.

Tolstoy believes that experience proceeds by mysterious and yet orderly currents. He believes, as I have said repeatedly, that there is a center, a truth to be seized, an objective ground to experience, from which or to which, in some mysterious ways, we can be deflected or attracted. Experience is not chaotic—neither for individuals nor for nations—though the direction may be difficult if not impossible to perceive. The war may disarrange life and blow patterns into designs difficult to gauge, but as such it has only done more quickly what is always being done. There is no chaos in the movement of nations and none in the movement of men. The axes hold steady. The most that Tolstoy will concede to chaos is "incomprehensibility," that is, designs forever beyond the understanding of the intellect, although not out of reach of immediate consciousness.

The various strands of Pierre's life come together to form a pattern that began in the first pages. He has either been unaware of this pattern or has misinterpreted it, as he is surely doing in his increasingly wild conceptions of himself. His plan to save Russia by killing Napoleon is the result of one such self-conception. His interpretation of the apocalypse and especially his reading of his own role in providential history is a grotesque yet accurate caricature of man's attempts to pierce through to the logic of events. Indeed, Pierre seems at this climactic juncture of Russia's fate and his own to embody extremes of various sorts, a tendency that was apparent in the ease with which he tumbled from hope to despair and back to hope. As the crisis sharpens and as Russia moves closer to victory or defeat, so too does the inner life in Pierre sharpen. He seems to reflect in his own life something of the inner chaos of events, the loosening up of what is fixed and steady in Russia's national life. There is something bizarre and unsteady in his life, as he moves from dispassionate observer of the battlefield of Borodino, to manager of his estates, to plotter against Napoleon, to hater of the French, albeit good-natured friend of Captain Ramballe. Tolstoy is preparing Pierre for his spiritual rebirth in prison, and one of the conditions of his rebirth is that what has been fixed and ordered must become unfixed and disordered; the old patterns must dissolve for the new to appear. Andrey's control of his life and of experience was always firmer than Pierre's; although Andrey changed under the pressure of experience, he also remained the same.

In order to become a new Pierre, he must divest himself of the old. He must cease to be Pierre Buzukhov, inheritor of a great fortune, husband of the most beautiful woman in Saint Petersburg, habitué of the English club, Freemason, and philanthropist. He must lose for a time wealth, rank, nobility, and even his name. He must divest himself also of a pretension to truth and special destiny. Pierre's moral change begins at the battle of Borodino. There Tolstoy calls attention to his inappropriate dress by noting his wide-brimmed hat; for his clothes, like his inner self, are at odds with the event he is beginning to participate in. Later, when he is beginning to see reality and to experience true happiness, he has only a tattered shirt left of his old clothes. The outer divestment parallels an inner divestment—of illusion, intentions, searchings for meaning. Pierre does not give up fully his old self until he sees the French execute some prisoners. A spring of some kind in him breaks, and his habitual world falls apart. He no longer believes in himself, or in God, or in the harmonious structure of the universe. Falling into what looks like skepticism, he is actually performing an act of humility. Pierre has descended to despair and skepticism many times before, but this time the fall is deeper and more complete. On other occasions the readiness with which Pierre came to believe again was a sign that his despair was not complete. In prison he confesses to a general, final, and irrevocable despair before the irrationality of the world. One cannot fail to note at this point that Andrey too, at Austerlitz, confessed to the incomprehensibility of the world, as does Pierre here. Yet for Pierre such an acknowledgment is the condition and prelude of his spiritual regeneration, whereas for Andrey it led to a reinforcement of his cynicism. What is the difference? It lies, I believe, in the fact that Andrey refused to let go of his claim on the world; he saw that the world was not knowable but did not see that it was not his right to know it. The spring never broke in Andrey; it just grew tauter. What breaks inside Pierre is the false self with its subjective demands, claims, and illusions about truth. Once that breaks, he is ready to receive the truth rather than make it.

What Pierre gives up is unambiguous: the outer man defined by his clothes, property, name, money; and the inner man defined by his conceptions of good, right, God, love, and countless other beliefs and emotional commitments. What he gains is not easy to understand, even though it is put forth as one of the central visions of *War and Peace*. Not that Tolstoy does not tell us what it is: it is happiness, peace with oneself, inner harmony, satisfaction. But these are only abstractions. If we insist on asking what it is that Pierre learns, Tolstoy gives us an array of outrageous paradoxes, consciously formulated and impudently put forth: Pierre is most free when he is imprisoned; happiest when devoured by lice and devouring horseflesh; and most at peace with himself when his friend and teacher is dying from disease and later is executed by the French. It is in the face of such paradoxes that E. M. de Vogüé threw up his hands. That Pierre, the aristocrat, should have been enlightened by a simple peasant was beyond Gallic logic: "At this point I despair in making my compatriots understand what is being said; I repeat only what is. The wise, civilized, noble Bezukhov seeks to be taught by this primitive creature; Pierre has finally found his ideal of life, and his rational explanation of the world is embodied in this simple soul."[18] Tolstoy is not saying, as he has been so often interpreted as saying, that Pierre's happiness depends on the privations. Nor is he saying, as de Vogüé seems to understand, that the truth is to be found in peasants and simple souls. Rather, Tolstoy is saying that nothing material is necessary to attain happiness. When Pierre returns to his properties after the war, he is as free and happy and self-possessed as he was in prison. The happiness is wholly inner; neither opulence nor privation can destroy it or create it. But opulence may make it harder to see and privation easier. What Pierre learns in prison and what he embodies briefly is embodied fully in Platon Karataev; what Platon Karataev embodies, Natasha lives; and what both embody is what Andrey glimpses on the battlefield of Austerlitz and in the best moments of his life.

Critics have had no hesitation in telling us what Pierre has learned from Platon, and what Platon embodies and symbolizes. And they have done so with remarkable unanimity. Romain Rolland's characterization of Platon is representative: "He has a Russian heart. Russian fatalism, peaceful and heroic, is personified in this poor peasant, Platon Karataev, simple, pious, resigned, smiling in suffering and in death."[19] Hagan's characterization is even more typical: "He lives close to the soil; and he is a model of love, self-sacrifice, and submission to the will of God."[20] Noyes speaks of his "all-loving self-effacement";[21] Fausset, of his being "a personification of self-lessness";[22] and Redpath speaks of his "spirit of self-sacrifice,"[23] which is shared by "Pierre, by Natasha, and, in the course of time, by Andrei."[24] So it goes: for Western critics almost without exception Platon is always pious, sacrificial, Christian, and all-loving. The Soviets, disliking Platon, use other terms, but they say something of the same thing: that Platon is passive, unindividual, and foolishly humble.

There are, however, problems with the conventional characterizations of Platon and especially with the Christian truths he is supposed to embody. There is nothing self-sacrificial, humble, unselfish, or Christian about the truths that Pierre takes from Platon. When Platon falls ill of fever and his strength begins to fail, Pierre keeps aloof from him, tries not to think of his moans, and is careful not to come close enough to smell his decaying flesh. Ivan Karamazov confesses to Alyosha that he could never understand the Christian love that reputedly moved "John the Merciful" to put his mouth to a freezing beggar's mouth festering from disease. Neither could Platon, nor Pierre, nor Tolstoy. When Pierre hears the shot that kills Karataev, he does not interrupt his ruminations about how far it is to Smolensk; when he sees the soldier who apparently killed Platon running by him with a smoking gun, he thinks—trivially—how the day before yesterday the soldier had burned his shirt while drying it over a fire; and when the full realization of Platon's death comes to him, he thinks of a summer evening he once spent with a beautiful Polish lady on the veranda of his house in Kiev.

Pierre's seeming moral hardness and insensitivity and lack of love is nevertheless the vital condition of the new spiritual power he has attained. It is the way Platon—Tolstoy reminds us—would have acted if Pierre had died. Platon, we are told, has no attachments, friendships, or love as Pierre understands those things. He loves no one in particular. Despite the affection Platon feels for him, Pierre knows that Platon would not suffer a moment's grief at parting from him. What kind of self-sacrificial Christian loves no one in particular, has no friendships and attachments, and feels affection for another only when he is in his presence? Platon Karataev does not live for others, but for what is before him: for what he can feel, see, hear, and touch. He is so unreflective and so "immediate" in his reactions to life that he is almost without memory: he does not know how old he is; he never knows what he is going to say when he starts a sentence; and he cannot remember what he has said after he has said it. It is true that there is a ritualistic trust in God and a fatalistic streak in Platon. Thus Platon marvels how well everything turned out when he went into the army, even though he looked at it first as a misfortune. His favorite story, too, is about the false imprisonment of the merchant for a murder he had not committed. The trust in God's will is, of course, an item in traditional Christianity, but Tolstoy is making some serious modifications of traditional Christianity in the person of Platon, as he does in other parts of the novel, and these modifications question such traditional virtues as "self-sacrifice" and "living for others." Platon loves only what is before him—what the incomprehensible force acting in immediate time moves him to love. Lasting ties, friendships, love, as well as their opposites, hate and enmity, are subtle impositions of personal measures on what is unmeasurable. Imposing such personal measures is what Andrey does when he decides that the world is not knowable; what Pierre does when he decides that he knows what is best for his peasants; what Sonya does when she "loves" Nikolay forever and by that fidelity preempts what he will be and what her feelings will be in the future.

Tolstoy has perceived—dimly in the early works but clearly now— that there is a coercive force at work in even our brightest ideals, as there is in such traditional Christian virtues as love, friendship, sacrifice, fidelity, and humility. He has perceived that there is an impulse in human beings to constrict the world of others and themselves according to some fixed and personal measure. There is no doubt that this is what Pierre learns from Platon, and it is the very opposite of what the tradition of criticism on Tolstoy has asserted: Pierre learns self-affirmation rather than self-denial, a living for self, rather than a living for others, a trust in the immediate, unknowable flow of circumstances even if such trust violates what the traditional virtues of lasting friendship, love, and affection demand. If there is any doubt that Tolstoy is making such a serious modification of traditional Christian virtues, one can turn to his treatment of Princess Marya, who is the embodiment of such virtues and who by the practice of such virtues seriously restricts her life and that of her father.

Princess Marya

Princess Marya has been universally admired for her spirituality, patience, and self-sacrifice. R. F. Christian praises her for her "gentleness, deep faith, long suffering, humility and addiction to good works."[25] Fausset praises her "integrity of a single religious faith,"[26] and Hagan says resoundingly, "To live in accord with the Order of God is, essentially, to share the vision of Karataev, Princess Mary, her God's Folk, and ultimately, of Pierre and Prince Andrew—to practice an ethic of love, self-sacrifice, and cheerful submission to whatever life may bring."[27] But none of these critics, or others, have put the same emphasis on the undercurrent of unreality and unintentional cruelty that runs through her temperament. The prince is unforgivingly cruel to his daughter in the daily ritual of punishing geometry lessons which hover between comedy and terror, and in the daily texture of his relations with her. But Marya, too, is cruel to him, though less obviously. She reflects in her unvarying and unreal self-sacrifice her father's unvarying and unreal resistance to change, and she reflects and reciprocates his cruelty. Indeed, she plays an important part in provoking her father's cruelty to her by refusing to admit her father to be what he is: a brusque, punishing, frustrated, and arbitrary old man, as well as a courageous, strong-willed, and honorable man. For her he *must* always be good, honorable, and without fault. His violent outbursts and abuse of his daughter spring partly from his impotent frustration before the image the daughter has of him as always the same. Her unrealistic faith in the old man is the wall she has built around him, which, he, sensing it, attempts to rend by fury and cruelty. The father, at least unconsciously, wants the daughter to assert herself. Her invariable humility is itself a provocation to assaults against it. Both father and daughter are locked in a relationship in which the unreal identity of each is reinforced by the unreal identity of the other—a classic Freudian neurotic situation. Although Tolstoy never plumbed the depths of the human psyche, as did Dostoevsky, his genius and that of Freud's had to meet in the universal patterns of humankind. Both father and daughter have unreal views of the world and unreal views of each other. The father's unreality is more obvious and direct.

Old Bolkonsky has built a fortress outside himself and inside himself against contingency and others, most of all against those he loves. He is no Prince Vassily or Count Rostov. He is intelligent, strong-willed, disciplined, honest, and direct. Yet his insistence on commanding reality and believing things to be as he wants them to be leads him increasingly to estrangement from life, sterility in human relations, and cruelty not only to strangers but also to his loved ones. Rejected by the world—he had been exiled during the reign of Paul—he has in turn exiled the world. His ceaseless energy and compulsive exactitude are not only weapons to control the conditions of his life; they are also defenses against what threatens him. All vices for him spring from idleness and superstition, and all virtues come from energy and intelligence. As a tribute to energy he endlessly turns snuff boxes on his lathe; as a tribute to intelligence, he ceaselessly works out problems of geometry. Most of all he has walled himself off from chance. Everything is fixed and regular to the split second in his life. He sleeps from twelve to two, receives guests only at two, and gives Princess Marya a geometry lesson at the same time every day. He never departs from his schedule no matter what the occasion. Whenever he enters a room, somewhere a clock chimes. Life may change outside the walls of Bleak Hills: fops like Prince Vassily may gain court favor; peacocks like Napoleon may frighten present-day generals; the idle and the stupid may turn the wheels of public service in the capital—but none of this will affect the life of Bleak Hills.

Not even the news of the death of a beloved son is permitted to disarrange what Nikolay Bolkonsky has built. On the morning he receives news of his son's probable death, the prince goes for his morning walk as usual and he turns his lathe as usual. But the control is too much. When he turns to scream the words of Andrey's death at his daughter, he lets go of the lathe, and it comes to a grinding halt. Princess Marya is to remember its dying creak long afterward, because the lathe and its insistent whir are a sign of the control that her father has imposed on his life and on the lives of others. It is like the secret axis on which his world turns; when it stops turning, so does the world that he had constructed. The love he bears his son is a chink in his inner fortress, as is the love for his daughter. The tie to the daughter is closer and the socially available defenses weaker. He can rely on the convention of honor, on the suppression of emotions between father and son and on his son's strength too. Even so, his voice is shrill and disturbed as he grabs for the rhetoric of honor and shame in bidding his son good-bye, when Andrey leaves for the Austrian front. The battle against his daughter's love and his for her is sharper and more unrelenting, so that only the daily bruising by insult and humiliation can keep it at bay. The drawbridge to the outside world can be kept up, and the manor house at Bleak Hills can rest in dreamy remoteness from the events of the day; but there is no defense against the contingency within the castle. The intensity of Bolkonsky's rage against his daughter is a measure of his feeling for her.

Whatever Marya's motive, she exercises likewise an intolerable control over the prince, condemning him to abstraction and constriction in the unchanging image she has of him. She mirrors, too, in her belief in the other world and in her attempts at self-sacrifice the same unreality about the world that does the prince. Her retreat into suffering faith and the solaces of the other world are defenses against the pain and sterility of her present world. Her faith, which permits her to bear the barrenness of life that the prince has subjected her to, permits her also to find reasons by which she can persist in her worship of him. Only his death liberates her from the punishing pattern of love and cruelty. It is only when her father is dead and she is alone, and circumstances press in upon her during the peasant revolt, that she responds to what is actually in her and not what she would like to have in her. And what is actually in her, as she shyly admits to herself in unguarded moments, is a desire to live happily in this world; for though she speaks of heaven, her heart dreams in secret of the earth and of children, husband, and hearth. It is no accident that the new Marya, born of and responding to the movement of circumstances, is the woman who touches Nikolay's heart, breaking down his habitual responses. Nikolay himself is able to respond to the disconsolate and suffering Marya because she is at that moment a prisoner of the rebellious peasants. She is a damsel in distress, Nikolay is the heroic and rescuing count. Her distress appeals mightily to his romantic nature. Sonya had oppressed him with the fidelity of her word and her unvarying sacrifice and had never understood that what Nikolay, in his unvarying romanticism, wanted more than anything else was to perform sacrifice rather than receive it.

There is no doubt that Marya becomes a different person after her father's death. Before his death too, she is unmistakably cruel in her treatment of Natasha, when Natasha visits her father during Andrey's absence. Bolkonsky is petty, vicious, and gleefully insulting, but Marya too, less openly, is cold and unkind to the hapless Natasha. This is Marya's tribute to her father but her own action nevertheless. Nor is she displeased to learn that the engagement is terminated because of Natasha's faithlessness. I am of course not judging Marya as vicious. No one can deny the fund of basic generosity, fairness, and kindness, not to say of compassion and willingness to suffer, that we find in her nature. It is because her nature is such that the distortions that come from it are significant. Tolstoy is perhaps being deliberately provocative in challenging our conventional set of values, though, to judge from critical opinion, his challenge has gone unnoticed. He is saying that the fullness and beauty of life will not be found in conventional Christian values. Princess Marya is not his ideal—as many have taken her. Her actions and qualities are not an example of one of the best moments but a subtle deflection from that radiant core where life beats full. No one by any stretch of the imagination can find moments of plenitude and happiness in the life she leads at Bleak Hills. These qualities are to be found in Natasha, and Natasha and Marya are opposites in temperament and response to life. Even the images of heaviness and slowness that characterize Marya's temperament are in contrast to the quickness, lightness, and constant movement that characterize Natasha.

Natasha flits from boyfriend to boyfriend. She is a creature for the pleasures and feelings of this world. She is undoubtedly Tolstoy's finest flower, and it is to her—and especially at her most sacred moment at the ball—that one must go to seize those qualities that define the unknown *x* that the young Nicholas of *Childhood* was already searching for. What Andrey sees in the face of his wife and in the sky at Austerlitz, the feeling he has when he first sees Natasha, the words he speaks to Pierre on the ferry, and what he perceives in himself when seeing the little girls stealing plums in his last visit to Bleak Hills are all adumbrations of what is to be found in Natasha at the ball, as are the qualities of Platon and the knowledge of what Pierre had learned from Platon in prison. Tolstoy has taken leaf after leaf from his onion, and what is left is Natasha—especially Natasha at the ball. Princess Marya may inhabit a circle near to the radiant core, but only Natasha stands in its center.

Natasha

We may find fault with what Tolstoy does with Natasha in the epilogue: fattening her waist, deadening her wit, narrowing her views; but no one would want her different at the ball when she is unable to see herself in the mirror at the top of the staircase because the intensity of her inner life has misted her eyes and blotted out her vision of outer life, or when she sits outside Moscow sunk in private sorrow for a love lost and a beloved rediscovered and watches without seeing an empire burning. We meet her first in Tolstoy's sacred place, in the bosom of her family, and at the sacred time when she is beginning to feel herself to be a woman. She bursts onto the scene by violating social decorum, breaking in upon her parents, burying her face in her mother's lace kerchief and hiding a doll in her petticoat, overflowing with excitement and life over some inconsequential joke. She infects those about her with good feeling, dissipating the stern rebuke that had formed itself on the countess's lips. A few minutes later, hidden in the potted shrubbery of the conservatory, she watches with girlish curiosity as Nikolay kisses Sonya. In imitation, she tries to coax Boris to kiss her; then, impatient with his reluctance, she kisses him.

As in this opening scene, she is always in movement. When her brother Nikolay comes home in 1806 after the battle of Austerlitz, she throws herself on his neck, and even more impulsively on Denisov's neck, hugging and kissing him to everyone's embarrassment. When she interrupts her mother at prayer, she cannot stand still, grimacing, sticking out her tongue at herself, leaping into bed, and playing hide and seek with the covers. Her movement is contrasted with the immobility of Sonya and the heaviness of Marya's step. Marya believes in God, dreams of dedicating her life to the godfolk, and is restrained from a life of penury and sacrifice only by the equally weighty virtues of honor and respect for her father. Marya is heady with virtue; Natasha is light with the inconsequence and frivolity of her actions. Tolstoy seems to underline the triviality of the scenes in which Natasha bursts with happiness as if to emphasize that life needs no reasons to overflow. She lives in what is before her. Life is never kept at a distance by intellectual, religious, or philosophical conceptions. The movement is outer and it is inner. No viscosity of the soul fixes her in unvarying attitudes, either of envy or of sacrifice, of fidelity or of desire. Nikolay and Sonya may seal the future with their kiss, but Natasha seals nothing but the moment. She knows who she is in the moment, and she gives nothing to the past or the future. Yet, as we know, she can go wrong. She steps into the magic core of Tolstoy's world at the ball, and most decidedly steps out of it with her betrayal of Andrey. At the ball she shows us how it feels to be "right"; in the betrayal of Andrey she shows us how that right relationship can be corrupted and what corrupts it. It is these two situations that span the complexity, beauty, and vulnerability of Natasha, and by extension, the axes of Tolstoy's moral world.

In preparing for the ball she gives herself to what is before her— dresses, hems, shoes, and coiffures. She immerses herself completely in the tasks at hand so that the ball itself is an abstraction. It is not real for her until she is in the place itself, that is, until her senses are touched by the colors, sounds, textures, voices, and atmosphere of the ball itself. She thinks of the ball for the first time only when she is in the dark swaying carriage. In the carriage she tries to imagine the flowers, the music, the dancing, the tsar, but thoughts and images are no substitute for reality. She cannot believe in what she imagines until she is there. It is only when she steps out of the carriage and onto the red carpet, when she climbs the staircase and the colors, sounds, and objects are actually before her, that her mind and imagination and inner self become one with the reality around her. Imagined reality or abstract conceptions are not enough for her. So thoroughly is she in what is outside her that when she looks into the mirror at the landing of the staircase, she cannot see herself in the reflected maze of dresses and figures. It is as if Tolstoy wanted by this image to signify Natasha's absorption into the immediate sensuous reality about her. She is, in a sense, everything reflected in the mirror.

Natasha is from a social point of view unimportant: this is her first ball, and the Rostovs are on the lower rungs of the social ladder. When an aide unceremoniously pushes them against the wall to make room for others, the true measure of their importance is taken. It is not the importance of the Kuragins, particularly of Princess Ellen. But if Princess Ellen is the queen of Saint Petersburg, she is not Tolstoy's queen. In Tolstoy's eyes Natasha outweighs Ellen, the great statesmen, and even the tsar himself. Tolstoy contrasts the lacquerlike hardness of Ellen's shoulders and the fullness of her breasts with the thinness of Natasha's arms, her barely outlined bosom, and the frailness of her shoulders. She is still a child in the temple of wickedness. Tolstoy underscores the child in the emerging adult when Natasha picks up her arms to embrace her father as he comes toward her, and then, remembering that she is a young lady and not a child, lets them drop.

Mme Peronskaya is the guide for the near rustic Rostovs, pointing out to them who is who in Saint Petersburg society. She is our public voice. When she speaks, Natasha is silent. The public world about Natasha and the world within her are contrasted, as are two kinds of vitality: the noise and hubbub of the outside world and the beat of Natasha's pulse and heart. Tolstoy uses the same word, *blesk* (glitter, brilliance), for both the social world and for Natasha. Mme Peronskaya's chatter about the public world fills the air around Natasha but does not reach her. The intensity of her inner world is such that it obliterates the outer world. She cannot see clearly: the light and sheen "blinded" her; and she cannot hear clearly: the sounds of voices, steps, greetings "deafened" Natasha. The glitter (*blesk*) of the outer world becomes the glow (*blesk*) of the inner world. The English translations have not preserved Tolstoy's careful annihilation of hearing and sight. The Russian bristles with meaningful ambiguity in the phrase: "Svet i blesk eshche bolee oslepil ee" (the light and sheen blinded her all the more). In Russian the word *svet* means both world (here specifically the world of high society) and light. Literally the glare of the lights, jewels, and dresses have "blinded" Natasha, but metaphorically it is the social world that blinds her, in the sense that her sight becomes closed to it. She has no need of its light, because another kind of light burns in her. As Mme Peronskaya's voice drones on, there is no indication that Natasha hears or sees anything that is pointed out. She hears and sees only what concerns her: "Natasha heard several voices asking about her and felt people looking at her." Mme Peronskaya points out the Dutch ambassador, Princess Ellen, Anatole Kuragin, Boris Drubetskoy, and the host and hostess who bob up and down like marionettes, greeting every entering guest with the same words, "Charmé de vous voir." It is as if the droning voice of Mme Peronskaya and the repetitive gestures of the hosts were externalizations of the mechanized spiritual life of those present.

Dead to a dead world, Natasha awakens only when a real feeling touches her, the feeling for a friend, Pierre. She sees Pierre slouching through the crowd, walking as through a marketplace. Even the slouch is important, for awkwardness in so much decorous regularity is a touch of spiritual life. Mme Peronskaya is not Natasha's guide, but Pierre is. As her eyes follow him, he takes her to a handsome dark man of medium height in a white uniform, Prince Andrey. It is appropriate that a real feeling should take her eyes to a real friend, who then takes her to what will be a real love. Andrey, at Pierre's request, rescues her from a young girl's terror of not dancing at her first ball, and Natasha rescues him from the weighty deliberations of the previous day's proceedings of the State Council. Her charms take him to thoughts and feelings that his habitual attitudes can only dismiss as nonsense: he catches himself thinking, as he sees her at a distance, that if she goes first to her cousin and then to another lady, she will become his wife. The nonsense itself is a sign of the spiritual change Andrey is undergoing under Natasha's influence. One of the effects of Natasha's infection of others takes the form of changing their normal way of acting, thinking, talking, and perceiving. She disarranges Andrey's life, Pierre's life, and even Boris's life, making him forget for a while that his mission in life is to marry an heiress.

Everyone is charmed at the ball by the mysterious vitality that flows from Natasha. Yet she notices no one. She does not notice Princess Ellen's success, that the tsar has talked for a long time with the French ambassador, that such and such a dignitary has talked with another dignitary. She does not notice when the tsar arrives or when he leaves. She notices no one; yet everyone notices her. She seeks to impress no one and impresses everyone. Tolstoy tells us that she is at that highest point of happiness when a man becomes completely good and does not believe in the possibility of evil, misfortune, and sorrow. With Natasha and through her, Tolstoy is saying that one is good because one is happy and not happy because one is good. We know that we are in the presence of some sacred truth: the mysterious plenitude of life seems to consist in Natasha's intense absorption in the present and some extraordinary sensitivity to the concrete and sensuous life about her. We know Natasha is in full center of Tolstoy's magic circle and that the concentric circles about her vibrate with increasingly less intensity as they recede from the center. What is the center?

We will find no explanation of it in the tradition of enthusiastic praise for Natasha. Everyone acknowledges that Natasha is charming, beautiful, vital; that she is Tolstoy's fairest creation. Noyes goes so far as to call her the finest female creation in all literature. Since Turgenev's initial dislike of her, it is hard to find any critic who does not like her. But despite this veritable orchestration of praise from Western and Soviet critics alike, there is virtually no explanation as to what she represents, apart from such adjectives as "instinctive" or "natural." Even the usually acute Merezhkovsky lapses into the general rhetoric of indiscriminate impressionism in her presence: "How tenderly and firmly is tied the knot of her human personality! Of what evasive, fine, and various gradations of spiritual and physical life is woven this 'chastest model of purest charm!' "[28] Bayley has sub-chapters on almost everything in *War and Peace*, but none on Natasha, implying that her character needs little explanation or commentary. The same is true of Steiner. Only the Soviet critic Bocharov in his excellent small work on *War and Peace* seems attentive to the mystery and complexity of Natasha's character. He notices that she has a way of breaking down their habitual way of seeing things. But like Bychkov and other Soviet critics, he is driven to see her as in some way an embodiment of the people, and by that he means a Soviet heroine.[29]

R. F. Christian's work on Tolstoy, while original, judicious, and always well documented, tends to reflect much of what one would call general opinion on Tolstoy. Especially significant is Christian's attempt to formulate the "focal idea" of *War and Peace*. He believes this idea to be exemplified by Natasha and the right characters in the novel:

> It is not easy to express in words the focal point of Tolstoy's novel. Broadly speaking it is the contrast between two opposite states: on the one hand selfishness, self-indulgence, self-importance, and the attendant evils of careerism, nepotism, vanity, affectation and the pursuit of purely private pleasures; on the other hand, a turning outwards from the self, a groping towards something bigger, an endeavour to surmount individualism, a recognition that the cult of the self is an unworthy alternative to the service of one's neighbours, one's family, the community and the country at large. Most people, Tolstoy appears to be saying, are preoccupied most of the time with their own selfish cares.[30]

I wish to take special note of the positive and negative poles of what R. F. Christian takes to be Tolstoy's moral axis. That axis is put forth in fairly conventional terms. Tolstoy is against "selfishness, self-indulgence, self-importance" and he is for something that surmounts "individualism, a recognition that the cult of the self is an unworthy alternative to the service of one's neighbours, one's family, the community at large." In short, Tolstoy is against the self and in favor of self-denial. Yet as we look at the high moment of the novel and at the embodiment of the truth that moment contains, we find the very opposite: nothing characterizes Natasha more at the ball, and indeed before the ball, than an intense and consuming absorption in her self. It is Sonya who denies herself in her unvarying and barren fidelity to Nikolay. Natasha is oblivious to the tsar, to all the great dignitaries about her, and to everyone about her, indeed. She has neither memory, nor distraction, nor plan, nor calculation. She is wholly self-absorbed, and in a strange way it is this absorption that draws others to her. Tolstoy has dressed Natasha and Sonya alike for the ball, yet no one is drawn to Sonya, the embodiment of self-denial and service to others. Despite a tradition of critical opinion that has insisted on formulating Tolstoy's value center in a conventional Christian and humanistic manner, Tolstoy seems to be saying the very opposite. He seems to be saying that life beats full *when one lives for oneself*, and beats less full *when one lives for others*. What is more, Tolstoy characterizes the other "good" moments of *War and Peace* in the same way, that is, by intense absorption in oneself and at the same time, paradoxically, in the world about one.

Nikolay is totally in the wolf hunt; he doesn't hear the cry of the dogs, does not feel his gallop across the fields, nor does he see the place over which he gallops. He sees only the wolf, and feels only himself in the experience. He has forgotten the deteriorating financial situation of his family, the burden of keeping his word to Sonya, the hypocritical ideals of his regiment. The intensity of self blots out the world, as the world was blotted out for Natasha at the ball. When Pierre returns to Moscow from captivity, he no longer sacrifices himself for his peasants or looks for the meaning of life. He experiences an inner freedom and happiness which manifests itself in relationship to others as a lessened awareness of their needs and a greater awareness of himself. When the princess grows unexpectedly fond of Pierre, Pierre's "artifice" consists, Tolstoy tells us, "in seeking to please himself by drawing out human qualities in the bitter, hard, and in her own way, proud princess." People are drawn to him, as they are to Natasha at the ball, because he lives for himself.

Yet one can retort, with justification and considerable textual evidence, that some of the most unattractive characters in the novel live for themselves. Surely Prince Vassily, Anna Mikhaylovna, Boris, Princess Ellen, and others live purely for their own advantage. If Natasha's living for herself is in some way an element in the right relationship to the world, how do we account for those repulsive characters who also live for themselves? They do not truly live for themselves. Boris is hypocritical, sycophantic, self-seeking, but his feelings are not his own; they are the feelings society approves of. His thoughts, conversation, and actions are prepared for him. He says what he thinks will give him advantage, not what he actually feels like saying; he does what is expected of him by others, not what he actually feels like doing. The selfish person does not live for himself but at the expense of others, and in that sense he lives for others. Natasha lives for herself at the ball. Princess Ellen lives for others: for the prurient desires she can awaken in them, the envy she can inspire, the advantage she can manipulate. Prince Vassily calculates who he will be in a certain situation, what must be said to certain people, what he should feel under certain circumstances. Prince Vassily is never Prince Vassily; he is never himself; he is whatever decorum and advantage dictate.

Natasha—at least at the ball and in her golden moments—is never dictated to from the outside. She is always what the inside moves her to be, and by being herself she permits—in contrast to the selfish person—others to be themselves. Her self-absorption draws Andrey to her, and as he comes to see himself and the world with a similar self-absorption, she is drawn to him. Why this should be so is similar to why people are drawn to Pierre after the war and why Pierre is drawn to Platon. The kind of self-absorption that Tolstoy dramatizes in Natasha at the ball, in Pierre after prison, and in Platon implies a relinquishment of control over and subtle coercion of the world about one, respect for the uniqueness and inviolateness of the beings of others. The more one lives for oneself, the more one permits others to live for themselves. What Andrey sees in Natasha is a being of mystery and charm, because she is for a time untouched and unlimited by his conceptions of what life should be. For a time, too, Andrey, under Natasha's influence, lives his own center, free of the past and the future and unlimited by his conceptions. Up to this point, except for the best moments, Andrey has not permitted himself to be more than he could think and judge. It is Natasha who permits another Andrey to appear, and for a time he becomes a new, different, and unknown person to himself. But only for a time, for the hold of old habits is too great. His ingrained habit of holding experience at a distance infects his relationship with Natasha; in suggesting that they wait a year he is holding his love for her at a distance.

Natasha's betrayal of Andrey may seem like some gratuitous irony on the part of Tolstoy, for he takes his finest creation and permits her to fall and to betray her prince charming. Something of Tolstoy's distaste for romantic situations is surely there: he has brought the two heroes of his novel together in almost a fairy tale way. The prince comes riding into the garden of the maiden (Otradnoe) and listens to the beauty of her voice through almost magic casements (the evening at Otradnoe), and then falls in love with her at the king's ball. The situation is conventional and romantic enough to provoke Tolstoy's contempt. There is something savage, too, in the way he makes her fall. Natasha's head is turned as quickly as a bar maid's by the glitter of false society and by the most contemptible of men, Anatole Kuragin. But something more than general ironical dispositions and reflexes of Tolstoy and something more than general literary categories are involved. There is a logic: what happens follows from the way Tolstoy has conceived of Natasha and Andrey and of the sacredness of life that Natasha embodies. *It is not Natasha who betrays Andrey, but Andrey who betrays Natasha.*

That betrayal begins with Andrey's suggestion that they wait a year before announcing their engagement. Andrey does this from the best of motives. He does it to please his father, but he also does it for Natasha's good: to give her time to test her love and to reflect coolly in his absence about the wisdom of her engagement. He believes he is acting from just and unselfish motives, but he is actually looking at the love from his own point of view. His habitual way of seeing experience as something to be analyzed and tested is assumed to be best for Natasha. He asks her, in effect, to see the world as he sees it. As an older man it would be easy for him to stand a year's delay, but Natasha is not Andrey, neither in age nor in temperament. She does not look upon experience as something to be "postponed." Such a postponement is an implied rejection of her by her beloved, a rejection she comes to feel more and more acutely as time passes. The rejection is confirmed and made explicit by Andrey's father and sister.

Natasha aches to give Andrey a love that is concrete and full, new with every shift of feeling and circumstance; yet Andrey asks her to love an abstraction. When Andrey is gone, the love is gone; the world for her, in the absence of her lover, passes like arrant nonsense. Her mood in Andrey's absence is caught by Tolstoy in the description of a day passed in the winter of 1810-11, a year of postponed reality for the Rostovs and for the nation itself. Beyond the horizon looms the collapse of the Rostov fortunes, Natasha's betrayal of Prince Andrey; and beyond the domestic drama, the engulfment of Russia itself in war. Natasha, bewildered and aimless, looks desperately for a person and not an idea. On the third day after Christmas week she tells her mother, "I want him at once, this moment." But he isn't to be had, and the long day must somehow be filled. It is filled by restless movement and inconsequential events. Running up to the dancing master Vogel and his wife, Natasha listens dreamily to a discussion whether it is cheaper to live in Moscow or Odessa. She sends Nikita for a cock, Misha for some oats, and Fyodor for some chalk; persuades Petya to carry her on his back downstairs, fingers the strings of a guitar, picking out a phrase of an opera she had heard with Prince Andrey, and goes off repeating senselessly the word "Madagascar." One action seems as good as another, for all activities are nonsense in the absence of her lover. For Natasha, only the world of Andrey is real. The rest has as much sense as the word "Madagascar," that she senselessly repeats and as much coherence as the different acts she drifts from in her restless mood.

It cannot escape our attention that the germ of corruption lies in Andrey's "good" impulse to live for someone else, for his father and, in his view, for a maturing Natasha; and to live also for something other than what is before him, that is, for the future and for some abstract test of experience. The love is gathered into the net of the old Andrey—the dutiful son, mindful of honor and justice, reflective about the consequences of his action. When he was falling in love with Natasha, his mind was filled with nonsense and his heart was filled, to the exclusion of everything else, with the immediate feeling of her mysterious presence. Andrey's suggestion that they wait a year is, among other things, an acquiescence to "public" values. This is clear in his attempt to mollify his father's disapproval of the engagement, an attempt which proves to be a thoroughly useless gesture since the father is not prepared to be mollified under any circumstances. Bolkonsky's vulgar, grotesque courtship of Mlle Bourrienne is a caricature of his son's love; his reception of Natasha a gratuitous insulting of her. The impulses in Andrey that lead him to "sacrifice" his love for honor, filial duty, and sober reflection are impulses that take an immediate, personal, and tactile feeling, and change it to something abstract and immobile. The removal of experience by the mind and consequent control of the experience is the same process that is at work in society's codification of experience. It is a question of degree.

It is society and its values that celebrate the ritual of false attraction and temptation and lead to Natasha's fall, but it is the social values in Andrey's act of giving into his father's request and to his conception of "honorable" postponement that empties her of true feeling and makes her susceptible to false feeling. The celebration of the triumph takes place appropriately for Tolstoy in the temple of wickedness, the opera, for art for Tolstoy is the corrupt and corrupting instrument of society. Tolstoy's signal that Natasha's real love is to be turned into false love is the presence of false love triumphantly crowned at the opera in the persons of the red-necked Julie and the proud possessor of her fortunes, Boris, overseen by the soulless engineer of their union, Boris's mother. Tolstoy had given us, before this and by way of contrast with Andrey's and Natasha's love, a description of the love of Boris and Julie.

Julie's and Boris's love is a public love, in which the conventional and general emotions that have been codified and made available for everyone's use are wearily expressed. They hunch over albums of mournful sketches, read poetry, and have long discussions about the nothingness of all earthly things. Julie plays mournful nocturnes on her harp and reads *Poor Liza* to Boris. They suffer together and feel melancholy together, but they actually feeling nothing of what they imitate. Boris feels only that Julie is repulsive and that he needs desperately her estates and forests; Julie feels only an unnatural desire to hurry through the forms of courtship and on to the ecstasies of conjugal love. Knowing what her Penza estates are worth, Julie makes Boris pay for them with all the conventional protestations of love and imitated feeling. Their love affair is a ghastly pantomime of true feeling, and such public imitation of feeling is what Natasha will adopt—without the conscious cynicism—in the absence of true feeling and the concrete presence of her lover.

Neither Natasha's absent lover, nor her absent heart, nor her innocence, nor her simple-minded father are shields against the weapons of society at the opera. At first the artificial lights—and they are described as glancing off the hard stones and metals of the dress of those present—light up nothing in her heart or even in her eyes. She still lives within, and her black eyes stare blankly at the scene. She is vaguely conscious that the Countess Bezukhov, very naked, plump, and bejeweled, has entered the next box and spends a long time settling her gown. She notices abstractly the near-naked women, the gay uniforms, the artificial light and warmth. But what she sees has little to do with what she feels. Her thoughts are all with her absent love and the bitter rejection by Andrey's father and sister. The Count Rostov, who should be her defense against the world's wickedness, leads her toward it, first by pointing out this and that person, later by engaging the Countess Bezukhov in conversation, and finally, in what is a climactic gesture, by leading Natasha into Ellen's box.

Tolstoy's satire of what goes on on the stage is devastatingly bitter. It is something he will do again, but no better, in *What Is Art* and also in *Shakespeare and Drama*. Tolstoy alienates our sympathy by what one might call an extreme realism. It is a kind of faithful and stupid realism, where the viewer refuses to go along with the illusion that art demands. Later the technique Tolstoy uses here will be named and explained by Shklovsky and other formalists as "estrangement" or "deconventionalizing" (*ostranenie*), but it would be a perversion of Tolstoy's intention to believe that he is merely performing an exercise in literary form.

Tolstoy uses Natasha's attitude toward the nonsense that is going on on the stage as a measure of the change that is going on in her. At the end of the first act she is "alternately ashamed and amused at the actors." Before the performance is over, Natasha will be applauding as wildly as the others. Another measure of the moral change she undergoes is her growing interest and intimacy with Ellen and Anatole Kuragin. Before the first act Natasha is abstractly aware of the person and dress of Princess Ellen; toward the end of the first act she notices Anatole Kuragin, who goes to his sister's box and whispers his appreciation of Natasha to Ellen. During the entr'acte, while Kuragin stands before the footlights staring at Natasha and making comments to Dolokhov, she becomes more and more conscious of him, and even turns her head so that he can see what she thinks is her best profile. Natasha begins to imitate those around her, especially the Countess Bezukhov. What the heart feels to be shameful becomes easy and natural when the world approves. She talks to Boris with a gay and coquettish smile; she smiles at those around her with a smile similar to Ellen's.

As the opera goes on, Anatole's intimacy with Natasha Rostov becomes more and more explicit, the opera becomes more and more grotesque, and the Countess Bezukhov becomes more and more friendly and more and more naked. Between the second and third acts, Count Rostov holds a conversation with the Countess Bezukhov and introduces her to his daughter. The Countess Bezukhov in turn invites Natasha into her box to see the rest of the performance. When Natasha passes into the box of the Countess Bezukhov, she passes symbolically into the habitation of wickedness. At the end of the third act the audience goes wild about Duport, a dancer who gets 60,000 rubles a year for leaping and twirling his feet. Ellen turns to Natasha and asks, "Isn't Duport admirable?" and Natasha answers "Oh, yes." As the opera ends, the moral transformation of Natasha is accomplished.

Surrounded by falseness, encouraged by example, she is led to accept what the world approves rather than what her heart approves. In the absence of the real, she is unable to recognize what is unreal. James Farrell, in his curious book *Literature and Morality*, asks of Natasha's fall: "In what, then, does the *wrongness* of her action consist?" He answers his question by saying that she has violated convention and has "grievously contravened the social code of honor"; that "the natural desire of humanity for happiness has come into conflict with the regime of social order."[31] The interpretation represents a misunderstanding of Natasha's relationship to society. Society is not Natasha's opponent in the fall but her abettor; society does not oppose her affair with Anatole but encourages it. The consummation of the affair with Anatole is not a victory for "the natural desire of humanity for happiness" but a victory for the meretricious feelings that society has encouraged.

In the days following Natasha's night at the opera the Countess Bezukhov completes what she and Anatole had begun. Anatole attempts to corrupt Natasha because his life is directed by self-pleasure and whimsy; Ellen, because her life is directed by envy and spite; and both, because Natasha is different and better. Society has taught Anatole to turn love and sense into rapacity and sensuality, and Ellen to turn beauty into profit. Ellen breaks in on Natasha while, half naked, she is trying on a dress and takes her to a shameless soiree and to Anatole. The art of Mlle George's poetry reading is more corrupt than the art at the opera—Mlle George recites poetry about her guilty love for her son—and Anatole is more brazenly corrupt in word and gesture. He confuses Natasha's young heart with the touch of his lips and the lies of his words. The world's duplicity is greater than her power to discern it. She believes what she is told with her habitual intensity and sincerity. She will continue to believe it until she hears from Pierre himself that Anatole is married. Then she feels her remorse, her shame, and her guilt for the hurt she has inflicted on Andrey with the same intensity. Crushed by shame, she believes she is worthless, that her life is over. It is Pierre who rekindles the embers of self-respect in her breast by words that may be the most beautiful in the novel: " 'Everything over?' he repeated. 'If I were not I, but the most handsome, the most intelligent and the best of men, and if I were free, I would this moment be down on my knees and ask for your hand and your love.' " The gesture is romantic and the words are romantic, but Tolstoy does not let us forget that Pierre is still Pierre. After speaking these words, Pierre rushes breathlessly out of the house, trying unsuccessfully to find the armpit of his coat.

Andrey begins the corruption of Natasha's love, and society brings to completion what he began. The connection between the honorable impulse of Andrey and the corruptions of society must be understood in its full implications if we are to understand what it is that deflects Andrey from the "truth" he seeks so agonizingly. Despite his contempt for society and conventional modes of behavior and perception, he has nevertheless been tied, though subtly, to the same modes of perception. He has rejected again and again society's values, but he has not rejected the intellectual and perceptive sources of those values. He rejects with scorn the "known" values of society, only to replace them with "known" conceptions of their uselessness and harmfulness. In each case his view of life and his part in it is circumscribed by what his mind can conceive: first by the adoption of collective knowing and then, in his rejection, by his own "knowing." He is never an "unknown" Andrey to himself and the world about him is never "unknown" to him. The repetition of conventional values he adopts for a while—marriage, glory, politics—are replaced by the repetition of his own negative values of skepticism and cynicism. His withdrawal into "honor" after Natasha's betrayal is yet another example of the triumph of convention. Andrey never learns to live for himself. One way of describing his deflecting force is to say that he is always living for an "absent" Andrey—one put at a remove in the abstractions of honor, judgment, or fidelity to some rule of the past or future. The selfish person is one who lives for others, but on Tolstoy's strange axis the faithful person will also be living for others; and on that strange axis the selfish and the faithful may meet.

One will want to say that there is a good living for others as well as a wrong living for others, and that when Tolstoy shows that a certain kind of living for others distorts life, this is the "wrong" kind. But Tolstoy refuses stubbornly to make such a distinction and insists rather on showing us repeatedly that what we normally call the right kind of living for others (sincerely felt self-sacrificial acts) distorts life as much as does the wrong kind of living for others. There is a remarkable similarity between the mechanical, expected, repetitive, and predictive way in which Prince Vassily meets life and the way that some of Tolstoy's "good" characters meet it. Sonya may be a very different kind of person from Prince Vassily, but her unvarying fidelity has the same kind of mechanical, predictive, and desiccating influence on her life. Indeed, her "fidelity" manipulates and coerces Nikolay almost as effectively as does Vassily's machinations, as is evident from Nikolay's reluctance to leave his regimental life and his discomfiture at the thought of his vow to Sonya. Nikolay Rostov's relationship to Sonya and their future together has been preempted by the unfailing fidelity they have vowed to each other; Sonya can only be what her fidelity has dictated; Nikolay must always be what his word has promised. Prince Bolkonsky must always be, at least in Princess Marya's mind, the best, kindest, and most honorable of men, and the world must always be knowable in Prince Andrey's eyes. "Nothing is forever" may be one of the most beautiful and surely the most eloquent line in *War and Peace*, but like so many of the truths that Andrey tells, he tells it in the wrong spirit, that is, bitterly. Nothing is forever because reality is movement and change, and the impulse to lift oneself above that change is, as Platon Karataev tells Pierre, like lifting a net from the water and leaving only empty interstices. Whatever throws a dam across the movement and change of life commands it to be something it is not and by such commands impoverishes life.

These commands are of great number and may be of great subtlety. Such impules as grief, regret and compassion, as I have shown in my discussion of the early novels, may be silent commands to reality to be something other than it is and to what the individual and group want it to be. Sacrifice, social reform, and living for others may be similar commands. Thought itself and any concept may be such a rampart against change and as such a distorting and desiccating element. I say "may" because thought can also be something that does not lift itself above circumstances and directions of life; it may become a consciousness moved by the incalculable circumstances and directions of life rather than attempts to move them. In the final analysis the poles of Tolstoy's world seem to spin on what "moves" and what is "moved." There is a consciousness that raises itself above circumstances and by such abstraction is stricken with emptiness, and there is a consciousness that is moved and is full. There is a sacrifice that holds itself above change and the movement of life and it distorts both the giver and the receiver, and there is a sacrifice moved by the immediate circumstances of situation and feeling. None of this has anything to do with sincerity of intention or hypocrisy of intention, although it has everything to do with "intention." From *Childhood* on, Tolstoy has attempted to overcome the antinomies of flesh and spirit, reflection and experience, living for others and living for oneself. When I put forth "living for oneself" as one way of describing what is the "attracting force" of the magic circle, I am really speaking of a living for oneself that is not in opposition with living for others, as we see in that mysterious charm that draws others to Natasha at the ball while she remains absorbed in herself. So, too, the right kind of "necessity" is the right kind of freedom, which is perhaps Tolstoy's largest antinomy, and the one that he assaults with the greatest force and treats at the greatest length.

History

The point of the long theoretical discussion of history that dominates the later portions of *War and Peace* is to prove that necessity and freedom are resolved in the concrete historical act—the same point that Tolstoy has dramatized in the best moments of the domestic portions of the novel. Percy Lubbock was wrong when he said that Tolstoy was writing two novels without knowing it,[32] and the Soviet critic Bocharov is right when he says that there is only one novel in *War and Peace*, and that the same laws govern both the movement of individuals and the movement of nations and historical events.[33] Nowhere are the antinomies of freedom and necessity, which Tolstoy discusses at such length in the later chapters of *War and Peace*, and the resolution of these antinomies more eloquently communicated than in the hunt scene. The laws that Tolstoy formulates abstractly about freedom and necessity are the same that are shown to move the drama of the hunt.

Although we sense instinctively that the hunt scene is one of the high points of *War and Peace*, it is difficult to know why the hunt of the old grey wolf and its capture should be so moving. The scene has something of the impenetrability of Hemingway's *Big Two-Hearted River*, where one is exasperatingly in the presence of what seems to be a very special experience and vocabulary, and yet where one recognizes that something universal is being communicated. Hemingway's vocabulary of leaders, lines, strains, wet grasshoppers, and large trout is matched by the special vocabulary of the hunt with its special cries, terms for hounds, and elaborate rules. There can be no mistaking that this is one of Tolstoy's sacramental scenes. Tolstoy often signals such scenes by special images, such as the sky. Just as almost all of Andrey's "best moments" are signaled by a sky image, it is to the sky that Tolstoy draws our attention on the day of the hunt. We are told that there is a mist in the autumnal air and that the sky looks as if it is melting into microscopic drops of moisture, which are falling to the earth. Tolstoy pictures the sky as if it is touching the earth. He uses the same technique when Nikolay kisses Sonya in her mummer's costume; for an instant their tiresome love becomes true and vital, because the ever-same Sonya appears different in her costume to Nikolay. They kiss to the background of the sky touching the earth and of stars scattered in reflection on the snow. On the day of the hunt the twigs are covered with glistening drops of dew, just as a dew illuminated by moonlight signaled the special experience of Andrey's reaction to Natasha's excited voice at Otradnoe, and as a dew-illuminated garden signals the love and happiness flowing in both Sergey's and Masha's hearts in *Family Happiness*.

The enigmatic character of the hunt scene has led critics—when they have bothered to explain it at all—to symbolize and allegorize it. Bocharov, who has concerned himself with the inner relations of *War and Peace* more than any other Soviet critic, sees the scene as connected with the rest of *War and Peace*. But the only connection he makes is to read it as an allegory of the historical struggle of the people. The point is not as far-fetched or as doctrinaire as it sounds, since Bocharov makes a good case of how "hunt" imagery permeates many scenes of heroism.[34] Still, there is a considerable stretching in such an interpretation and, more important, very little explanation why "hunting," whether real or symbolic, should create such a beautiful experience. The feeling of beauty comes from our recognition that we are touching that inner circle where life beats in its plenitude—a recognition present in the best moments of *War and Peace*. What the hunt scene shows us in dramatic fashion is how it feels to live for oneself and at the same time for others, or how it feels to be free and determined at the same time.

The beginning of that confluence of freedom and necessity is seen in the decivilizing process that takes place in the preparations for the hunt. The usual patriarchal distinctions disappear, and a more primitive and natural order supplants them, an order that comes from the nature of the task and the circumstances before them. Danilo the serf gives the orders, and Ilya Rostov the master accepts them. The "primitivizing" of a scene is something that one would expect from

Tolstoy, and it is something he has done and will do not only in the stag's lair scene in *The Cossacks* but also in *Master and Man* and in the mowing scene in *Anna Karenina*. The point is, of course, to regress from the excrescences of civilization, but it is not—as I have cautioned before—to recommend some uncivilized state as desirable. Tolstoy does not extol the noble savage. What follows the reversal of hierarchies is no immersion into "chaos" or "disorder"; rather, the scene is just as ordered, decorous, and ritualistic as a ball. What characterizes it is to a large extent the absence of anything arbitrary. There is the sense of everyone knowing his place and doing his job without command or coercion, almost silently, as if language were a social instrument that separated one from the immediate experience. Tolstoy often signals the importance of an experience by the half-disappearance of normal discourse, as if such discourse were an obstacle to true communication. The asseverations of love of Sergey and Masha in *Family Happiness* and of Kitty and Levin in *Anna Karenina* take place with abbreviated language. There and here Tolstoy wants to convey the sense of things taking place by themselves. "Every dog knew its master and its call. Every man in the hunt knew his task, his place, and the part assigned him. As soon as they had passed beyond the fence, they all moved without noise or talk, lengthening out along the road and the field to the Otradnoe forest."

What Tolstoy is attempting to describe is how it feels to be personally and intensely absorbed in an experience and yet to be part of a group. Nikolay and others are doing what they want to do; yet what they want is what others want and what the circumstances necessitate. Tolstoy is describing a free necessity, which is an at-one-ness not only between the individual and others but also between the inside of the individual and the circumstances he finds himself in. When this happens to Nikolay, he experiences one of the happiest moments of his life. And it happens when he catches sight of the old wolf. This moment is expressed in the Garnett translation in this way: "A stroke of great good fortune had come to him, and so simply, without noise, or flourish, or display to signalize it." In the Russian, "Sovershilos' velichayshee shchast'e—i tak prosto, bez shuma, bez bleska, bez oznamenovaniya," the word *shchast'e* means both "happiness" and "luck." Although "happiness" is probably the better translation, the word has something of the "unintendedness" that "luck" signals in English. The word *shum* is literally "noise," but it is probably being used here in the sense of "trouble" or "commotion," since Tolstoy wants to convey the ease with which the moment appears. The happiness comes by itself; it is not planned, caused, or coerced. It is simple and natural and it does not draw attention to itself (*bez bleska*). Nikolay ardently wishes the wolf to appear, but when it appears, there is no distance between wish and reality. They are one; the tension is gone, the distance is closed, and there is no inner and outer. The wolf in Nikolay's prayers and wishes is the wolf in his perception. But it is one thing to show such a confluence of necessity and freedom and another to explain it, and this is what Tolstoy attempts to do in his much-discussed and much-criticized theoretical chapters.

In the philosophical chapters Tolstoy attempts to explain what he means by freedom and necessity, and he does so with a language that becomes more and more abstract and more and more remote from the dramatic portions of the novel. As a consequence these philosophical chapters have been universally belabored. An early Russian critic called them "disgusting"; [35] Turgenev found them wearisome; [36] Flaubert threw up his hands in consternation; [37] Lubbock spoke of a theory drummed into the reader with merciless iteration, desolating many a weary page"; [38] Janko Lavrin spoke of the history as "encumbering the narrative to the point of weariness"; [39] and for Noyes the chapters were a blemish and the theory "of no importance except as coming from Tolstoy." [40] A year after the first French translation of *War and Peace* appeared (in 1874), C. Courrière wrote what was to be a characteristic comment: "Why is it that the admiration one feels for something so beautiful must be ruined by the philosophical theories of the author? In this gigantic struggle between two worlds and in this great displacement of humanity, Count Tolstoy has seen only a conjunction and series of accidental causes having nothing to do with human will. Napoleon, Alexander, Kutuzov, Bagration, and the French and the Russians are mere pawns on a huge chessboard moved by the hand of destiny. The author's fatalism is argumentative and doctrinaire; it reduces all the great events of the age to its small measure." [41]

The chapters have had few defenders, but Tolstoy himself defended his views as serious and important. In the rough drafts of the novel, Tolstoy says of his views on history, "What I have expressed in the epilogue of the novel, without quotations and references, is not the momentary fancy of my mind but the inevitable conclusions of seven years of work, which I had to do." [42] After publication he wrote in somewhat the same vein to Pogodin: "My thoughts about the limits of freedom and necessity and my view of history are not chance paradoxes, which I have taken up for the moment. These thoughts are the fruit of all my mental labor of life, and they constitute an inseparable part of that world view, which God knows with what labor and suffering I worked out and which has given me complete peace and happiness. Nevertheless, I know and knew that the tender scenes about young girls, the satire of Speransky, and trifles of that kind would be praised, because people are capable of understanding only those things. But no one will take notice of what is important.''[43] There is something spiteful and something of injured pride in these remarks. We need not, however, agree with him that his descriptions of ''young girls'' are trivial, and we can still grant him that his thoughts on freedom and necessity have not been taken seriously enough.

His position on history has been reduced to the antiheroic view of history, and his philosophical position on free will and necessity has been reduced to something that has ordinarily been called *fatalism* or determinism, which in Western tradition suggests a view of the world like Calvin's or Zola's. Some of this may have been fostered by mistranslation, since Garnett uses the word ''determinism'' many times when Tolstoy says something else, and usually at crucial junctures. Here is one example. According to Garnett, Tolstoy says of Napoleon, ''In both cases his personal activity having no more force than the personal activity of every soldier was merely coincidental with the laws by which the event was determined.'' What Tolstoy was really saying was, ''. . . the laws by which the event was accomplished.''

The word ''fatalism'' used to describe Tolstoy's theory of history has not left the lips of critics from the time of publication until today. The critic Akhsharumov accused Tolstoy of fatalism shortly after publication of the chapters; Courrière spoke of ''doctrinaire fatalism''; Noyes spoke of ''blind fatalism' '' and so on. Yet Tolstoy said of fatalism: ''Fatalism for man is just as foolish as free will in historical events.''[44] Isaiah Berlin assumes with others that Tolstoy believed in a thoroughgoing determinism and looked on free will as an illusion. Berlin's remarks on fatalism and determinism are not, as in the case of the other critics, a casual judgment but are a thoroughgoing consideration of the implications of freedom and determinism for the structure and coherence of the novel. If Berlin is right—that a thoroughgoing determinism informs Tolstoy's remarks in the philosophical chapters—then there exists an irreconcilable dilemma at the core of Tolstoy's thought and art.

The dilemma is this: all the variegated inner and outer life that Tolstoy traces with such unsurpassed accuracy, fullness, and freshness is nevertheless "illusion" because such life presupposes moral consciousness and moral consciousness presupposes free will, and Tolstoy exposes tenaciously and repeatedly the illusion of free will. Here is one of Berlin's many statements of this central theme:

> On the one hand, if those feelings and immediate experiences, upon which the ordinary values of private individuals and historians alike ultimately rest, are nothing but a vast illusion, this must in the name of truth, be ruthlessly demonstrated, and the values and the explanations which derive from the illusion exposed and dis-credited. And in a sense Tolstoy does try to do this, particularly when he is philosophizing, as in the great public scenes of the novel itself, the battle pieces, the descriptions of the movements of peoples, the metaphysical disquisitions. But, on the other hand, he also does the exact opposite of this when he contrasts with this panorama of public life the superior value of personal experience, the "thoughts, knowledge, poetry, music, love, friendship, hates, passions of which real life is compounded"—when he contrasts the concrete and multi-coloured reality of individual lives with the pale abstractions of scientists or historians, particularly the latter, "from Gibbon to Buckle," whom he denounces so harshly for mistaking their own empty categories for real facts. And yet the primacy of these private experiences and relationships and virtues presupposes that vision of life, with its sense of personal responsibility, and belief in freedom and possibility of spontaneous action, to which the best pages of *War and Peace* are devoted, and which is the very illusion to be exorcized, if the truth is to be faced.[45]

Berlin adds, "This terrible dilemma is never finally resolved." He assumes that the vividness, variety, and dramatic intensity of charac-ters and scenes depend upon the presence of moral consciousness, that there is no moral consciousness without free will, and that Tolstoy demonstrated repeatedly that there is no free will. The reader may question Berlin's assumption that no moral consciousness is possible without free will, but the assumption is, I believe, valid. The difficulty does not lie there.

It is true that Tolstoy rails against the "great man" theory of history and against the view that men have the freedom to move historical events. It is equally true that he speaks of events and the lives of men as governed by law and necessity: Napoleon's fleeing army carries within itself—like a melting snowball—the elements of dissolution; the Russian retreat to the advantageous position at Tarutino takes place "by itself," that is, an army in retreat will necessarily follow its sources of supply, no matter what is decreed; the burning of Moscow is "bound to take place," given an abandoned city with a preponderance of wooden structures and the presence of an undisciplined, marauding army. But if Tolstoy believes in a thoroughgoing determinism, what does he mean by *free* when he says, in *War and Peace*, "An innumerable collection of freely acting forces (and nowhere is man freer than on the field of battle, where it is a question of life and death) influences the direction taken by a battle, and that direction can never be known before hand and never corresponds with the direction of any one force"? What does he mean, too, by his repeated statements in the notes and rough drafts that man is free and that "Eastern fatalism" is nonsense? Tolstoy believes in some kind of law of necessity, but this law does not exclude a limited freedom. Here is one of many formulations to be found in the rough drafts: "Our view not only does not exclude freedom but necessarily establishes its existence, based not on reason but on immediate consciousness. Whatever might be the general laws governing the world and man, the infinitely small moment of freedom always is inseparably part of me."[46] But what is this freedom which is not excluded by laws of necessity?

It is not the freedom to move events. Tolstoy's argument against heroes as the movers of history is merely a special instance of the broader proposition that no one has the freedom to move history. In order for a person to "cause" history, the event has to begin with him. He would have to step out of space and time, and God alone can do this. Everyone lives in time and space, and everyone lives in history and never outside it. An act of will which is not conditioned by anything outside itself is an abstraction and hence unreal. It is an illusion, as is the belief of generals that they can direct the course of battles, and as are all those individual acts of the dramatic sections of the novel which are based on the premise that one knows what is going to happen.

If no one, then, has the freedom to initiate events, who or what causes events? According to Tolstoy, everyone and everything participating in the event causes the event. All the forces and conditions, both inner and outer, that are part of the event cause the event. Result y, then, is not caused by x or by x^2 or x^3 but by x^n. Tolstoy states his views on this point with uncompromising repetition throughout the theoretical chapters: "If many forces are acting simultaneously in different directions on any body, the direction of its motion will not correspond with any one of the forces, but will always follow a middle course, the summary of them, what is expressed in mechanics by the diagonal of the parallelogram of forces. . . . To find the component forces that make up the composite or resultant force it is essential that the sum of the component parts should equal the resultant. . . . The only conception by means of which the movements of nations can be explained is a conception of a force equal to the whole movement of nations.''

We seem to be back with the necessity that we have denied. Men do not cause events by their wills but are themselves caused by the totality of conditions that are part of the event. Is this not a throughgoing determinism? Even more, Tolstoy devotes considerable attention to the possibilities of discovering the laws that govern the emergence and operation of historical events, a concern that would seem to reemphasize his belief in the normative and hence unfree nature of events. His assumption that events are governed by laws and that these laws are at least partially discernible would seem to support all those who, like Berlin, have insisted that "fatalism" or "thoroughgoing determinism" best describe Tolstoy's view of history.

Reason is apparently capable of perceiving and formulating, at least in part, what is governed by laws. It is presumably the incalcuble complexity of those laws that prevents us from understanding how an event will take place. If the world is governed by laws and men have a faculty by which the laws may be discerned, then it is reasonable to expect—no matter how elementary man's knowledge may be at the present time—that men will eventually understand fully the laws that govern phenomena. Theoretically, this would seem to follow even though practically it might be impossible. It was this consideration that led Berlin to hypothesize that by some incredible calculus men might theoretically understand the laws that govern history.

Nevertheless, Tolstoy expresses unmitigated scorn for those who attempt rationally to discern the laws that govern phenomena. His most bitter satire, after all, is reserved for the military leaders who believe that they can formulate the laws of battle and predict the course of a battle. Similarly, Tolstoy turns scathingly on those practitioners of science who look upon life only from the point of view of reason, find no place for free will, and believe that "the life of man is expressed in muscular movements that are conditioned by nervous activity." On one hand Tolstoy leads us to believe that the world is governed by laws which are at least potentially discernible by reason, and on the other hand he is bitterly critical of all attempts—in both theoretical and dramatic chapters—to discern and formulate those laws. Can man, by the use of reason, discern the laws that govern historical change or not? Tolstoy seems to give different and contradictory answers.

While seemingly championing the belief that laws governing historical phenomena exist, and even encouraging their discernment, Tolstoy is scornful of all efforts to predict events. It would seem that only ignorance prevents us from knowing the laws that govern phenomena. Once known, the laws must hold for all phenomena whether past, present, or future. Yet it is clear, without the slightest laboring, that Tolstoy, in both theory and drama, is uncompromising in his scorn for those who believe that they can predict events. His argument is as follows: Men cannot predict events because they live in time, space, and circumstance. An individual will always see event x from his point in time, space, and circumstance y, and the direction of x can be understood only when it is seen in the whole series of events of which it is a part. Tolstoy puts it this way: "Only the expression of the Will of the Deity, not depending on time, can relate to a whole series of events that have to take place during several years or centuries; and only the Deity, acting by his will alone, not affected by any cause, can determine the direction of the movement of humanity. Man acts in time, and himself takes part in the event." Tolstoy seems to believe in strict historical limitation of view, and it is this belief that moves him to look with contempt upon those historians who attempt to arraign history. Those who criticized Alexander's actions fifty years later and accused him of reactionary politics argued nonsensically that history should have been something other than it was and that they had an invariable measure by which to judge Alexander's acts. Alexander did, Tolstoy tells us, what the times and his nature demanded. There is no such thing as good or bad history and no measure by which historical personages may be tried.

Still, if our strictly limited point of view and consequent inability to understand the direction of events explain why we cannot predict the operation of the laws that govern phenomena, it would seem that the same strict historical limitation would prevent us from discerning and understanding any laws. Yet in other arguments Tolstoy seems to assume that men can discern and understand these laws. One can summarize the difficulties encountered thus far in this way: Tolstoy tells us that "free will" is an illusion as we commonly conceive of it, but he tells us man is "freer" in some conditions than in others and that he always has some irreducible element of freedom as part of his nature. Events are governed by laws, and it is within the cognizance of man to discern these laws, but those who attempt to discern them—

generals, men of science, historians—are idiots. Man is strictly limited by his "historicity" and cannot step out of history to judge it. In short, man is free and he is not free; laws govern and do not govern history.

At this point we can dismiss his theory of history as nonsense—and some have done this—or we can disregard contravening evidence and choose either necessity or freedom for Tolstoy. When this has been done—Isaiah Berlin has done it—the choice has been made, almost without exception, for thoroughgoing determinism. Yet it is impossible to choose determinism for Tolstoy since he himself explicitly denies it in the very chapters under discussion. Tolstoy says: "But in neither case, however we shift our point of view, however clear we make to ourselves the connection in which man is placed with the external world, or however fully comprehensible it may appear to us, however long or short a period of time we select, however explicable or unfathomable the causes of the act may be to us, we can never conceive of complete free will, nor of complete necessity in any action."

Could there be a more direct, explicit refutation? How is it possible—in the face of such a statement—that distinguished critics have for so long insisted that Tolstoy believed in determinism? It can only be that they disregard or reject what Tolstoy says in support of freedom and accept for personal reasons what he has to say about necessity. The answer to these puzzles lies, I believe, in a set of crucial definitions Tolstoy makes. I am referring to Tolstoy's extended definition of the two faculties of man, reason and consciousness (*soznanie*). The correct understanding of these two terms will permit us to know how man can be free and yet unfree, bound by necessity and yet free of necessity. And it will permit us to dispel the dilemma that Isaiah Berlin has found to lie at the core of *War and Peace*. The word *soznanie* might also be translated by "experience" or "awareness." Since the English word "consciousness" is not sufficiently differentiated from "rational process," the crucial opposition between these two modes of cognition is obscured. The French word *conscience* is a better translation. The constituent parts of the Russian word are the morpheme *so* and the radical *znanie* (knowledge). The force of the morpheme *so* is that of "withness" or "linkage," and one might conceive of the meaning of the word as knowledge attended by being *with* or *at one with* the object of cognition. The fact that English slang has evolved the expression of being "with" something may be testimony to the lack of such a concept in standard English.

Consciousness (*soznanie*), then, is a form of knowledge or awareness radically different from rational knowledge. "Consciousness" is immediate, personal, present, and experiential. Reason is abstract, general, and impersonal. For consciousness the world is "subject," for reason it is "object" (*predmet*). Garnett translates *predmet* as subject and confuses the whole opposition. Reason denies the freedom of man; consciousness affirms it. The opposition between the two is complete and unqualified, and Tolstoy tells us that it is impossible to affirm which is true. The last point is the most important, because, if we accept the evidence of reason, there cannot be a single instance of free will; everything is governed by laws. If we accept the evidence of reason! But there is no indication that Tolstoy sees the evidence of reason as real and the evidence of consciousness as illusory, no indication that determinism was real and freedom illusory. There are considerable and explicit indications to the contrary. Tolstoy is at pains to deny that one can affirm one to be true and the other to be false. In the rough drafts of *War and Peace* he says: "The consciousness that I am free is a consciousness that cannot be proved and cannot be disproved by reason."[47] To reason, the evidence of consciousness is wholly false; but to consciousness, the evidence of reason is wholly false. If Isaiah Berlin chose between the two, Tolstoy did not.

In the face of Tolstoy's repeated statements both in the text of the novel and in the rough drafts that neither reason nor consciousness are by themselves true and that man is free and he is bound, we can accept his discussion of the rational discernment of the laws of history only hypothetically. But if both reason and consciousness, necessity and freedom, are hypotheses and Tolstoy does not choose between them, does he then leave us with a dilemma that he refuses to resolve? Are we left with a choice, but no underpinnings for the choice, an either-or but no firm indication that one or the other is right? Such an unresolved formulation of the claims of necessity and freedom would be a more accurate assessment of Tolstoy's view of the problem than the categorical choice that Berlin and others have made in favor of reason and a consequent determinism. Yet Tolstoy has, I am convinced, resolved the problem, but has done so by denying the opposition of reason and consciousness and substituting for that opposition another one: reality and unreality. Both necessity and freedom are "unreal" and both are "real." They are unreal when each is asserted to be exclusively true.

The totally free choice assumes that the individual can step out of the nexus of space and time and initiate an act abstractly; the totally rational view of the world assumes that men can step out of space and time and conceive of the whole series of events. In both, man plays at being God. In both the world is turned into an object, for the abstract "free will" treats the world outside itself as an object just as surely as does the absolute reason. Total freedom and total necessity meet. The real act, however, cannot be either, for man does not live outside of history, but in history. Since he lives in history, he cannot step out of history to initiate events (unreal freedom), nor can he step out of history to judge history (unreal necessity). Those who attempt to command and those who attempt to arraign history are fools. They are foolish because one can know—really know—only one's own point in time and space. The more limited man becomes, the more real he becomes and the more effective he becomes in discerning the direction of reality. Paradoxically, a restriction of one's acts and one's view of events is really a widening of one's power over events. If the reasoning behind such a view is not immediately evident, it is clear that Tolstoy dramatizes such a situation again and again in the dramatic portions of *War and Peace*. It is Tushin, the obscure battery commander, and not Bagration the general who "moves" and "effects" events at the battle of Schongraben; it is the anonymous people who, giving no thought to the salvation of Russia but only to their private interests, save Russia. Personal acts and not public concerns move history because they are real acts, being responses to immediate circumstances and immediate time; public concerns exceed in their generality what one is immediately in touch with. One cannot "freely" move history, but one can move freely in history by responding to the actual events one finds oneself in.

If one conceives of real history as a nexus of conditions that are constantly changing, and if one accepts the fact that one's experience of such reality is restricted to one coordinate of that changing nexus, then it is clear that one will be closer to the actual movement of reality to the extent that one is responding to what is before one immediately. To the extent that one reflects, feels, and chooses on the basis of past moments or imagined future moments, or on the basis of abstractions that presumably hold for all moments, one will be at a remove from the real and ever-changing flow of circumstances. That is, one's choices will be based on illusion and not on reality. One will be most effective to the extent that one is most in touch with reality, that is, in touch with what is before one, what is outside one and inside one at any particular moment. Both "determinism" and "free will" are abstractions when they are held above the flow of actual and ever-changing circumstances. This is no different from what Tolstoy dramatizes in the novel. The Teutonic generals believe that they can predict what will happen, when according to Tolstoy one can know only what is happening and then only what is happening to oneself at a particular moment and in a particular place. This is why their scratchings on the blackboard are unreal and their commands are so much at variance with what actually happens. The finished products of society, such as Prince Vassily and Anna Pavlovna Scherer, are shown to behave like marionettes because they have removed themselves from actual reality by the regularity and predictive quality of the conventions they live by, which are always the same and consequently always at variance with changing circumstances. Natasha is in touch with real life at the ball because she attends to what is at hand and acknowledges the feelings she actually experiences as they are called for by the circumstances about her. She has immersed herself in herself, that is, in what she is actually in touch with. Platon Karataev, it will be remembered, is so much at one with what is before him that he forgets a thing or a person—even a good friend—that is no longer before him.

If we try to understand Tolstoy's real "necessity" without reference to a supernatural force, it must be something like this: man is limited by everything about him, but most of all by other people. Like a rolling sphere, he can go only a short distance without being deflected from the original direction by others. What limits him are the choices of other people. Other people are his necessity. A historical event is bound to be, not because of a law above the choices of people, but because a great number of people influenced by numberless conditions, inner and outer, create an event x. The choices create the event, not the event the choices. If we ask the classic question of whether or not the result could have been different, we ask something that cannot be answered, because history cannot be retried, or because, as Tolstoy says in the rough drafts, history is no longer history when we ask that question, but is rather the concept of history. The necessity of history may be indifferent to individual choice, but not to individual choices. Necessity is reality, that is, the compound of real life, the result of numberless choices, themselves influenced by numberless choices before them. One's free act contributes to necessity, and the totality of free acts is necessity. Freedom is necessity, and necessity is freedom.

The phrase "result of free choices" is important because it explains why Tolstoy can insist on "free choice" as an inevitable element in every historical act, and can also discuss the "laws" of history and their disengagement, while condemning every act of prediction. What has happened is different from what is taking place. Freedom is possible only in what is taking place; it does not exist in what has taken place. These are not my paradoxes. They are Tolstoy's: "The consciousness that I am free is consciousness and cannot be proved or disproved by reason; but the consciousness that I *was* free is a concept and therefore amenable to reason. If a man says: I know that I was free, he states a conclusion. I am free in the present moment; the past was present at the moment when I accomplished my act, and I was consequently free and I could consequently act as I did or differently."[48] What has happened has happened necessarily (as a consequence of free choice) and is consequently amenable to reason and to partial discernment of laws governing the events. These laws must be purely descriptive, however, and cannot be true universals that have predictive power. They are the consequences of free choices and not the determiners of free choice. Individual freedom, however, is always freedom qualified and conditioned by other free choices, and ultimately by the totality of free choices. Such conditioned and limited freedom is never perceived by reason and is always perceived by consciousness.

We can now understand why both in drama and in theory the sacramental moments are always individual, immediate, and in some special way "free." Freedom and necessity meet in the individual act, and only in the truly individual act. The more immediate, concrete, and individual the consciousness, the richer, fuller, and freer is the consciousness. These are more than paradoxes. One becomes conscious of the world to the extent that one permits it to rise in one's consciousness, and one permits it to rise in one's consciousness to the extent that one withdraws one's control over the world, whether the control is one of command, judgment, wish, hope, grief, or countless other subjective acts and impulses. True freedom then is for Tolstoy not the power to initiate events abstractly, as if one were exempt from space and time and from preceding conditions, but the consciousness of reality. The fuller and richer the consciousness (*soznanie*), the freer one is. Such a conception of freedom will appear strange only if one judges it from what is for Tolstoy the unreal conception of freedom as the initiation of events. Natasha is "free" at the ball because she experiences concretely and immediately what is going on inside and outside her, not because she makes some "free" choice. Her freedom is the richness and plenitude of consciousness, that is, the immediate experience of much reality. It is "freedom" in that she is not the captive of any moment of the past or future, nor of the fixities of grief, hope, longing. Her immersion in self is a repossession of self in its concrete and tactile relationship with everything about her. This is a kind of freedom one feels when one is most "alive" and most at one with oneself.

The more individuality, the more reality. The very pivot of Tolstoy's theory of history is the individuality of people and the concreteness of history. In the face of this it is something of a shock to read in Kareev's full, and presumably authoritative, study of Tolstoy's theory of history the following: "The whole philosophy of history of *War and Peace* in actuality comes down to denying the role of individuality and individual initiative in history: history for Tolstoy is mass movement, which takes place in a fatalistic way, and great people are only the tag ends of history."[49] Nothing could be more grievously wrong; no misunderstanding of Tolstoy's theory of history could be more resounding in its consequences. It is easy to see what led Kareev to such a misunderstanding, for the error is analogous to Berlin's misunderstanding: Kareev sees that Tolstoy rejects individual freedom of will in the sense of initiating and moving events and fails to see that Tolstoy formulates another kind of individual freedom as the very pivot of his interpretation of history.

The theoretical chapters of *War and Peace* deepen our understanding of the logic that runs through the motivation of the dramatic chapters and they imply and are implied by those chapters. It may seem to be a long way from the palpitation of Natasha's breast, the stumblings of Pierre, or the polished repartee of Prince Vassily and Anna Pavlovna to the discussion of history and the limits of free will and necessity, but the distance has been traversed by Tolstoy. Tolstoy's dramatic denigration of Napoleon, the tsar, and most military commanders finds its theoretical analogue in his arguments against the "great man" theory of history and in his argument against a certain kind of free will. In theoretical chapters he says that man is not free to step out of history and make reality. He says the same thing in the dramatic portions, and explores there the psychological consequences of believing in illusory freedom. He is concerned in the dramatic portions with how the belief in the illusion makes life sterile, and with the great numbers of ways by which men attempt to impose their will on reality. The ends that the lives of men serve, Tolstoy states in both theory and drama, are incomprehensible. In the drama he shows how the intentions, fears, expectations, and plans of men are defeated by a logic that is greater and more complex than their efforts at understanding. In the theory, this thesis is limited to the impossibility of man's judging history or formulating predictive laws.

In both theory and drama, life beats with real rhythm when it is not abstract, that is, when it is not obscured by illusory freedom or by illusory necessity, but when it is personal, immediate, and full. Neither Natasha at the ball nor Pierre after prison nor Nikolay at the hunt nor Andrey before the oak command, predict, generalize, or anticipate life. One is most free when one is most personal and most immediate, in Tolstoy's radical sense, because it is only then that one has given up the wrong freedom of commanding life and has permitted the world in all its complexity to arise in one's consciousness. One possesses the world by giving it up. By becoming oneself, the individual permits the world to be itself. One cannot predict events, but if, like Kutuzov, one permits them to be, their manifold relationships—at least as they are being made—rise in one's consciousness, and the shape of these relationships may be known to a limited extent.

Isaiah Berlin's dilemma does not hold for *War and Peace*. Berlin and Tolstoy make different assumptions about freedom. Berlin is wrong in giving Tolstoy a conflict and a muddle that he never had. Tolstoy knew what he was doing; he knew he was denying "free will" both in theory and in drama and at the same time dramatizing characters that were living and free. Berlin assumes that Tolstoy could have drawn the data of experience so vividly only if the characters were "free," understanding by "free" the freedom to choose what life will be. Tolstoy believed that such freedom impoverishes life and that his characters could live fully only when they gave up the freedom to choose what life should be and accepted the freedom to let life be what it is. Berlin fails to see what Tolstoy repeats more than once: the world is not governed by the iron laws of necessity; man *is* free. He fails to see that Tolstoy condemns one kind of freedom and extols another; condemns one kind of necessity and extols another. Natasha, Pierre, Andrey, Nikolay, and the variety and vitality of Tolstoy's world are not contradicted by Tolstoy's theories. Berlin's dilemma exists in *The Hedgehog and the Fox*, but it does not exist in *War and Peace*.

What Tolstoy had sought since *Childhood* he found, or thought he found, and he dramatized it magnificently. The last leaf of the onion was unpealed; the golden kernal was found. No terror of vacuity confronted him; there was a measure at the center of the universe, and life beat full. The dream Tolstoy had in the early diaries—the dream of ease and beauty and of a world that unfolded by itself and in which men were at one with themselves and the world about them—is realized in *War and Peace*. Men need not be in disharmony with the world. The physical processes that work silently in distant galaxies work too in the spiritual and emotional chemistry of the inner man. There are no existential voids for Tolstoy, but there is in the objectivity of those inner and outer laws a distance and impersonality that must give one pause. The indifference of the laws is masked by the intensity of the senses and the vitalities of youth and unmasked by the weakening of the senses. It is the reality of those processes, indifferent to consciousness and the human element in the universe, that is discovered, confronted, and struggled with in *Anna Karenina*.

Anna Karenina and *War and Peace* are two worlds, and only their greatness is similar. One is a culmination, the other a beginning. But that beginning is also an end. Tolstoy's conversion, the ten-year hiatus in creative writing, his preparations for martyrdom and his assumption of that role, the obsessions with sex and death which characterize all his later works—all these follow upon *Anna Karenina*, for the novel is already a harbinger of those momentous changes. Something light and happy goes out of his work and his life when we pass from *War and Peace* to *Anna Karenina*. No two novels could be more different. *War and Peace* is large and spacious, multicentered and man-centered. Men are in control. *Anna Karenina* is intense, focused in vision, and revealing of something dark and demonic in life. Men are not in control.

6 *Anna Karenina*

Anna Karenina is two novels, Anna's and Levin's. The novel about Kitty's and Levin's love is a familiar cartography, populated with people, situations, and values that we have met before. We are not surprised that the peasants resist Levin's attempts at agricultural reform, that conscious goodness such as Mme Stahl's will be disapproved, that the abstract intellectualism of Koznyshev, especially when it is used in the service of the public good, will be caricatured, and that true love will have something to do with bearing and bringing up children. Levin's novel has a pastoral quality, not unlike some of the scenes in *War and Peace*. The mowing scene reminds us of the hunt scene in *War and Peace*; like the hunt scene it celebrates mysterious self-absorption in immediate reality and the at-one-ness with others by way of that self-absorption. Levin's novel is a continuation of Tolstoy's art and a reaffirmation of his vision. The novel about Anna's and Vronsky's love is something we have not met before in Tolstoy's work. Anna and the destructive passions that she embodies are enigmatic. Her love is an eruption of something almost demonic into the calm world of Tolstoy. Her appearance at this juncture of Tolstoy's work and the persuasiveness with which she dominates the novel comes from something unsettling in Tolstoy's horizon—something he was loath to confront.

Anna Karenina was written at a time when Tolstoy was going through a series of personal crises. There were three deaths in his family in the early 1870s; there was the feel of death at Arzamas; and there was the fact that he was in his middle years with all the reassessment and changed consciousness that the diminution of sensuous vitality brings. We know from his letters and diaries that he found the writing of *Anna Karenina* difficult to sustain; he found the work unpleasant, he was impatient to finish it, and he considered the end product to be repulsive. All the evidence seems to indicate that he was writing something that went against the grain of his conscious beliefs but which was nevertheless true. It was about this time that he stated in a letter to Strakhov (his close friend and a sympathetic critic) about *Anna Karenina* that it was impossible to lie in art without destroying the art. He may have told the truth in *Anna Karenina*, but he didn't like the truth. What appalled him about Anna's fate and what appalls us in its reading is the change that occurs in her person. She changes from a beautiful, warm person to one who becomes increasingly querulous, petty, and vicious. We are so moved by compassion for her suffering that we tend to overlook the fund of sheer nastiness in her by the end of the novel. Something in the love she bears Vronsky turns her from life to death and from love to hate. It is this something that constitutes the chief problem for explication in the novel. And it was this something that constituted a threat to everything that Tolstoy had believed up to this point.

Tolstoy had, of course, depicted love and physical passion in the works before *Anna Karenina*: there are seductions, romantic flights, and even irrational actions following on the impulses of physical passion. But they are treated lightly, as if whatever interference they posed in the good life could be easily disposed of. Masha in *Family Happiness* is estranged from her husband by the unnatural life she leads in the city. Among the banalities she experiences and finally discerns is the banality of romantic love, but no tragic consequences ensue; she feels only repulsion for the passionate Italian and ends up wiser and happier in the embraces of her middle-aged husband. The seduction of the mother and the near seduction of the daughter in *The Two Hussars* are both trivial and foolish—in different ways—and both are treated as escapades rather than personal crises. Indeed, the sex is incidental. The important point is the depiction of the virtues of one generation and the decay of those virtues in another generation. Even in *War and Peace* Tolstoy shows no consciousness of the destructive consequences of passion. Natasha's head is turned by Anatole, and she suffers disgrace; but time and the ministrations to the needs of others bring her to "natural" health and the dissipation of further romantic fantasies. Tolstoy depicts Natasha's love for Anatole as momentary foolishness, not as a tormenting part of her makeup. Physical passion and the temporary derangements of orderly life that it entails are treated in the early works as "errors" that experience, proper conditions, and the counsel of others correct. Princess Ellen and the coarse sensuality she embodies would seem to be an exception. But that is precisely what she is, an exception—an evil, coarse, very stupid woman who has little place in Tolstoy's conception of life. He makes his nod to the existence of such creatures, showing his impatience with her by the sudden, unmotivated way in which he eliminates her from the novel and from his world.

There is no indication in Tolstoy's early works that a woman who lived in essentially beneficent conditions and one that was warm, intelligent, vital, sincere, and honest could be carried away by physical passion to the point of sacrificing her reputation, peace of mind, son, and even her life for the satisfaction of that passion. Tolstoy made his peace with the Betsy Tverskoys and Liza Merkalovs before *Anna Karenina*, but Anna herself was something new. Significantly, the early drafts of *Anna Karenina* show her to be a foolish, coarse woman. It is only reluctantly that Tolstoy comes to give her the redeeming moral traits that loom so large in the novel and which provoke so powerfully our sympathy. Yet it is as if in writing *Anna Karenina* Tolstoy perceived, as he had not done before, the full force of physical passion. Before she is carried away by her passion for Vronsky, Anna has been able to preserve her integrity in a corrupt society. Indeed, her passion is expressly differentiated from the banal passions of others in society, indicating that it is of a different order. If this is so, then nature itself, uncorrupted by false education, does not—contrary to what Tolstoy had long believed—automatically assure true forms of feeling. It appears, then, that it is not bad conditions that create false passion, but passion that creates false conditions. It is only after she is swept away by physical passion that the "unnatural" forms invade her life; that she flirts, lives abroad, exposes herself to foreign influences, disregards her maternal duties, uses birth control, and becomes dishonest, hypocritical, evasive, insensitive, and ugly in character. The very things that in other works would have explained why she had been swept away by physical passion become themselves the consequences and not the causes of the passion.

If then Anna's fate has not been caused by the corrupting influences around her, then the physical passion must have another source. But if the physical passion and its destructive attributes are something innate, something given, then they must be something in the order of nature. If this is so, then much of Tolstoy's edifice comes crashing down. It will not be enough to peal off the leaves of the onion to find the magic core; the core itself may be rotten. Tolstoy in the writing of *Anna Karenina* is at the point of a truly tragic stance, the acknowledgment that evil exists and is inextirpable from human nature. Up to this point Tolstoy had been an optimistic writer. No matter how much corruption and disorder he had found in human life, truth, happiness, and plenitude were in the order of things. It was only human stupidity and the cumulative codification of that stupidity in the conventions by which men lived that had clogged the pure springs of life. Is it any wonder, if the writing of *Anna Karenina* forced him to confront a situation that belied something essential in his world outlook, that he would feel a profound disgust with its writing and with art in general? He had, of course, almost from the beginning of his artistic career shown a suspicion of the ends of art and a distaste for his own part in furthering its ends. But never before had those feelings beset him with such intensity.

I am aware of course that, in the various explanations of why Anna degenerates as a person and commits suicide, the influence of a corrupt society is often put forth as a cause, as has been the tragic irreconcilability of love for both son and lover. But it is part of Tolstoy's magnificent art that he is able to engage our belief in what appear to be persuasive explanations, which nevertheless turn out to be untenable. Anna does not kill herself because God punishes her or because society punishes her, or because she cannot have both son and lover. She kills herself for reasons more obvious yet more mysterious than these. What makes her kill herself is the same force that at this point has such an unsettling and profound effect on Tolstoy's life and art.

The art is as different as the vision. One has the sense in reading *War and Peace* of watching different centers of a broad landscape come leisurely into focus. The sense of events uncoiling from prior events and the sense of character propelling events and hurrying to some predestined end is missing in *War and Peace*, indeed, in all the works written before *Anna Karenina*. The novel occupies less space; and its design is easier to grasp. This is why those of Jamesian and Flaubertian sensibility (as Percy Lubbock and F. R. Leavis) have preferred *Anna Karenina* to *War and Peace*. Tolstoy seems to have reacted to the less controllable aspects of Anna's fate by an increase in the control of his art. For there is more a conscious, even contrived use of structural niceties. As if in compensation for the enigma of the center, he increases his control of the periphery.

The control is apparent from the first pages in the relentless way in which Tolstoy pursues the developing love affair between Anna and Vronsky. The love affair from the first meeting at the train station to its physical consummation has a fateful character. Our first impression of Anna comes through Vronsky's reaction: Vronsky is compelled by some magnetism to take another look at her when she gets out of the train in Moscow, and Tolstoy's first description of her tells us why. Anna is described as someone in whom energy brims over into her brilliant eyes and smile. Vronsky notices the vitality in her being, even though she is regarded by her friends and her family as a woman comfortably settled in domestic life. Her mission to Moscow of domestic counseling tends to confirm the position she enjoys as someone wisely past the turbulence of life. Kitty, regarding her as an older confidant, draws upon her wisdom to help her with her romantic complications. We are confronted from the very beginning with two Annas: the settled matron past the turbulences of love, and the Anna of suppressed hunger for passion that attracts Vronsky at the first encounter. Tolstoy reinforces the "matronly aunt" image by various details. Dolly's children crowd about Anna, fingering her rings and the flounces of her dress. Anna responds to Kitty's excitement about the coming ball by an attitude of satiation with balls. The Anna who yearns for life beyond her role of wife, mother, and aunt is the hidden Anna who makes her first appearance at the ball.

Vronsky and Anna have covertly acknowledged an attraction at the railway station, but at the ball they come close to openly acknowledging their attraction for each other. Kitty, who has invariably pictured Anna in lilac, the color suited to a settled matron, is startled to see her dressed dramatically in a black dress set off by a single strand of pearls and a spray of pansies in her hair. The black dress with its sumptuous lace is something of an externalization of the luxuriant Anna that brims just below the surface of her settled manners and position. From their first meeting to the consummation of their love affair, Tolstoy will portray Anna as struggling against the "new" Anna that Vronsky has brought to the surface. Her protests are covert admissions. At the beginning of the ball, for example, Anna explains to Korsunsky, in response to his invitation to dance, that she tries to avoid dancing on such occasions. But as she finishes refusing Korsunsky, Vronsky approaches, whereupon Anna changes her mind and offers her arms to dance with Korsunsky, failing even to acknowledge Vronsky's bow to her. Tolstoy, the consummate psychologist and artist, records by that inconsistency another detail in Anna's growing attachment to Vronsky. Korsunsky is her protection against the attraction she feels for Vronsky and the force of the rebuff to him is the measure of the need to protect herself against him. Anna will seek protection in the early stages wherever she can from what she feels for Vronsky. Her decision to return to Saint Petersburg earlier than she had planned—a decision she pointedly announces to Vronsky at the ball—is a form of protection by flight. She needs her husband, child, and settled life as quickly as possible.

Although the drama of passion is barely engaged in Moscow, Tolstoy seems to communicate that deep in Anna's heart it has already been concluded. For it is during her trip back to Saint Petersburg that Tolstoy celebrates Anna's "fall" into passion and the consequent transformation of her values. I am referring to the scene on the train which symbolically records Anna's struggle between habit and passion and the victory of passion. It is a scene of intricately constructed parallelisms and barely concealed symbolizing. The scene—like the later one at the race where Vronsky breaks the horse Frou-Frou's back—begs to be dismantled. Tolstoy's intention is apparent, but the execution is, nevertheless, one of astonishing refinement. Once settled in her compartment, Anna wraps her feet in a plaid blanket and attempts to read an English novel of particular banality. The blanket is a protective detail and the novel a retreat into a make-believe world. But Anna is distracted from her reading by the bustle of people boarding the train and by various noises after the train has started. There is a tension between the make-believe, protective world in which she attempts to withdraw and the noises of the real world about her. She is distracted by the snow beating against the window pane, the sight of a muffled guard, and conversations about the terrible storm outside. In this context the storm is a symbol for the passion that rages in a deep level of Anna's being. Anna is separated from the storm by the window pane. Yet it almost touches her as it beats against the glass, and word of the raging storm is carried to her by the voices of other people. Her emotional ambivalence is accurately conveyed by the scene.

As she attempts to review what had passed in Moscow, a vague feeling of shame causes Anna to twist the knife in her hand. Trying to face the problem squarely, she concludes that she can find nothing to be ashamed of. But at the very point at which she exonerates herself from any shame in her relationship with Vronsky, the shame is intensified. Tolstoy is realistic enough to show us the limits of Anna's honesty. She attempts to face what is unpleasant but succeeds in avoiding it. The very vehemence with which she protests any possibility of other than ordinary relations between her and Vronsky convicts her.

As Anna turns to a form of unreality in her assessment of her own feeling, she returns to the fiction she is reading. But just as she cannot talk herself out of what she feels for Vronsky, so too she cannot force herself to be interested in the make-believe world of the silly English novel. Laying the book aside, she takes up the knife which she has been using to cut the pages of the book, touches the window pane with it, and then touches her cheek. The sensation of the cold knife causes her to laugh with delight. The knife may be taken as a detail signifying the destructive possibility of the passion, especially in a context that is manifestly sexual. The storm outside is communicated to Anna's cheeks by the instrument of passion; and what is communicated—the cold of the storm—relieves the flushed warmth of her cheeks and her passion. The storm outside relieves the heat inside. The imagery that follows this communication is almost coarsely sexual: Anna feels her nerves tighten as if on a screwing peg; her eyes open wider and wider; her fingers and nerves twitch; something within oppresses her breathing; shapes and sounds come to her in unaccustomed vividness. The symbolic acknowledgement of the claims of passion in her life seem to effect a transformation in her perception of the world. She does not know whether the train is going forward or backward; whether Annushka is her servant or a stranger; whether a fur coat on the arm of the chair is a fur coat or a beast. And most of all she does not know who she is: "Myself or another woman?" In effect a new woman has arisen within her and has been acknowledged by her—a division that is pursued to the bitter final days in which she commits suicide. It remains only for Anna to shake off symbolically the protective wraps of her former life and to go out boldly into the storm that is raging outside and inside her. In effect this is just what she does: she slips off her plaid and her cape, and the wind and snow burst into her compartment as an attendant comes in to look at the thermometer. As the train stops, there is a fearful clanging and shrieking, as if someone were being torn to pieces, and the room fills with a blinding dazzle of red fire. Anna feels as if she is sinking down; yet the sensation is not terrible but delightful. She goes out into the raging storm in search of relief from the heat of the compartment.

If the snow storm and the life outside the warm compartment symbolize the turbulence of passion, then Anna has moved in-eluctably in this scene toward the acknowledgment of passion. Through the snow on the window pane, the communication of the cold to her cheek by the knife, the bursting in of snow and cold into her compartment, she is led finally to what seems to be a conscious and willed decision to go out boldly into the storm. It remains only that she meet the object of her passion. And this is what happens. Outside Anna takes deep breaths; the chill of the air relieves the heat of the passion within. As she turns to go back into the carriage, she meets Vronsky. At the moment that Vronsky looks passionately into Anna's face and her face registers joy and pride in her power, the snow storm becomes more violent than ever, sending snow flying from the carriage roofs and tearing off some clanking iron from a roof. The scene is a masterpiece of constructed symbolic detail. There seems little doubt that Tolstoy intended the storm and its attributes to stand for the passion that Anna craves and yet fears, and intended the entire scene to record the unconscious and barely conscious transubstantiation of Anna's attitudes.

Although, on the journey, Anna acknowledges symbolically the claims of passion upon her being, she does not cease to struggle against what her heart has acknowledged. On her first day home she plays the dutiful wife. She does not go out; she waits for her husband to come home from his official duties; and when he returns, she forces herself to listen to an account of his brilliant official exploits. But her efforts do little to change what she feels. She has to fight a feeling of aversion for him—to argue herself into believing he is a good husband. She continues, too, to deny that she has any reason to feel guilty about what happened between her and Vronsky. Tolstoy gives us a little scene that illustrates how subtly Anna evades her true feelings. She unaccountably loses her temper at a dressmaker who has failed to have two dresses altered during her absence. Immediately after this uncharacteristic display, Anna once again goes over the events of her visit to Moscow, so as to assure herself that she had done nothing wrong in her relations with Vronsky. Once again she exonerates herself by convincing herself that her meeting with Vronsky was simply one of the trivial events of fashionable life. What does the display of temper with the dressmaker have to do with her self-exoneration? There is no doubt that Tolstoy wants these scenes connected, for not only do they follow each other, but Anna feels ashamed of herself after losing her temper as well as after exonerating herself. The shame is the tie. Anna has vented on the dressmaker the anger she feels toward herself and perhaps toward Vronsky. She displaces the shame she feels onto a trivial situation and another person. In effect she trivializes the shame as a way of protecting herself. It is in keeping with this form of evasion that Anna should go into the nursery to see her son after losing her temper. She spends the evening with him and puts him to bed. By her elaborate drama she protects herself against conscious acknowledgment of the true cause of her shame, but cannot annihilate the shame. The shame and guilt remain even though Anna attempts to relieve them by retreating to the habitual pattern of the guiltless mother.

With time, the defenses prove too weak and the attractions too strong. Anna's protests become weaker, her duplicities fewer, her desire more open. She chooses to move in Betsy Tverskoy's circle, which she had not frequented before because she knew she would meet Vronsky there. At one gathering at Betsy's, Anna and Vronsky become so absorbed in each other that they violate decorum. It is this violation that alerts Karenin. Karenin has taken no notice of Anna's growing intimacy with Vronsky until it has become a social impropriety and is reflected in the faces of others. Karenin's perception of Anna will always be mediated by group perception. He does not see Anna; he sees her indiscretion. Sensitivity to society, not to Anna, leads him to concern himself with Anna's behavior. Having perceived the attachment to Vronsky in conventional terms, later that evening he reminds her of her duty in conventional terms—of her duties to God and to the sacrament of marriage. This scene is often cited as evidence of Karenin's sensitivities and basic decentness. Yet it can be so read only if one shares the conventionalities Karenin lives by. Tolstoy is surely not presenting it that way. Karenin uses the general postulates of religion as justification of himself and as criticism of Anna, and most of all he uses them as a way of relieving himself of personal responsibility to Anna. He uses the Christian truths as he does administrative regulations. The scene is another instance of what Tolstoy has always been against: the generalizing of emotions and the consequent impersonalizing of them. Karenin does not see Anna the person, nor does he consult his own feelings or hers. He sees a generalized and official wife and mother, and he consults a system of ready-made values. The new Anna who has come into being on the train pretends to be ignorant of what he is saying and is unmoved by his counsel. She has lived by Karenin's rules and convictions, but Vronsky and his love have brought a different Anna into being. Her feelings, it is clear, have been severely repressed in her marriage with Karenin. It is natural that the repressed feelings should both frighten and attract her, as well as disorient her behavior. She is invaded by impulses which have not been directed by habit or reason. It is no wonder that they have the effect of creating another Anna. The presence of that other Anna is shown in this scene in her imperviousness to Karenin's appeal to the standards she has lived by, as well as by the enigmatic, frivolous, and elusive responses to his appeals. The new Anna and her old love are caught in the magnificent scene that brings the chapter to a close. As Karenin snores at her side, Anna stares, her eyes glowing, into the darkness, whispering to herself that it is late, late. Her old life is caught in the image of Karenin asleep by her side; the image of her new life is symbolized in the demonic glowing of her eyes in the darkness. There is both vitality and portent in the image. The glowing eyes are environed by darkness. It is too late for Karenin's counsel, but it is also too late for a great number of things. One will remember that when Anna throws herself under the train, Tolstoy takes us back to this scene, for the light that glows here in the darkness is extinguished by a huge, remorseless, impersonal force.

What Vronsky has pursued and what Anna has desired but dreaded, finally takes place, in one of the great seduction scenes of world literature. Matthew Arnold was right that Tolstoy pays no tribute to the Goddess of Lubricity.[1] It is a scene not of titillation but of torment. What is dramatized is not passion but the effects of passion: the terrible significance of the act for Anna and the frightened helplessness and astonishment of Vronsky. Vronsky stands over Anna with trembling jaw, and Anna sits with her head bent down. She slips off the couch and would slip onto the floor if Vronsky did not hold her. The jaw is a reminder of the predatory character of Vronsky, and the trembling expresses his weakness. Not knowing how to calm Anna, he can only mutter ineffectually, "Anna, Anna, for pity's sake." But his voice is to no avail, for the louder he speaks, the lower Anna drops her proud head. She asks God to forgive her, but the words die on her lips when she looks at Vronsky. She is too honest to ask forgiveness when she has no intention of giving up a guilty love. She rises and says to Vronsky: "I have nothing but you. Remember that." Vronsky is all that she has and he will be too little. His words cannot calm her, nor can his arm support her. He has nothing to offer her but his passion, and this is all that he offers her now. What is caught here in gesture and word will obtain between them throughout the novel—Vronsky's helplessness, Anna's suffering, the divergent significance that each attributes to the act. Tolstoy compares the consummation to an act of murder. By that comparison he presages the destruction of Anna and implies that the love itself will lead her to death.

After the love is consummated, Vronsky encounters opposition from his family and friends and "suffers" from his irregular position.

But neither Vronsky's love nor his suffering interfere with his appetite or his excitement about the coming horse race. We see him for the first time after the seduction scene on the day of the race and it is there that we have an opportunity to gauge the effect of the love on him. Tolstoy is careful to note that on the morning of the race Vronsky eats a beefsteak, that he had been paying attention to his diet, and that he is avoiding sweets and starches. There is room for many things in Vronsky in addition to whatever he feels for Anna. There is no room for anything else in Anna but the awesome emotions that have been aroused in her. We cannot conceive of Anna occupying herself with her figure and diet. We never see her eating; and no event could draw her away from her feeling for Vronsky and the guilt she feels toward her son. Anna gives everything to the love. Vronsky gives only what is proper and what he has to. He is sensitive to public opinion, to appearances; he is interested in other things. Anna is attentive to one thing only: her love for Vronsky and the painful situation attendant on that love.

When Vronsky sees Anna in the garden shortly before the race, he has an impulse to run to her but, glancing at the balcony in the belief that someone may be looking, checks his impulse. Tolstoy reminds us of the social check on Vronsky's love for Anna. In contrast, we first see Anna, after the seduction scene, alone in the garden with her forehead pressed against a cool watering can that she is clasping in her white hands. The face she raises to Vronsky is flushed and we can assume that she has pressed her forehead against the watering can to cool the fever inside her. The image is eloquent in its expression of Anna's emotional state. We know why Anna's face is flushed and why she is clasping the cool watering can. Vronsky does not. Seeing her flushed face, he asks her if she is ill. The question is a measure of his insensitivity. When he asks her what she is thinking of, Anna answers with heartrending simplicity, "Always of the same thing." Vronsky has been thinking of his diet, his mother, the remarks of his friends, his honor, the race, and Anna. But Anna has been thinking only of Vronsky and their love.

Since Vronsky is unequal to the passion and love that he has unleashed in Anna, the question must arise why Anna has fallen in love with someone so incapable of responding to her passion. Matthew Arnold was astonished that Anna should have been so irretrievably carried away by such a destructive passion, and that she should have been attracted to someone as unprepossessing as Vronsky.[2] A case can be made for Vronsky, however. By every conventional standard he does act honorably. He gives up his ambitions, permits himself to be excluded from the society he obviously enjoys, and alienates himself from his family, friends, and social milieu. He is willing to marry Anna, fight a duel for her, and leave Russia for her. He is, in short, willing to do everything that she demands. His desire to regularize his position and to have his child bear his name are understandable wishes by humane as well as social criteria. In the closing pages of the book he is a man victimized. Anna tortures him with her moods, her irrational demands, her baseless jealousies; she attributes false motives to him and punishes him repeatedly. He seems to be a model of understanding. By the usual standards, Vronsky, it would seem, acts more honorably than Anna has done. Yet most of us are on Anna's rather than Vronsky's side throughout the novel, and the reason we are so is one of the magic touches of Tolstoy's art. Giving everything to a destructive passion may not be in the eyes of many a sign of health. Vronsky is a social animal, and in the depths of his feelings he is not much different from Stiva Oblonsky. One can even argue that Stiva carries off his "passions" with a certain childish innocence; that one of his functions in the novel is to provide us with an alternative to Anna's searing, fateful reaction to life. Tolstoy, it is clear, satirizes Stiva, as he does Vronsky for the most part. But there is just enough of truth in the characters of both men to create some ambiguity about how reprehensible their actions are.

Our sympathy for Anna comes clearly from the suffering she undergoes, not from some superiority of character or love. The notion of some critics that her love is better than Vronsky's because it is more intense is a romantic notion which disregards how destructive her passion is. There is nothing pretty about Anna near the end of the novel and nothing admirable about the love. If Vronsky cannot satisfy her demands, it is because they are not satisfiable. He is to be sure in many respects a superficial person. Like Karenin's, his passions are small, but he is no scoundrel because he cannot satisfy Anna's demands for love. No one could, for Anna would contrive to keep them unsatisfied. If Anna has chosen Vronsky to keep the love unsatisfied, then *she* has used *him*, and not he her. Anna, to be sure, is totally absorbed in Vronsky, whereas he is only conventionally attached to her. If in the course of the novel he gives more and more to the love, it is because Anna's demands carry him off to regions he would prefer to avoid but is too weak to resist. The horse race shows us how totally absorbed Anna is in Vronsky and how his attention is taken by things other than Anna. But the aftermath of the race begins to tell us, too, how that total absorption by Anna is a way of victimizing Vronsky.

Tolstoy's technique in the description of the race has something of the contrived quality that I have spoken of as a trait distinguishing the art of *Anna Karenina* from that of *War and Peace*. Tolstoy consciously—even obviously—pursues an analogy between Frou-Frou and Anna. The rough drafts to the novel show us that he does this deliberately, since the drafts make it even more explicit than the novel that he wants us to see Frou-Frou as a surrogate for Anna. The analogy is already apparent when Vronsky visits Frou-Frou's stable before going to see Anna at Peterhof. Frou-Frou has a clean-cut head, bright spirited eyes, which express energy and softness, and a strong neck, which Vronsky pats. The combination of energy, softness, and nervous excitement, as well as the strong neck are descriptive traits that Tolstoy has used before for Anna. The sexual relation of Vronsky to the horse and metaphorically to Anna is made clear: Vronsky pats the horse on its hindquarters, calls her "darling"; her excitement infects him so that his heart throbs, and he has the desire to move about and bite. The analogy between Anna and the horse is made even more explicit after Vronsky makes his blunder and breaks Frou-Frou's back. As the horse writhes on the ground like a bird that has been shot—the same image that Tolstoy will use of Anna in describing her misery at seeing Vronsky fall—Vronsky is described in these terms as he stands over Frou-Frou: "With a face hideous with passion, his lower jaw trembling, and his cheeks white, Vronsky kicked her with his heel in the stomach." The "lower jaw trembling," one must recall, was the descriptive detail Tolstoy used for Vronsky when he stood over Anna at the moment after the consummation of their love.

During the running of the race, Anna cannot stay within the bounds of decorum. She clutches her fan convulsively, her face is set and white, and she sees no one but Vronsky. When he falls, she moans and begins to flutter about like a caged bird. When other drivers fall, Anna pays no attention to them, a reminder perhaps of the selfish consequence of passionate absorption in one person, a consequence that is made evident by her insensitivity to her husband. She does not understand that Karenin's loquacity that day is an expression of his inner distress. Here as elsewhere Karenin is pictured as attentive to the public image, and inattentive to Anna as an individual person. When he arrives at the race track, for example, he has a hard time distinguishing Anna in the sea of muslin, ribbons, feathers, parasols, and flowers. The detail is both natural and metaphorical since Karenin has always a hard time "seeing" his wife. One must, however, feel some sympathy for what seems to be a genuine concern on his part not only for proprieties but also for Anna when she breaks down in the stands and he attempts to shield her from public disgrace. To be sure, he is once again concerned with appearances, but appearances and genuine concern cannot always be separated. Tolstoy will show us later that Karenin can in crisis feel through and beyond social forms. We must feel sympathy for him also when, in the carriage, Anna tells him that she is Vronsky's mistress, that she is in love with Vronsky and that she hates Karenin. The declaration is honest but brutal; Anna adds no qualification, no excuse, and makes no extenuation of the facts. She makes the declaration with total disregard for Karenin's feelings. The following morning, as she packs and considers running away, a letter from her husband arrives, filled with religious admonitions, informing her that he expects things to continue as they have done in the past. It is only then that Anna feels the full helplessness of her position: her love will be imprisoned by appearance, environed by deception, and reduced to the "regular" and banal affair that society countenances. This, I assume, is the reason that Tolstoy has her go to Betsy's garden party after receiving Karenin's letter. There she gazes at what she has been condemned to: the illicit relations carried on so gracefully by Liza Merkalov and Safo Shtolts.

What is already gnawing at her is the desperate fear—which becomes so prominent later on—that once her love is reduced to the level of gracious and well-regulated affairs, she will lose Vronsky. Vronsky's ambition lies just below the surface of his attraction for Anna, and in a very real sense he would be happy to have his position regularized. It is the irregularity, as he expresses it on several occasions, that he finds repugnant, whereas it is the regularity that Anna would find repugnant. His position once regularized, Vronsky would be free to pursue his political ambitions. In effect, Anna would end up being tied to another Karenin, a possibility signaled by the fact that both men have the same first name. It is to impress upon the reader this possibility that Tolstoy pursues an analogy between Karenin and Vronsky at this point in the novel. While Anna is torn with guilt and terror at the consequences she expects to ensue upon her confession to her husband of her love for Vronsky, neither lover nor husband share her intense feelings. The day after the race, Vronsky is engaged in doing his "lessive," that is, going over his accounts and taking care of his debts, and Karenin is busy with his program for the investigation of the native tribes. Both Karenin and Vronsky find the tenacity and intensity of Anna's passion to be an obstacle to their normal interests. Karenin is a very ambitious man, and Vronsky is touched very quickly by the possibility of spectacular political success, which his old acquaintance Serpukhovsky embodies and offers him. Like Karenin, Vronsky reacts to the intensity of Anna's feelings only by conventional words, values, and acts. When Anna tells Vronsky that she had told her husband everything, Vronsky reacts by picturing a duel in which he would exonerate his social honor. His solution to the impossible situation is as much of a social solution as is Karenin's arrangement by which appearances might be preserved. Anna wants something desperate, violent, decisive, something on the level of what she considers her act and love to be.

For a while she adopts the position that both Karenin and Vronsky force on her—a "respectable" position in which she agrees to Karenin's condition that she not receive Vronsky in their home. The position she is placed in soon begins to tell on her, however. When we see her after several months, she has changed for the worse both physically and morally. She has grown stouter; her face is distorted with hatred; she has irrational fits of jealousy. One night on impulse, violating her promise to Karenin, she summons Vronsky to her house. Since Vronsky arrives just as Karenin is leaving, the men accidentally meet. The "accident" will appear to be less and less an accident in view of subsequent events. We can explain her fits of jealousy, her deliberate breaking of the rules she has agreed to, by the frustration of a woman living a love in conditions she finds degrading. But there is more to the accident. It is the first of a series of situations in which Anna will complicate her situation, provoking crises. From this first "accidental" complication to the agonizing last days, nothing distinguishes Anna's long, tragic deterioration more than this tendency to provoke complications, to reject what might be solutions to her terrible situation, to seek in its own way the death she finally embraces. If there is such a consistency to her actions, then the consistency tells us something about Anna's motivations. We can say, first, that Anna seeks such complications as a way of provoking Vronsky's attentions and to stem his drift away from her. It is a way of keeping the love and passion alive, although in a destructive way. The love weakens but the tie becomes tighter. The degeneration of Anna—the pitiful spectacle of a woman nourished on delusion, strife, punishment—comes from her efforts to keep the tie tight. Her self-destruction by suicide is the final attempt to keep the knot taut, even if it must be done by punishment, guilt, and self-destruction.

But the slide toward self-destruction is interrupted by Anna's near death in childbirth. Though Anna wishes to die in childbirth as a solution to her difficulties, she has not yet reached the point of actively seeking death. For a while the facts of childbirth and of near death bring her back to her basic self. Both she and Karenin grasp at something that is real in their relationship, and it is only Vronsky who comes off badly. As Karenin permits a better self to break through the layers of social control, Anna permits it to break through. There is no doubt that Karenin's feelings are genuine in the reconciliation scene, that his gratitude for what has been released in him and his consequent generosity to Anna and her lover are genuine. Karenin had earlier mouthed religious platitudes as he lectured Anna about her duties. Yet the religious joy he feels, in forgiveness, at what he thinks is her deathbed are true. The manner in which the emotion shows itself in Karenin is based on firm psychological evidence. Karenin is a well-disciplined person who has learned to control his emotions and who has become habituated to social control. Emotions for such a person are not easily expressed, except by way of permitted and ritualistic social forms, and when they do break through such social control, they are likely to be violent. It is only by such extra force that the repressive barrier can be broken. Needless to say, such an "explosion" will be at least temporarily disorienting. Karenin struggles with emotions he cannot control and which finally overcome him and his struggles. The blissful feeling that is released and which he tries to hold on to may, apart from its religious significance, be explained also as the relaxation of the struggle to keep his tensions unexpressed. It is perhaps significant that he sobs like a child, since the blissful emotion he feels at that point comes in part from sources deep in his being.

But Tolstoy shows how difficult it is for such genuine emotion to survive in the society that is portrayed in the novel, and how difficult it is to sustain that emotion in the face of momentum of past relations that reassert themselves once the extraordinary conditions are past. Once the danger of death is past, so that the normal relations can reassert themselves, Anna is still Anna and Karenin is still Karenin. Anna is still in love with Vronsky. Despite the gratitude she feels toward Karenin's generosity and despite her recognition of the spiritual heights Karenin had scaled, she still dislikes her husband. Karenin tries to hang on to the blissful feeling of forgiveness, as Anna tries to hold on to the feeling of gratitude toward her husband, but the force of society will insist that things be as they were before.

Tolstoy tells us that besides the spiritual force controlling Karenin, there is yet another force, a brutal one which controls life. It is the force of society, that is, the expectation of others. Betsy is its embodiment: in Betsy's presence Karenin cracks his knuckles, bows stiffly, becomes cold and rigid; in Betsy's presence Anna begins to hate her husband again. After Betsy leaves, Anna cannot wait to get rid of Karenin; she tells Stiva Oblonsky that she hates him for his virtues. Karenin, confused and dismayed before Anna's irritation with him, is nevertheless willing to accede to anything that she might desire. He is willing to give her a divorce and her child as well, or to keep her as wife and let her keep her lover. His statement that he is willing to accede to everything means that he is willing to give her a divorce and her child too. Anna rejects all these offers, even while acknowledging his generosity. *Anna doesn't want a divorce; Anna wants Vronsky.* This statement may appear to be a contradiction, since quite obviously Anna will have Vronsky if she becomes divorced and marries him. But she does not want what the divorce will bring; she must know on some level that such "having" will no longer be the same "having." She goes abroad with Vronsky without a divorce and without her son, her only explanation being that she could not take advantage of Karenin's magnanimity.

The most persuasive and most commonly accepted explanations of Anna's motives and sufferings have to do with the irreconcilable love she feels for son and lover and the impossibility of having both. Yet at the point of her near death and Karenin's magnanimity she could have had both. Her reasoning that she did not want to take advantage of Karenin's magnanimity is evasive reasoning. She is not above hurting Karenin and, indeed, hurts him now, for by not accepting what his forgiving heart offers, she rejects him once again. *Anna does not want the son*, or, perhaps more accurately, she does not want the son if it means losing Vronsky; a regularized position in which she would be once again wife and mother would mean losing Vronsky. Tolstoy makes all this quite clear in what he tells us about Anna's feelings when she is in Italy with Vronsky. In Italy, where she has her lover but not her son, she has never been happier. When she made the rupture with her husband to leave with Vronsky, she justified her causing grief to Karenin by telling herself that she too would suffer in being separated from her son. But Tolstoy tells us that however Anna meant to suffer, she is not suffering, and he is careful to tell us that she does not even miss Seryozha. This is not to suggest that Anna does not love her son. Still, the irreconcilable conflict between love for the son and lover may be a simplification of Anna's motivations. One can dismiss her happiness in Italy and lack of yearning for her son as the temporary consequences of novelty and first feelings of delight in living with Vronsky. But other things lead one to see Anna's love for Vronsky as all-consuming and her love for her son as less powerful and perhaps even at times a pretext to provoke the love of Vronsky. It would be consistent with Tolstoy's views that a destructive passion would weaken the ties of motherhood. There is, finally, Anna's admission to herself on the last day of her life, while she struggles to understand what is happening to her, that she had not loved her son as long as her love for Vronsky was fulfilling. The passage is important enough to quote and to point out a serious translating error on the part of Garnett, who renders the passage to mean something significantly different from what it is saying: "Seryozha?" she thought. 'I thought, too, that I loved him, and used to be touched by my own tenderness. But I have lived without him, I gave him up for another love, and did not regret the exchange till that love was satisfied." The word "till" (*poka*) in this construction, should be "while."

Anna can live without her son and she can live quite happily also without society, as the sojourn in Italy shows. For many critics an unjust society is the cause of Anna's misery. There is every indication in the novel, however, that social conditions, whatever their form, are essentially irrelevant to Anna's misery. If Anna lived in a society that permitted love to flourish without the hypocrisy of her particular society, would she too flourish? I do not think so. Such easy love would probably be a greater threat to Anna than the constraints of her society. If she fears that Vronsky will cool toward her—and there is considerable evidence that she does—then it is the constraints of society that work to her favor, as a permissive society would not. Vronsky does have a social conscience even if he lacks a moral conscience. Feeling the "irregularity" of his relationship with Anna, he suffers from it, both for himself and for Anna. The love between Anna and Vronsky earns social opprobrium because it violates decorum. If Vronsky feels considerable discomfort because of social rejection, Anna too, it would seem, incurs considerable suffering through such rejection. But there is evidence that Anna needs a rejecting society—even its insults and cruelties. There is a very revealing scene after her return to Russia from Italy that underscores this need. Anna insists on going to the opera in a low-cut dress with the Princess Oblonsky, a person of doubtful reputation. By going out openly in society when her cohabitation with Vronsky is known, she exposes herself to public humiliation. Vronsky, horrified by

Anna's intention, is astonished at her inability to understand what she is doing. Anna does understand, of course, but she purposely misunderstands. She knows that she is throwing down the gauntlet to society. Yet Anna wants to be humiliated, cut off from society, because by so doing she will also cut Vronsky off from society. There is no hint that Vronsky understands the price that she is willing to make him pay in order to have him as she wants him. Vronsky's reflexes are always social. Part of his "tragedy" is that he seldom understands Anna: He knows neither what she is doing to herself nor what she is doing to him.

Fearing the loss of Vronsky's love more than anything else, Anna sees social respectability as a threat to that love. After she is insulted by Madame Kartasov, she blames Vronsky for what has happened. In a sense she is right. He had with his love brought into being an Anna that he could not satisfy; because he cannot satisfy that love, Anna is driven to ever more extreme measures to provoke his love. She will take his love in any form that he will give it, but she will not take his indifference. After a terrible fight about the Kartasov incident, Vronsky calms Anna by trite asseverations of love, which Anna drinks in with shameless thirst. She will do what is necessary to tie Vronsky to her. Her tireless ingenuity, whatever form it takes, has but one end. It becomes ever clearer that Anna's enigmatic and increasingly desperate actions may have little to do with the loss of her son and social rejection but very much to do with a dread of losing Vronsky.

When Dolly visits Anna's and Vronsky's country estate, she finds an Anna who devotes herself completely to Vronsky's interests. Anna spends a great deal of time making herself attractive to him; she reads on every subject that interests Vronsky; she interests herself in Vronsky's agricultural activities and in the hospital he is building. She lives for him, Dolly notices, and not for the child Annie. When they visit the nursery, Anna has trouble finding one of the child's toys and seems unfamiliar with the surroundings. Anna also horrifies Dolly by stating that she has no intention of having more children, because pregnancy will make her less attractive to Vronsky. It would seem that she would extend such devotion to meet Vronsky's deeply felt desire for a divorce so that his child and other children might bear his name. Yet she has been so evasive on this point that Vronsky asks Dolly to bring up the subject. When Dolly does so, Anna says she doesn't want to talk about it, but adds in contradiction that she thinks about the divorce every day, and that Karenin will not give her a divorce because he is under the influence of the Countess Lydia Ivanovna. She claims finally that, even if Karenin did grant her a divorce, he would not permit her to have

Seryozha. While Anna's remarks outwardly suggest that she would like a divorce but is convinced that the possibility is remote, they may also be taken as the answers of someone searching for reasons for avoiding a divorce. Her belief that Karenin will not grant her a divorce because he is under the influence of Countess Lydia Ivanovna is a mere supposition; and her statement that a divorce would be futile because Karenin will not grant her her son is beside the point, since she does not have her son in any case. Anna really does not want a divorce; her evasive replies are a sign that she does not want to face up to the real reason why.

Why, then, does she a short time later write for a divorce and accompany Vronsky to Moscow to wait upon Karenin's decision? To ask for a divorce does not, of course, mean that Anna wants one or expects to get one. It is no accident that she decides to take the step when the chances of concessions from Karenin are few, and when she feels Vronsky is falling out of love with her. Her decision to ask Karenin for a divorce is a stratagem to justify going with Vronsky to Moscow. He had announced to her that he would have to leave her for a while to take care of some business matters, and she had angrily insisted on accompanying him. When he coldly insists on going alone, she impulsively announces that she will write to Karenin for a divorce and, by that strategy, gains the right to accompany Vronsky. Anna will use any weapon she has to keep Vronsky close to her: the weapons of beauty, flirtations with other men, devotion to his interests, even hurt, humiliation, and guilt. Anna is not above, for example, ignoring a child or using it if it furthers her possessive claims on Vronsky. She ignores Annie shamelessly, yet uses her to summon Vronsky back from the provincial elections by falsely asserting that the child is seriously sick. She cannot flout Vronsky's desire to marry her and give a name to his child without endangering the tie between them. By taking steps to secure a divorce she commands Vronsky's gratitude and by taking the step when Karenin is likely to make no concessions, she can reasonably hope to keep Vronsky separated from the public acceptance he so devoutly desires.

During their stay in Moscow, Anna flirts shamelessly with every man she meets, and her relations with Vronsky worsen. The strife that had entered their lives occasionally and which was always assuaged by Vronsky's embraces now becomes unrelenting. Anna seems to lie in wait for pretexts to hurt Vronsky; the moments of civility become fewer and briefer, the moments of reconciliation and expressed tenderness less and less satisfying. Anna by any conventional standard is responsible for the bitterness in their relations. She is convinced without rational cause that Vronsky's love has weakened, that he is interested in other women, that he is to blame for all her difficulties. She is irrational, punishing. In moments of lucidity she recognizes that he is not in love with anyone else, that he is still in love with her. We feel indignation at Anna's unreasonableness, but we feel great sympathy for her suffering. Most of all we feel shock to see the Anna who entered the pages of the novel exuding life, warmth, and sensitivity, now so cruelly transformed.

There are few scenes in world literature as painful to read as Anna's last day on earth. She is environed by emptiness. Within her is an abyss which she is helpless to fill. For her Vronsky alone can fill it, but he has left her—after the inevitable quarrel—to see his mother about business matters. As she waits for the word from the servant she had sent to summon Vronsky back, Anna attempts to fill the vacuum of time about her and in her. She cannot recognize herself in the mirror; she cannot remember whether or not she has done her hair. She can no longer coherently connect what she thinks with what she does and says. The world about her, including her own person, appears alien. The details that flash on the retina of her mind as she goes to see Dolly are, I believe, there to emphasize Anna's disconnectedness with the world about her. Life has become like a film that she watches but is not part of. She sees signs, people, dresses; someone bows to her; but none of what passes in front of her has any meaning to her. The visit to Dolly and the meeting with Kitty are as meaningless as everything else. Anna doesn't know why she has come or what to do. Tolstoy again projects Anna's inner state onto the world outside her, and what she sees is ugly. Back home, not knowing why she has returned, Anna sets off to the railway station in an effort to catch Vronsky. On the way to the railway station she has a moment of lucidity: she understands that Vronsky will not deceive her, that he has no schemes about Princess Sorokin, that he is not in love with Kitty, that he will not leave her. The moment of lucidity sets off the darkness of the irrational impulses that are overwhelming her. In that moment, Anna understands that what is driving her to destruction has nothing to do with the many pretexts she has given herself. *She even admits that a divorce and the return of her son would not really change anything*.[3] The feelings that Vronsky and she have for each other would not change, the shame would be the same, the contempt of other women would not diminish.

When Anna gets out at the provincial station and the coachman gives her a note from Vronsky nonchalantly saying he will be home at ten, Anna is engulfed with a feeling of desperate aimlessness. The world recedes from her. She exclaims, "My God, where am I to go?" Tolstoy could not have chosen a more appropriate setting in which to dramatize Anna's desperate lack of goal. The station itself is a background for people who are going somewhere. Anna is going nowhere and has nowhere to go. People rush past her, greet each other, embrace, pursue their destinations, reach out for each other. But Anna stands on the platform with nothing inside her or outside her; she stands on the edge of her being. It is then that she sees the approach of a heavy freight train. The platform shakes, reflecting physically the dizziness Anna feels. Tolstoy increases the tension: as Anna tries to fling herself under the wheels of the first car, she is held back by the effort to get rid of the red bag she is carrying. On her second try, she succeeds, and the candle which had illuminated her brief life is extinguished forever.

Why does Anna kill herself? The question asks why Anna degenerated from the life-loving, generous and humane person we first meet to the tormented, punishing, strife-ridden and strife-giving person she becomes at the end. One will want to exonerate Anna—to blame society, her husband, Vronsky, and surely to blame the conditions of her love. Good reasons can be found to exonerate her; Tolstoy gives us many. But although he loves Anna and weeps for her, Tolstoy is convinced that she is wrong and that the love she bears for Vronsky is wrong. To show that she is wrong he gives us a picture of the right kind of love in Kitty's and Levin's love. The contrast between those two loves embraces the structure of the novel. Tolstoy has worked out the contrast in a deliberate way. While Anna is falling in love with Vronsky, Levin is being rejected by Kitty. When Kitty and Levin are falling in love, Anna is on her deathbed, attempting to reconcile herself to Karenin, struggling to give up Vronsky. As Anna and Vronsky leave Russia to begin their restless and aimless travels, Kitty and Levin are married. When Anna and Vronsky return to Moscow to make one desperate attempt to get a divorce and resolve their situation, Kitty is having a baby, finding new bonds of love and companionship with Levin. When Anna kills herself, Levin finds the secret of life in the words of an ignorant peasant. By and large the novel describes the deterioration of Anna's and Vronsky's love and the growth toward maturity of Kitty's and Levin's love. Both couples face some of the same situations, but the situations separate Anna and Vronsky and they bring Kitty and Levin together. Kitty, like Anna, experiences irrational outbursts of jealousy; like Anna, she feels unloved at times. Levin, like Vronsky, feels put upon by the demands of his beloved. Yet, while jealous outbursts increase the strife between Vronsky and Anna, they give Levin insight into the complexities of Kitty's soul. After Levin returns late and tells Kitty that he has been drinking at the club with Oblonsky and Vronsky and has met Anna, Kitty is convinced irrationally that her husband is in love with Anna. But the assurances of Levin assure Kitty, and the assurances of Vronsky that he is not in love with Princess Sorokin do not assure Anna. Later that night, when Kitty begins her labor, one of the important bonds between the couple becomes manifest.

To account for the difference between Kitty's and Levin's "right" love, and Anna's and Vronsky's "wrong" love, one may say that the former is "natural" and the latter "unnatural." But it is not so easy to say why one is natural and the other is unnatural. The good marriage for Tolstoy is free of the vanities of social life, fixed in mutual obligation of practical work, characterized by devotion of the partners to each other; most of all it is based on the birth and rearing of children. Levin's and Kitty's union fulfills, or at least comes to fulfill, all of these conditions. But in large measure so does the union of Vronsky and Anna. They are surely devoted to each other, at least before the union begins to sour; Anna has a contempt for society and Vronsky comes to say that he has; they have a child; and for a time at least they are both engaged in practical work—Vronsky, like Levin, with the circumstances of agricultural work, and Anna in helping him in his work. Yet each of these conditions comes to separate them rather than to unite them. Some incalculable element converts some of the same things into a warm, growing relationship for Kitty and Levin, and some incalculable element converts the love of Anna and Vronsky into a destructive, humiliating relationship. Kitty's and Levin's love ends, of course, in marriage and enjoys the approval of the society about them. There can be no doubt that the illicit relationship makes the love of Anna and Vronsky harder to maintain. But it is inconceivable that the legality of the one and the illegality of the other should explain the rightness and wrongness of the loves. Tolstoy makes it amply clear that he has nothing but contempt for much of what is approved by society. It is equally clear in his description of Anna's love that something deeper than the violation of convention lies at the basis of the destruction which overcomes that love.

This incalculable element cannot be the cruelty of the society in which Anna lives, nor the condition of irreconcilable love of son and lover, for the reasons I have already explained. Even less can it be what the epigraph suggests: that Anna suffers because she has sinned. Karenin thinks about God, but Anna does not. During her last day on earth Anna does not think about society, divorce, sin, or her son; she thinks only about Vronsky and his lack of love for her. Her last words are: "I will punish him and escape from everyone and from myself." She kills herself, at least as she explains it to herself, in order to punish Vronsky. This is not the first time that the thought of death has been linked in her mind with punishing Vronsky. It is, in fact, a repeated refrain. At the time of the quarrel about when to leave for the country, she solaces her "horrible shame" with the thought of death: how, if she died, Vronsky would repent, pity her, love her, and suffer for her. She smiles with satisfaction at the thought of his feelings after she is dead. If she is killing herself in order to punish Vronsky, then the motive is in keeping with what she has been doing to him throughout the affair. Since the consummation of their love, she has been punishing him by her fitfulness, her refusal to get a divorce and regularize their position, her jealousy, as well as by direct taunt and insult. "Where love ends hate begins," she tells herself as she prepares to end her life on earth, implying by this a necessary transition from one to the other. If Anna cannot have Vronsky by love, she will have him by hate. Many of her irrational actions are explainable as attempts, pleas, stratagems, by which to compel, if not Vronsky's love, at least his attention. If nothing else will turn Vronsky to her, perhaps the pain and guilt from her death will, if only in memory. All of this, while explaining why Anna acts and speaks as she does, does not explain why she would want to cling to Vronsky with such compulsive possessiveness. Nor does it explain why she hates herself as much as she hates Vronsky. For she is convinced that she is a shameful and corrupt woman. When, after the quarrel on the subject of when they should leave for the country, Vronsky comes to her tenderly and tells her that he is ready to go whenever she wants to, she cries out in tears, "Throw me over, get rid of me," for "I am a corrupt woman." Only the desperate, passionate caresses which she showers on him are able to still for a little while the hate she feels for herself. On the day before her suicide, after Vronsky's departure, she imagines his saying to her all the cruelest words that a coarse man would say. The next day, on her way to see Dolly, she catches herself in her thinking by noticing, "Again you want humiliation." The ugliness she sees around her on that day is surely the ugliness and hate she feels in herself.

The shame, as well as the desire to punish Vronsky and herself, come for Tolstoy from the nature of the love itself. It is the love that is wrong, not Anna or Vronsky or Karenin or society. And what is wrong with the love, for Tolstoy, is that it is contaminated and corrupted by sexual passion, whereas Kitty's and Levin's love is not so contaminated. Tolstoy insists rather coarsely on the physical basis of Anna's love. The imagery used to describe the suicide is sexual: the huge railway car throws Anna on her back; the peasant who appears at this point and who has appeared in her dreams is probably a symbol of the remorseless, impersonal power of sex. As he beats the iron, he pays no attention to her. In an early instance of the dream that she recounted to Vronsky, the bearded peasant (who mutters French phrases) runs into her bedroom. Vronsky too associates his dream of the peasant with the hideous things that he had to witness in conducting the visiting foreign prince about town. The last agonizing hours she spends on earth are also filled with sexual references. There is the explicit acknowledgment that she cannot live without Vronsky's caresses; she shudders with the imaginary physical caresses on her back as she stands in front of a mirror examining her hair. She sees the world about her as dirty, and such dirt is associated with shame and with the self-hate resulting from the slavery of sex. She reacts to children buying ice cream by the bitter acknowledgment that she has lived only for her dirty appetites, as do all people. On the train she mentally undresses a stout woman dressed in a bustle and finds her hideous.

It is the nature of physical passion that works for the destruction of Anna's and Vronsky's love, brings them to hatred of each other, brings Anna to hatred of herself, makes their relationship more and more spectral, breaks down the communication between them, brings them into a situation where they cannot speak frankly to each other, makes them avoid certain subjects, and forces them to surround themselves with other people so as to make each other's presence tolerable. Kitty's and Levin's relationship, on the other hand, is free of passion: they argue, work together; they feel close and at moments drift apart; they love each other and the love grows and prospers, but there is no indication on the part of either that the body of each is in some way the basis of their closeness. Kitty's and Levin's union is uncontaminated by sex. They draw closer to each other because they come to respect a certain distance; the constant refrain of Levin's understanding of Kitty is her difference from what he had imagined her to be. He comes to see and respect a center in Kitty different from his own and he permits her to work out her own relationship to children, work, the household, and people, just as she permits him his absorption in his agricultural theories and practice. The work of each is serious in a way that the activities of Anna and Vronsky are not. Vronsky's hospital, agricultural management, machinery, and painting strike us as pretexts; and Anna's care of the English children, her writing of a children's book and her absorption in agricultural books are patently pretexts. Anna herself recognizes this in her scorching analysis of her relationship with Vronsky on the last day of her life, when she calls their activities pastimes (*zabavy*). Vronsky never enjoys the kind of total absorption in work that Levin enjoys when he cuts hay with the peasants.

Tolstoy sees sex as a massive intrusion on a person's being and a ruthless obliteration of the sanctity of personhood. Both Anna and Vronsky feel coerced and manipulated by the other. The stronger Anna loves, the more she coerces and the more she alienates. The corrupting power of sex seems to be an extreme example of what Tolstoy has always been against: the attempt of the individual to make the world one's own and the consequent impoverishing and desiccating effect that such coercion has on the world about one. The truth he reaches in *War and Peace* consists of the consciousness of the plenitude of life that one attains when one gives up one's control of the world. The centers of being of others with all their radical uniqueness come into consciousness only when one permits them to so arise. The right love also, for Tolstoy, comes into being under the same conditions. And although it happens for Kitty and Levin, one cannot avoid the feeling that the love is there to assure Tolstoy that what he has believed in is still valid: that one can find wisdom, happiness, peace, fulfillment, no matter how powerfully Anna's story seems to argue the existence of something in nature that makes these things impossible.

Such an explanation of Anna's deterioration and death is consistent both with Tolstoy's view of life and with the course of Anna's actions in the novel. Anna's is a possessive love. Feeding on its possession, the love alienates or destroys what it attempts to possess. Tolstoy signals this in the seduction scene, when he compares the act of physical love to an act of murder; this is for him no idle conceit, for possessive love does kill what he considers to be the fount of a person's being—something sacrosanct, radically individual, belonging to no man but only to the self-in-God. Vronsky resents Anna's invasions of his personality, reacts unfavorably to her attempts to coerce him into undivided attention to her; yet his very resistance provokes Anna to demand more and more. The duel of control and resistance leads

Anna to more and more hysterical attempts and to resentment too, because of his refusal to give himself entirely to her. Suicide thus becomes the final attempt to control his being by way of guilt. Tolstoy has built into the structure of the novel a fairly probable course for Anna's actions that is in keeping with his personal distaste for sexual love. He has in short been able to generalize what is personal and for many a bizarre view of sexual love, and to incorporate it into his general views about what desiccates life and what makes it flourish.

What is more, with his immense talent he has been able to dramatize the course of such a love so that it appears persuasive in its consequences. All this is Tolstoy's reading; yet it is not the only reading that the text will support. There is, of course, a presumptive validity to what the author has on some discernible level of structure led the reader to believe; yet the reader is not bound to accept—and, indeed, in some cases must not accept—the author's intentional structure as the definitive structure of the novel. I am talking about an intentionalism that one can discern in the novel, not one pronounced by the author in letter or diary. Wimsatt and Beardsley disposed of the latter some decades ago, but the "intentional fallacy" disposed of one kind of intentionalism and obscured another.[4] The personal predilections, even eccentricities, shape the inner relations of the text in an inescapable way. The author's text is only one of many. Otherwise the text would be the prisoner of a special personality; no matter how great, it would still be limited and fixed in a special time. Anna's fate continues to provoke in us powerful feelings of compassion and mystery for reasons other than those Tolstoy has worked into the structure of the novel. Tolstoy has drawn a powerful portrait of a woman tortured and torturing, loving and hurting and being hurt. The portrait moves us as powerfully as it did Tolstoy's contemporaries, but for different reasons—reasons supported by structures in the text. Tolstoy's views on sex were already extreme at the time he wrote *Anna Karenina*; they are bizarre today. If Anna's terrible fate is the consequence of her sexual love and its evil nature, as Tolstoy would have us believe, and if this were the only explanation that the text could support, then I do not believe the novel would continue to move us as deeply as it does. There seems little doubt that in reading *Anna Karenina* we are in the presence of one of those great texts, the structure of which is multiple and which in its richness can support a great number—perhaps an inexhaustible number—of explanations.

The compulsive nature of Anna's love and the delusional nature of her mental life as the novel progressives would lead us, for example, to look for some psychoanalytic explanation of her motives. Anna is a driven person who becomes increasingly impervious to rational argument and objective evidence and increasingly incapable of discerning with reasonable accuracy the reality about her. It is some inner need that directs the course of her actions, feeding her delusions and distorting the reality about her. Tolstoy has instinctively perceived that Anna uses the reality about her to camouflage a hidden reality. He gives us what appear, but only appear, to be explanations of why she acts as she does: the cruel society, the irreconcilable love of son and lover, the social shame before her actions, the conscious guilt at having hurt her husband, the fear of being abandoned by Vronsky. But Tolstoy has signaled that in the end these are all pretexts or rationalizations for something else.

Tolstoy explains the delusions as consequences that proceed from the nature of sex, which he looks upon as destructive of the sanctity of being. Perhaps, but not necessarily. A consequence in one system of explanation may be cause in another. What is painfully apparent on the last days of Anna's life is that Anna's misery does not come from the threat of abandonment by Vronsky, but that the threat of abandonment is a consequence of some other cause. Anna courts abandonment by insulting Vronsky and pushing him to hate her. Although Vronsky is not involved with other women, Anna insistently and obsessively needs to feel that he is in love with someone else. Vronsky does not hate her or see her as a corrupt creature (as she repeatedly charges him with thinking), but Anna needs to feel that she is hateful and corrupt. Why does Anna want to be hurt? to feel humiliated? and why does she court and propel the very things she fears and loathes? If not from external causes, then from inner causes, and from drives that seem unmodifiable by external circumstances. Nothing is more obvious than the "trapped" nature of Anna's feelings. If these destructive drives are so deep and powerful, they can only come from early experiences.

We know nothing about what led her to marry Karenin, but we do know that Karenin is twenty years older than she, and that his whole manner is one of public and private authority. One of the elders of society, he is something of a father to Anna. If Anna feels abused by Karenin's emotionless relationship to her, we might entertain the hypothesis that some psychic need was being satisfied when she chose him for her husband. This hypothesis takes on some credence when we see that Vronsky, for whom Anna abandons Karenin, in many ways resembles her husband. From Vronsky too Anna suffers from the threat of abandonment, and from a coldness that she discerns in him and projects onto him. That Anna should have been swept away by someone as unprepossessing as Vronsky—which astonished Matthew Arnold—becomes less mysterious when one entertains the hypothesis that Vronsky may be precisely the kind of person Anna needs: that she has chosen someone who will not meet the demands of her love and someone who will—with good form and a sense of honor—abandon her for social and political standing.

What I am suggesting is that Anna neurotically chooses someone who will hurt her, that she courts the feeling of being unloved, and chooses a situation in which she will feel shamed and corrupt. It matters not a bit that her sense of abandonment and emotional abuse is in good measure imaginary. The delusional nature of her hurt signal to us how compulsive and unchangeable her needs are. The need to be abandoned and hurt and the need to feel corrupt and hateful must come from sources deep in her being and early in her upbringing. Though we know nothing about her childhood, we do know that the sense of corruption precedes rather than follows upon the self-destructive acts she engages in. We also have some hints in the text itself that the drama in its most painful stages is related to her childhood; at least elements of childhood feelings invade her reflections at certain moments. On the night before her suicide, Anna waits in her room like a petulant child for Vronsky's return and for proof of his love by a visit to her before going to bed. She waits like a child waiting to be tucked in for the night. On the morning of the day of the suicide she kisses her hand as a mother will do to a hurt child. When she commits suicide her last thought is of herself as a child. We know also from the text that Anna suffers from the delusion that Vronsky loves another woman, who, in the last days, becomes increasingly his mother. Vronsky's mother, who becomes the obstacle to their moving to the country, is for that moment at least the cause of Vronsky's abandonment of her. It takes only the mildest of displacements to shift the cause of being unloved and abandoned by Vronsky from Vronsky's mother to her own mother. And if Vronsky represents for Anna's psyche a repetition of Karenin and the paternal image, then Anna in her last delusional hours reenacts a drama of terrified child facing abandonment by the father because of the intervening and hateful mother.

Once one begins to reason in this vein, a host of statements, actions, and ruminations begin to develop in a way different from the way Anna's fate is usually explained—whatever the range and variety of explanations—and different too from the way I have explained Anna's motives. I am not suggesting that *Anna Karenina* is best read as a psychoanalytic drama, but I am suggesting that one of the reasons the novel escapes the constricting force of Tolstoy's bizarre views on sex lies in the fact that multiple novels can be constructed from the order of dramatic events given. This is to say that the author's intentionalism—however deeply we see it imbedded in the text itself, and whatever term we wish to use for such a presence, whether "implied" or "realized" author—has a limited control over what we read and should have a limited control over what we accept. The emotions we give to *Anna Karenina* come from sources in part different from those that feed Tolstoy's passion.

We have, of course, an obligation to discern what the author has put into his work, but it will do his work and him no credit to limit its power to the sometimes eccentric views of the author himself. If a great work is "universal"—and I think *Anna Karenina* is universal—then it expresses and escapes even the deepest recesses of the author's creative being. This study is devoted to tracing out the special "mythology" of Tolstoy's view of reality and man's proper relationship to it, as Tolstoy has confronted this relationship in his fictive hypotheses. But I believe that such a "mythology" or personally structured experience is something that we must displace if we are to bring the structure into reasonable alignment with our understandings. *Anna Karenina* is powerful evidence for the spiritual and emotional biography of Tolstoy at this juncture of his life, for it shows how mightily Tolstoy attempts to integrate his increasing aversion to sex into a structure of experience that he had formulated so beautifully and coherently in the early works, especially in *War and Peace*. It is because he has trouble integrating Anna into his structured world that so much of her escapes his understanding and control. Kitty's and Levin's love is there to reassure us and especially Tolstoy himself that everything he believed in before *Anna Karenina* is still true. Tolstoy takes Levin to the fountain of truth again. But because it is a truth we have seen before it is less persuasive, especially when seen against Anna's fate.

The truth that Levin comes to is the truth that all the heroes of Tolstoy's novels come to: what Olenin glimpses and what Pierre and Natasha experience for a while, and what Karataev epitomizes: that one is in touch with reality when one empties oneself of wishes, desires, thoughts, plans, intentions. The world about one, incalculable in its movement and complexity, becomes one with oneself when one permits it to be. A good part of Levin's story, for example, has to do with plans and failures in his dogmatic attempts to bend life and people to his will. His plans are continually frustrated by the peasants, much as Pierre's reform intentions are sabotaged by the realities of peasant life. The peasants wreck Levin's machinery, disregard his instructions, steal his hay, and are uninterested in his reforms. They are like the recalcitrant element of life which refuses to give itself to the abstractions of Levin, as life had refused to give itself to the abstractions of Olenin, Prince Andrey, and most of Tolstoy's heroes up to this point. Levin comes to learn the most precious of Tolstoy's truths: that reality gives itself to one when one ceases efforts to possess it. Perhaps nowhere in the novel is this expressed more beautifully than in the "sacramental" scene of the hay mowing. In that scene Levin experiences, if only for a day, what the feel of reality is; and if the scene is no effective answer to the destructive impulses in people that Anna has introduced, Tolstoy's art is so great that one feels that it is an answer.

Levin's right relationship to the land and life is contrasted with his brother's wrong relationship. His brother Sergey Koznyshev has come to the country to relax. He comes to the country not to fill his being but to empty it. The beauty of the season and the imminence of the practical work of harvesting have absorbed all of Levin's sensibilities. He takes part only half-heartedly in the argument with his brother about the relative merits of working for the public good and working for one's own self-interest. Tolstoy, one might note in passing, is very much on Levin's side when he insists that the mainspring of action is self-interest, as he is on Andrey's side against Pierre in a similar scene in *War and Peace*. As in *War and Peace* he uses "self-interest" with no pejorative overtones. What he means by the term is living concretely, for one's immediate self rather than for an abstract self. It is the "public good" and abstractions of that kind that separate man from the immediate reality about him and conceal a predatory self-interest.

As Levin mows with the peasants, he forgets about the idle argument he has had with his brother. The mowing is real, and the argument appears unreal. Levin learns something on the day of the mowing that he had not learned from the book he was writing or from his plans to reform himself and the peasants. He learns that one does not understand the peasants and the land by conscious analysis but by becoming at one with the land and the peasants. The peasants he

works with are not functions of his understanding; they are real
people who work more skillfully than he and who have identities and
centers just as he has. As the day goes on, his consciousness of what he
is doing becomes progressively obliterated. With that obliteration
Levin becomes at one with the scythe, the workers, and nature. At first
he tires easily, but as he gives himself to the job, mowing with the
same rhythm as does the older peasant, the job becomes effortless.
When the work is going smoothly, Levin thinks of nothing, wishes for
nothing, and hears nothing but the swish of the scythe. As soon as he
becomes conscious of what he is doing and tries to do it better, the
mowing becomes more difficult and the row is badly cut. We are
confronted once again with the phenomenon that one's personal
effort interferes with one's right relationship with the world. Levin
"understands" the world about him when he is at one with it, and he
is at one with it to the extent that he ceases to separate himself from it
by thought, desire, and will.

   Tolstoy expresses this unity of self and surrounding by some
brilliant stylistic strokes. Levin takes a short nap after dinner—a tuft of
grass for his pillow—and when he awakens the world is changed for
him; he feels himself to be at one with the world about him, and the
union of inner and outer is caught in the style itself. Tolstoy speaks of
the "slanting rays of the evening sun" (*na vechernikh kosykh luchakh
solntsa*.) Since the Russian word for "slanting" (*kosoy*) is a homonym
for the word for scythe (*kosa*), the natural image of time is identified
stylistically with the instrument of work "scythe." The river is
described as gleaming at its bends like steel bands, so as to remind us
again of the gleaming steel of the scythes and to suggest the unity of
tool and the natural image of the river. The same verb "gleaming"
(*blestet*) is used for river, meadow, and scythe. The tool and the world
acted on are one, as are the action and the actor. As dusk falls, Levin
loses sight of his fellow workers. Only the sounds of the men urging
each other on, the clank and hiss of the scythes, the sound of the
whetstones are heard, like some natural chorus. At the beginning of
the day Levin had been very conscious of the names of the peasants
and of their personalities, but at the end of the day only the common
sound of the group united with nature in work remains in his
consciousness. As the day progresses, he loses consciousness of himself
as different from them. It is the immediacy of the work and of the
common task that effects this. Tolstoy speaks of the work as "boiling"
at this point (*rabota kipela*); the image is that of the mist coming from
the meadows, uniting stylistically the work with the natural surround-

ings. Levin's sacramental moment consists in his temporary loss of concerns and cares of a world that goes beyond the immediate situation and the submergence of his being in collective work and in the immediate surroundings. Permitting the world and the peasants to be what they are, he has permitted himself to be what he is. For that day Levin does not feel himself as a "postponed" being, someone who has alienated himself in future Levins or in past Levins, or a Levin who is imprisoned in his conception of who he is or should be. He is a concrete being, who is at one with himself, those about him, and the physical world about him. Tolstoy not only states that nature, man, and his activity are one; he makes them one in image and word.

When Levin returns home, he finds that his brother Sergey has spent the entire day inside going over reviews of his work and studying miscellaneous papers. Sergey's only response to nature is to scold Levin for letting flies in. He attempts to dredge up the previous day's argument, but Levin is uninterested. He does not contest his brother's distinctions, and the whole problem seems trivial in comparison with the reality he has lived that day. Levin has been able to achieve the unity with the land and the peasants which he was not able to do by his plans for them. It is a good moment because Levin "follows" and does not "lead," permits himself to be and does not force himself to be. The communication between him and his brother Koznyshev is there by way of contrast between "false" communication and "true" communication. One is false because it consists only of words and ideas; the other is true because it consists of one's whole being uncoerced by the willed communication of words.

The mowing scene is something of a confirmation of the epiphany that Levin experiences near the end of the novel after all his searching for the truth. We will remember that Levin goes reeling down the road from the impact of a peasant's distinction between one peasant who lives for his stomach and another who lives for his soul. According to Levin's interpretation of this, "He said that one must live for one's own wants, that is, that one must not live for what we understand, what we are attracted by, what we desire, but must live for something incomprehensible, for God, whom no one can understand nor even define." Levin, it is to be noticed, interprets *nuzhdy* (needs or wants) by desire and the need to understand. Since these are presumably what keeps one from the truth, they are examples of the force that have kept Levin from the truth and have condemned Anna to live in falsity. Levin has been kept from the truth by his effort to understand; Anna by living for her desires.

Despite the feel of reality of the hay-mowing scene and its undeniable beauty and expressiveness, one is left with the feeling that Anna has won the day, that all of Levin's searching and finding are insubstantial if they do not confront the destructive power that Tolstoy has located in Anna's physical passion. The Levin plot has something of an air of a fable, beautiful but remote, whereas Anna's plot has the air of pressing reality. When Anna and Levin meet briefly near the end of the novel, it is Anna that sweeps Levin temporarily into her orbit and not the other way around. He is captivated by her beauty and intelligence and thoroughly won over to sympathy for her difficult position. But Anna is untouched by Levin. When he leaves her presence, she ceases thinking about him. Levin lives in the secure, rationally dominated world Tolstoy had constructed before he discovered Anna, while Anna lives in a world ruled by demonic passions which, one is convinced, would sweep away any consideration of the wisdom that is embodied in Levin's life. Tolstoy bravely puts forth Levin's life as an alternative to the moral center of Anna's world, but he dares risk only the briefest of encounters between these two worlds.

After *Anna Karenina* and the ten-year hiatus in his creative work which followed upon his religious conversion, Tolstoy wrote principally only about two things: sex and death. The two were associated in his mind. Sex for him serves death, as it does in *Anna Karenina*, almost in eerie anticipation of the Marcusian interpretation of Freud, in which the sexual impulse is seen to be in the service of the death instinct. Tolstoy saw sexual passion as degrading, and destructive of man's spiritual self. Many of his works after the conversion, at the time of his renewed interest in creative writing, are campaigns against the corrupting attributes of sex, as *The Devil, Father Sergius* and *The Kreutzer Sonata* eloquently show.

The *Kreutzer Sonata* was to summarize Tolstoy's feelings of disgust with sex. Absent from this novel is the sympathy Tolstoy had felt for Anna in the grip of passion. The dogmatism and intractability always just under the surface of his views burst forth to bludgeon the reader. Love, or what the world called love, was for him not only stupid but degrading and repulsive. It was more than that: it destroyed everything human in people and in the end destroyed the people themselves. There are hints of this in *Anna Karenina*, though the compassion with which Tolstoy treats Anna's life mitigates what she does to herself. Anna is wrong and Levin is right; there can be no doubt about that; but even if wrong, she is still to be loved and

pitied. In *The Kreutzer Sonata*, however, there are no such miti-
gations: those who give themselves to sex are lunatics and ugly, vicious
people, and the world which encourages such love is ugly and vicious.
Even in marriage, sex is repulsive and destructive. The point of the
narrative of Pozdnyshev is to show how sexual love degrades a human
being, thus arousing hostility to others and to himself. Pozdnyshev
kills his wife not because she may have had an affair with Trukhachev-
ski—whether she actually did is never made clear—but because he
himself has slept with his wife. Those critics who have argued for or
against the reality of Pozdnyshev's wife's fall have missed the point,
for it really doesn't matter whether she fell or not. It is quite probable
that the wife's fall is a product of Pozdnyshev's deranged imagination,
but it is the immoral act of sexual relations with his wife that has
brought him to such derangement.

The agitation Tolstoy felt about the question of sexual relations had
its effect on the construction of the novel. Eager to spew forth the
various arguments he has and has had about sexual relations, he fails
to connect the diverse points, some of which are directly contradictory.
He argues, for example, against the corrupting influence of society
because of its view of sex: its hypocrisy, commercial exploitation of
women and men, and the pervasive air of deception that it encourages. The argument against the way men and women are brought
up in society would seem to indicate that these corruptions can be
remedied and that a love other than that which obtains in society can
be imagined and perhaps even established. Indeed, the old trades-
man's defense of traditional views on marriage and the relations
between men and women lead us to believe that there are better ways
of arranging these things in society than those which are practiced. Yet
in the end Tolstoy makes clear that sexual relations, whatever their
form, are destructive of man's spiritual nature. But if this is so, then
his railing against the specific abuses in society are undercut, because
there is no remedy except to give up sexual relations altogether, even
for the purpose of bearing children. This is the most bizarre part of the
novel. One cannot doubt that Pozdnyshev's views are Tolstoy's own,
for Tolstoy wrote an afterword in which he outlined in uncompromising expository form what he was trying to say in *The Kreutzer
Sonata*; what he says is essentially what Pozdnyshev has said. In *Anna
Karenina* Tolstoy perceived for the first time the destructive power of
physical passion. His inability to explain its place in the world he had
created up to then produced that troubling ambiguity of attraction
and fear that we feel in the presence of Anna's enigmatic fate. It was

Tolstoy's incertitude that abetted the peculiar suspension of judgment characteristic of the novel. By the time he wrote *The Kreutzer Sonata* he had come to terms with the new force and was once again the dogmatist bent on annihilating what he could not answer.

The Kreutzer Sonata shows, if nothing else, that Tolstoy was not able to distance his disgust with sex sufficiently to turn the theme to the service of art. He is more successful in *The Devil* and *Father Sergius*, but not as successful as he will be in handling the theme of death, which is pervasive in his later works. Death had haunted him from his earliest works—one will remember the mother's death in *Childhood*—but it had not invaded his consciousness with the same power as it does in the works after *Anna Karenina*. Reality had always been unknowable for him. Indeed, the acknowledgment that reality is unknowable,—the acknowledgment made by Pierre in prison—was the condition of the right kind of experiential knowing by way of an absorption of self in the immediate, but incomprehensible, flow of sensuous data before one. Death, however, brings to Tolstoy the terror and consciousness that there may not be any direction to the flow of historical reality and that sensuous immediacy may be spectral. But he refuses to give in to this fear. His faith that there is a right experience, which exists in nature and is accessible to man, remains unaltered. Imitation, art, society, intellectualism continue to distort experience, as do the subjective impulses of grief, regret, and compassion as well as the myriad attempts to bend reality to our needs.

The way to that right experience continues to be by absorption in oneself and not in things outside oneself, but the self one lives for now is a divine self. The answers to the king's three questions in this tale of 1903 are much the same that Tolstoy gave in the early tales: one attends to what is at hand at the present moment. Only the injunction to do good would be new, for in the earlier works, if one absorbed oneself in what was at hand, one would do good without effort or consciousness, as Natasha and Pierre do in their sacramental moments. The injunction to do good, with its implication of conscious effort, indicates some doubt on Tolstoy's part that goodness comes by itself. Tolstoy is being increasingly assaulted with terrors—real or imagined—that he had not faced in the works before *Anna Karenina*. Although this awareness of certain tragic aspects of life comes very much to the forefront of his works now, what is even more noticeable is the reaffirmation that life can be true and good.

7   *The Death of Ivan Ilych*

The years from *Anna Karenina* to *The Death of Ivan Ilych* are momentous for Tolstoy's moral and spiritual development. They are the difference between the "first phase" and the "second phase," between the Tolstoy who captivated his readers with the power of his craft and his fictive vision, and the Tolstoy who captivated not only the Russians but the world with his theological and spiritual visions. No other author in the history of literature presents a change of such proportions as does Tolstoy during these years of spiritual crisis, with their isolating aftermath and the renewed creative energy. After having created two of the world's greatest novels—*War and Peace* and *Anna Karenina*—as well as a score of important other works, he puts down his pen, withdraws into himself, repudiates his craft and gives up all his normal pursuits in order to find the truth that his mind craves. There are some who have doubted that the spiritual crisis was sincere. Those who have seen only posture and calculated effect in the spiritual searchings are not unlike those who have seen only Tolstoy's reserve, distance, and irony in his analysis of the values by which civilization moves itself and have failed to see the insistent thirsting for belief. The spiritual crisis of these years was real, even though the man could not—at least in subsequent years—keep from playing the roles that the public projected on him.

What happens after the years of personal crisis and search for religious truth is a new career, in some respects greater than the first, certainly one which had a broader impact upon his age. The pedagogical bent had always vied with his immense artistic talent and had finally won out. Tolstoy becomes something more than a writer: he becomes a religious leader, sage, a modern prophet. His pen now addresses itself not only to the problems of art but also to the political, social, cultural, and economic problems of Russia and the whole world. If his pedagogical bent expresses itself with a vengeance in his new career, his artistic instincts come back to the surface, and he creates a new art—different from that revealed in the works before the conversion, but just as beautiful and just as powerful. The works are less happy, more preoccupied with death; the odor of sin and corruption is everywhere. Tolstoy knows the truth now, and the fiction is less hypothesis and more exposition. There is an impatience with the circumstances of probabilities, an essentializing tendency to Tolstoy's understanding of men and their conditions. Men and the world, he is convinced, are everywhere the same, and the differences are not important. He writes mostly about death and sex, purity and corruption. Everywhere men meet the same problems; everywhere the answers are the same. The artistic task he sets himself is to exposit in fiction a few simple, encompassing truths. In order to do this he denudes his fictive world of everything that competes with the simple truth, baldly stated. As such, the fictive world is a hieroglyphic; sensuous detail so copious in the early works is now sparse and translucent. The details point to things beyond themselves.

Tolstoy pictures corruption and salvation in his fictional works while expositing them in his economic, political, and cultural essays. The ties between the essays and the fiction are close and many. The overt subject matter may be different, but Tolstoy's opinions on conscription, government corruption, the evils of private property, and nonresistance to evil have their subterranean passages to his parables on life and death. Except for *Resurrection*—which was written under special circumstances, with a special end in mind—little of the specific matter of his social opinions reaches his creative works. The ties are there nevertheless. In the expository essays he immerses himself in time; in the fictive works he reaches for eternity. His fictive works are beautiful parables, shorn of the limiting details of time and fact, verbal icons raised above the qualifications of history.

But the two kinds of writing turn on one axis—that of coercion and freedom. If one goes through the opinions Tolstoy pours out on every conceivable subject during this period, and strikes through the gestures and the increasingly public man, then one finds a Tolstoy who, as in the early works, is against every form of coercion and for every form of freedom. Men must not serve the government, because the government *forces* its citizens to pay it tribute, to serve in the military, and to do its will; the church is evil because it *forces* its adherents to worship, *coercing* them by fear and superstition to do its will. Private property is evil because it is a form of power by which one man *owns* another. Modern art (since the Enlightenment) is corrupt because it is a class art, that is, an institution by which one group of people imposes its will on another. Whether it is religion, economics, art, or politics, Tolstoy's answer is always the same: the individual by himself is capable of recognizing the truth; his reason—when untouched by false education and the manifold corruptions of church, government, society, history, and fellow man—is a vehicle that conducts the truth to him. All truth comes from the inviolate individual; all error comes from those who would violate the sanctity of the individual, whether of others or themselves. One does not need teachers, priests, government officials, or even one's fellow man. If some of this appears to be in opposition to Tolstoy's often-voiced ideal of brotherhood, one must pause, because Tolstoy's brotherhood is not what we think. Or at least the path to his brotherhood is not by way of the community. Indeed, man reaches brotherhood by freeing himself from his fellow man. The truths that Tolstoy preached during this period are of consummate simplicity, yet also of complexity. They are direct yet mysterious. Nor are they so different, except in points of emphasis, from those he put forth in his early works, where he had celebrated the individual as his own source of salvation and had censured imitation of others, the codifications of emotions and beliefs, as the source of corruption. The truth was to be found within man and not outside of him, then as now.

Tolstoy tried to kill his art in the eighties but could not. The gold continued to flow from his pen into such works as *The Death of Ivan Ilych*, *Master and Man*, and *Hadji Murad*. Tolstoy could not resist the increasing demands of a public partly of his own making for statements on pressing contemporary problems. But some part of himself—even while resisted and contemned by the public man—reached into eternity through his art. There was a second Tolstoy after the conversion, and a second art. The second art was different from the first but the same in quality. Tolstoy could only be a great writer, even though he was the only writer who tried not to be.

The Death of Ivan Ilych was Tolstoy's first published work after his conversion. It was written after almost a decade of immersion in theological reflection and writing, and indifference to the writing of fiction. More schematic and deliberate than the early tales, it is more pruned of descriptive and analytic detail. The density of circumstances is largely absent, and it reads like a distillation rather than a representation of life. Disdaining the verisimilitude that such density often confers upon an artistic work, Tolstoy makes his appeal by way of formulaic selection of essential detail. This gives the tale the air of a chronicle or parable. Such a manner could easily lead to abstract moralizing; yet, though the moralizing is there, the details and skeletal action have been so skillfully chosen that the distinctly uncontemporary mode of narration succeeds in an astonishing manner. There is, too, in *The Death of Ivan Ilych*—as there will be in the tales that follow—a punishing quality about Tolstoy's moral passion. He seems now more certain of the truth—more eager to castigate those who do not live by the truth. These are unpromising attitudes for the production of great art, but Tolstoy does not hesitate to express them. It must be remembered too that these are the years when Tolstoy's views on the uselessness and perniciousness of Western art, his own included, are maturing. The passions for moral truth and pedagogy cannot overcome his art, but they themselves are conquered and turned to the purposes of great art. It is to the art that we must turn in order to see how this had been accomplished.

The art of *The Death of Ivan Ilych* has affected widely diverse audiences and lent itself to various modes of dissection. The story is great enough to support the weight of different critical perspectives. It has the "transparency" that Roland Barthes has put forth as a mark of the greatest works of literature, permitting us to speak about it with the different critical languages of time, place, and critical intelligence. The Freudians, for example, have had little to do with Ivan Ilych, and Tolstoy's narrative manner as well as his philosophical convictions would seem to leave little terrain to work over. Tolstoy abjures ambiguity and symbolization; the intent of the narrative style is to lay everything out as clearly as possible. Nevertheless, Ivan Ilych's life may be described as a system of determined evasions of love, human contact, and self-knowledge. Because he has arranged his life in a rigid, ritualistic manner, it is easily unhinged by unexpected events, however trivial. There is nothing of the flexibility of interaction with reality that is the mark of a healthy man for Freud. Freud spoke of "love and work" as the two qualities of the healthy person. But Ivan Ilych has never learned to love and never learned to love work. He follows his career—in his father's footsteps—as one would a military campaign, with ramparts thrown up to keep him from contact with reality or human emotions, whether those of others or his own. It would take only a shift of vocabulary to see his rigidities and evasions as neurotic flight and defense.

Indeed, one can read this short novel as Ivan Ilych's attempt to appease one father and his discovery of another. Identification with his father and alienation from himself and real life by way of that identification constitutes the essense of his emotional life. He follows in his father's footsteps quite literally, imitating the relentless march toward the sinecure his father occupied and toward which his father has launched him. He is a "good boy," not only the *phénix de la famille*, but also the "good boy" in the greater family of the bureaucratic and social circle in which he makes his career. He looks to his surrogate "fathers" with the same kind of attentiveness and pleas for approval as he had done apparently with his own father. Doing what is expected of him, he is rewarded for what he does. When he reflects on the various advantages of marrying Praskovya Fyodorovna, the most important is the approval of his superiors. What he does and what he feels have already been chosen for him. His greatest reward is to become one of the fathers—to enjoy what they had enjoyed.

In such a reading, Ivan Ilych's sickness would be a sign of his health, for the sickness (the bruise on his side), like a visitant from another world, would represent the return of the repressed, and as such would be perceived as painful. It is perhaps no accident that the pain that penetrates his body awakens in him memories of his childhood—of a sensuous and very personal nature. The personal life from which he had been deflected by identification with the life of the fathers is what returns to his consciousness; this for Tolstoy is a sign of health. The pain, which alienates him from the life of his fathers, returns him to his own forgotten, personal, and individualized life. This return is accompanied by what one would call "childhood" situations: Ivan Ilych is scolded by his doctors and by his wife; he becomes progressively helpless; Gerasim has to carry him from chamber pot to sofa as one would a child. One can even go so far as to say that he "progresses" back to "birth," for the symbolism of the black bag and the issuing into light is put in terms of birth pangs and giving birth.

The tale would seem too—in its evident philosophical and Christian intentions—to offer little for Marxist analysis; yet I am persuaded that it will bear a refined Marxist analysis—something that the Soviets have never given it. If we consider the tale in the light of Marx's propositions about the alienation man suffers in a commodity culture, the possibility of such a reading becomes evident. Things, it must be admitted, are prominent in the story, and Tolstoy plays stylistically on the density and power of possessions. Ivan Ilych is not ready to start his career—after being trained like a seal for it—until he has been provided with a portmanteau, an inscribed medallion for his watch chain, new linen, a traveling rug, and toilet accessories. He wants Praskovya Fyodorovna as much for her property as for her pretty face and correct social position. Things determine Ivan Ilych's feelings, his relationship with people, his pain and pleasure, his happiness and misery. His life has been environed by things: he is tucked in with them when he goes off to his first job; his marriage begins with conjugal caresses, new crockery, furniture, linen; his highest moment comes with the furnishing of a new house; and his fall comes from reaching to hang a drape. The whatnots, antiques, dishes, plates on the wall, bronzes, and upholstery which Ivan Ilych has bought, arranged, hung, and installed bring him and his wife and daughter to ecstasy and temporary harmony. But the same objects bring Ivan Ilych to irritation with every spot on the tablecloth, and to an explosive quarrel with his wife about expensive cakes left over from a party. Most of the characters in the novel relate to each other by way of what they possess. What they think, say, feel, and value has been congealed in what they own. They have become commodities, as is patently evident in the way the doctors handle Ivan Ilych's pain and the way that Ivan Ilych's dearest friends look upon his death. His death is an opportunity to be exploited, something to be measured by benefits or advantages. Indeed, the whole work may be read as a series of exploitations by Ivan Ilych and of him.

The novel lends itself magnificently, too, to a "formalist" or close linguistic analysis, for Tolstoy's art is rich in calculated linguistic effects. The power of the first line of the chronicle proper is unsurpassed in simple beauty: "Ivan Ilych's life had been the most simple and the most ordinary and therefore the most terrible" (*Proshedshaya istoriya zhizni Ivana Il'icha byla samaya prostaya i obyknovennaya i samaya uzhasnaya*). The line gets much of its beauty and power from the control the words exercise on the chronicle that follows. A range of possible meanings of the word simple (*prostaya*), in English and Russian, is artfully exploited. There is the intended meaning of "without complexity," but the word can also mean something left out, and there is also the hint of "foolish." The most powerful influence of the line comes from the juxtaposition of "simple" and "ordinary" (*obyknovennaya*) with the word "terrifying" (*uzhasnaya*).[1] For if there is a dominant emotional effect in the novel it is the juxtaposition of common life with uncommon horror. We ordinarily expect horrible consequences from horrible causes. The horrible fate of Dostoevsky's characters, for instance, come from horrible crimes and guilts; even Anna Karenina's terrible fate comes from such proportionally terrible acts as leaving a husband and child for a guilty love. But Ivan Ilych's life is ordinary, structured on a few simple contrasts which are repeated with monotonous appropriateness: what is pleasant or unpleasant and what is proper or improper. In the course of the story the contrasts are confounded, so that the novel is based largely on a series of reversals. During the course of the tale, pleasure becomes pain, what is proper becomes what is not proper, approval of society becomes disapproval, the solidity of things becomes the spectrality of things, Ivan Ilych's well-regulated life becomes unregulated, and the common pleasure becomes the uncommon horror. The development of the story consists essentially of the progressive growth of Ivan Ilych's consciousness of the horror that lies below his well-regulated, pleasure-dominated, proper life. The story moves toward what the opening lines announce: the end is the beginning, and the beginning is the end. It is in keeping with this structure of ironic reversals that Tolstoy gives us the death of Ivan Ilych before telling us about his life.

Before Tolstoy gives us the chronicle of Ivan Ilych's life, he tells us what it was worth, how it should be judged. Irony is his weapon of judgment; we know immediately what we are supposed to be for or against. We are supposed to be against the predatory self-interest barely concealed beneath the routine expressions of condolence. The contrast between the conventional forms and private feeling is something Tolstoy has done many times before, but here he is doing a great deal more. The announcement of Ivan Ilych's death comes in one of those respites from judicial labor that Ivan Ilych loved so much, as is commented on later in the novel—when he was able to smoke, drink tea, talk about politics, general topics and most of all about official appointments. That is, we learn about his death in a situation that recalls one of the pleasures he enjoyed while he was alive, and the scene is the first of a series of identifications by which the life of Ivan Ilych before and after death is compared and analogized. The opening scene which presents Ivan Ilych in death is at the same time a representation of his life.

Tolstoy meticulously re-creates in the opening scene the atmosphere, conditions, values, and modes of behavior by which Ivan Ilych had lived, and the recreation in dramatic form is a judgment on Ivan Ilych in death. Life as Ivan Ilych had lived goes on after he is dead. As Ivan had a passion for bridge, so Pyotr Ivanovich, weariedly performing the duty of paying respects to the dead, hurries away to meet the impish and impious Schwartz for a game of bridge. As Ivan Ilych had taken from Praskovya Fyodorovna only the conveniences of board and room, so Praskovya Fyodorovna in her tearful conversation with Pyotr

Ivanovich reveals a predatory concern only with the monetary convenience she can gain from her husband's death. Ivan Ilych had labored to furnish his house with whatnots, antiques, dishes and plates on the walls, and Tolstoy goes to the point—in his recreation of Ivan Ilych's life—of drawing our attention to some of the commodities that had ruled his life and which continue to exist after his death. The room in which Pyotr Ivanovich talks to Praskovya Fyodorovna is filled with furniture and bric-a-brac that Ivan Ilych had collected. Pyotr Ivanovich's attention is explicitly drawn to the upholstered furniture in pink cretonne that Ivan Ilych had consulted him about and to the antique clock that Ivan Ilych had liked so much.

As Ivan Ilych treated people before death, so they treat him after death. The "worth" of his colleagues was their capacity to advance his welfare and his pleasure, and the "worth" of Ivan Ilych in death is the opportunity his passing gives to others to advance their welfare and pleasure. He treated people impersonally and was indifferent to their vital interests. This was most evident in his relationship with his wife, with whom he talked at times only when a third person was present. She pays him back in death. We learn of his death in the opening scene by way of the formal obituary that Praskovya Fyodorovna has written, which Fyodor Vasilievich reads to his colleagues in the judicial chamber. The conventional expression of sorrow in the obituary is the precise correlative, in impersonality, of the actual emotions Praskovya Fyodorovna has toward her deceased husband. The items of description in this opening scene are a duplication of the kinds of feelings, human relationships, and objects in which Ivan Ilych had lived. Tolstoy is saying that Ivan Ilych's life is the ironical factor in his death.

The dramatized beginning casts its shadow over the chronicle that follows. We know that Ivan Ilych's life will be shallow, impersonal. The form of the narration that follows reinforces this judgment. Large blocks of Ivan Ilych's life are expressed in a few paragraphs, and Tolstoy deliberately mixes matters of consequence and inconsequence so as to reduce all the events to a kind of undifferentiated triviality. He tells us, for example: "The preparations for marriage and the beginning of married life, with its conjugal caresses, the new furniture, new crockery, and new linen, were very pleasant...," mixing love and furniture in similar grammatical form and brevity. Later, the death of two children is reported in a subordinate clause, while the main clauses are retained for an account of the father's troubles.

The narration of the first seventeen years of Ivan Ilych's married life—an accounting of moves, promotions, successes—reads like an inventory rather than a life. The sameness of the events makes it difficult to remember what is individual, significant, or striking. Events of a significant personal nature do appear in his life, but Ivan Ilych manages, by adhering closely to the proper and decorous rules of his society, to avoid them. During the first months of her pregnancy, Praskovya Fyodorovna interrupts the even course of properness and pleasantness by irrational bursts of jealousy, by demands for his attention, and by coarse and ill-mannered scenes. But Ivan Ilych evades such pleas for sympathy by spending more time away from her; he evades her pleas as he evades similar pleas of the accused in his courtroom. All this is done in the name of good breeding, conformity to public opinion. The law of the society, to which Ivan Ilych subscribes enthusiastically, is the law of pleasantness and properness. What is disagreeable and improper has no place in this mode of life, and when it obtrudes itself—as had Praskovya Fyodorovna's behavior during pregnancy—it is ignored or relegated to irrationality.

Ivan Ilych's meaningless life takes on meaning only when the disagreeable that intrudes on his life cannot be ignored. When he is passed over for promotion, he is jolted out of mechanical complacency and projected into anger and self-evaluation. By happenstance, this intrusion in his well-planned and decorous life is quickly erased when Ivan Ilych manages to obtain a position better than the one he had been denied. His life resumes its decorous, pleasant course, but another disagreeable event, more fateful than the first, intrudes upon his life. He "falls," and the ambiguity of the word and its biblical connotations were probably intended by Tolstoy. The "fall," to be sure, is appropriately trivial: from a ladder and while he is occupied with the objects that are the explicit badge of his place in society. Ivan Ilych has climbed only as high as the drapery, but the fall is as deep as the abyss of death and the agonies of consciousness before death. This second accident with its attending misery brings Ivan Ilych to a kind of spiritual rebirth, to irritation, reflection, self-evaluation, and finally to an awareness of himself and of others. Little by little the pain, which penetrates his usual activities, excludes him from the unpainful lives of his associates, bringing him to isolation and to confrontation with that isolation. The pain in his side makes him different from others; it individualizes him.

The pain grows to affect his dinner, his bridge, his relations with his wife; it spoils his work and his enjoyment of his furniture. His pleasant, decorous life becomes unpleasant, indecorous. At first it affects only his outer life, but gradually it affects his inner life; it overcomes the resistances of self-satisfaction and self-exoneration and leads him to self-assessment and self-incrimination. Ivan Ilych comes finally to see that his life has been wrong, but he comes first to see that the lives of others are wrong. He notices that no one really cares that he is in pain. They ignore his pain; when they cannot ignore it, they trivialize it; and when this is no longer possible, they blame him for it. It is Ivan Ilych's pain, not theirs, and they want to be touched by it as little as possible. They give only what they have always given, which is what Ivan Ilych had always given when confronted with someone else's pain and someone else's appeal for compassion and love: pretended compassion and love, that is, the conventional forms of polite interest and concern. As Ivan Ilych earlier defended himself against involvement in his wife's pain by blaming her (she was irrational) and absenting himself, so now Praskovya Fyodorovna defends herself against involvement in his pain by blaming him (he was irrational in not following the doctor's orders) and by absenting herself with her opera, social life, and involvement in her daughter's coming marriage.

To the measure that Ivan Ilych's pain mounts and his behavior becomes disagreeable, the indifference of those about him becomes more determined. The weapons they use to protect themselves against his pain are the weapons that Ivan Ilych used to protect himself from everything unpleasant. Schwartz continues to be impish; the bridge games go on; his wife, daughter, and the daughter's fiancé go to the theater and carry on the foolish conversations about art. Indeed, the tempo of enjoyment of those close to him seems to mount in inverse relationship to the increase of his pain. When he is about to lapse into the final day of unceasing pain, the daughter announces her engagement to the young examining magistrate, and the pleasure of Praskovya Fyodorovna and the daughter is at its apex.

Ivan Ilych comes to see their indifference and cruelty and he comes to blame them. He does not blame himself—not, at least, until the very end. Several times during his illness the thought comes to him that perhaps he has not lived his life well, but each time he dismisses the idea as nonsensical. He comes far enough in his forced, slow reassessment to admit that there had been little happiness in his life, and what there has been took place in childhood and has been decreasing ever since. But it is not until his final hours that Ivan Ilych sees the truth of his life. Undoubtedly the struggle he puts up in the black bag is a symbol of the struggle he maintains to justify his life. He slips through the bag and into the light only when, in his final hours, he stops justifying his life and listens, specifically when he himself feels pity for others: first for his son, who has come with eyes swollen with tears, and then for his wife.

It is hard to make artistic sense of Ivan Ilych's conversion, of the symbolism of the black bag, and the truth that he sees in the last moments of his life. The gradual reassessment of the worth of his life that he makes under the bludgeon of pain, the frustrated demands for compassion, the polite indifference to his plight from others, and his terrifying aloneness before impending death are all psychologically believable and well done by Tolstoy. But it is another matter to believe in the "revelation" that Ivan Ilych experiences when he slips through the bag and to believe artistically in a spiritual rebirth.

There is another difficulty, too, present throughout the long ordeal of Ivan Ilych's sickness. Ivan Ilych himself poses the problem one night about a month before his death when, exhausted by pain, he weeps "because of his helplessness, his terrible loneliness, the cruelty of man, the cruelty of God, and the absence of God." He cries out to God: "Why hast Thou done all this? Why hast Thou brought me here? Why, why dost Thou torment me so terribly?" The problem is correctly expressed in his anger against the senselessness of the suffering he undergoes, the lack of proportion between whatever he has done and what he has been forced to suffer, and against the contingency, accidentality, and senselessness of his fate.

If we ask with Ivan Ilych why he had to be bludgeoned by pain, we cannot say it is because he lived his life badly, although Tolstoy seems to be saying that. Even if we suppress the perfectly normal rejoinder that all the others in the society have lived lives just as badly but do not suffer, we still cannot find in any moral calculation a connection between the badly lived life and the physical pain. The life is not that bad, and the pain and terror are too much. The life is too trivial for the pain to be so great. We can make sense of the psychological pain—the loneliness, the suffering from lack of compassion, the humiliation of being treated as a thing by those about him—because these follow on the kind of life that Ivan Ilych has led. The lives of others in the society, like Ivan Ilych's, are trivial and terrifying, for reasons that are artistically believable. But we cannot make sense of the physical pain that Ivan Ilych suffers, nor, for that matter, why he and not others must suffer such pain.

If Tolstoy insists on the psychological suffering that Ivan Ilych undergoes after the "fall," he insists even more crudely on the sheer

physical pain that Ivan Ilych endures. The unremitting howling of
Ivan Ilych in the last three days of his life is a detail so monstrous that
only Tolstoy's art could make it palatable. We know why Ivan Ilych
suffers loneliness, fear, anger, resentment, depression after the "fall"
but we do not know why he has to die. I believe that Tolstoy is
conscious of the gulf between Ivan Ilych's behavior and his fate, and it
is precisely the irrationality and the utter inexplicability of the gulf
that he wants to express. Death exists, and it is the truth. It is
something that Ivan Ilych has not believed in and that the others in his
society do not believe in. But it is the reality, nevertheless. The
"pain" they so assiduously avoid, of which death is a summation,
comes to be referred to as *ona* in Russian ("it" in the feminine
gender), that is, both to pain (*bol'*) and death (*smert'*). It is this
pain-death that makes Ivan Ilych's former life increasingly spectral,
and that unmakes the pleasure he has guided his life by.

I am suggesting that it is the refusal to accept "death" as part of life
that leads to the sterility of Ivan Ilych's life and the lives of those about
him. Why this is so is something that follows upon Tolstoy's
conception of death. The society is built upon a pursuit of well-being
and an avoidance of discomfort. "Self-pleasure" is the law of society.
The avoidance of "pain" and ultimately death explains the series
of abstract and impersonal relations that obtain in the story. One
protects oneself from involvement in the pain others suffer by
formalizing and thus impersonalizing relations with others:

This process is illustrated in the relations between Ivan Ilych and his
wife, in his indifference toward her pain in pregnancy and her later
indifference toward his pain in his mysterious illness. Each blames
the other. His friends act similarly; they want nothing to do with
his pain, and when it obtrudes on their lives, they trivialize it,
formalize it, and deny it. Ivan Ilych may be irrascible, annoying, and
embarrassing, but he is not dying. They will not accept his pain as part
of their lives, nor will they accept his dying.

It is Gerasim alone who acknowledges the truth. He accepts the fact
that Ivan Ilych is dying and cheerfully acts to make him comfortable.
He breathes the health of youth and natural peasant life, lifts up the
legs of the dying Ivan Ilych, cleans up after him with good humor, and
in general shows him a kind of natural compassion. Expressly con-
joining Gerasim's health and vitality with his acceptance of death,
Tolstoy seems to be saying that death and life go together. But it is not
immediately clear how they go together.

Death is for Tolstoy the supreme irrational event: an event

impervious to human desire, understanding or the manipulation of will. It is also the summation of whatever is disagreeable in life—of every pain, sickness, and accident. Ivan Ilych's plea for justice from a seemingly cruel God may arouse our sympathy, but for Tolstoy the plea is an attempt to bring death into the realm of human understanding. There is no logic to Ivan Ilych's sickness and death, no accounting for the intrusion of such pain into his well-ordered life, and surely none that he rather than someone else be picked out for the special bludgeoning. The fact cannot be understood or justified. But it does make a difference, apparently, whether we acknowledge death. If we ignore it, then our lives are struck with sterility; our relations with others and ourselves become impersonal.

Why this should be so is not immediately clear, since the consciousness of death may lead to a whole range of attitudes, including despair and stoicism. It may lead and has led to the impoverishment as well as to the enrichment of life. The special tie that Tolstoy seems to see now between the conscious acceptance of death and fullness of life can be explained in part by turning back to his early work. Although *The Death of Ivan Ilych* signals a change in Tolstoy's view of the world, it also reaffirms the continuity of his thinking and his art. In the early writings, through *War and Peace*, Tolstoy had celebrated submission to the accidentality of circumstances and had satirized the attempt to control circumstances either by an outright act of will or by making subtle demands upon life. The withdrawal of control over life and the humility before the infinitude of circumstances was what revealed the manifold beauty, wealth, and significance of life; now, in *The Death of Ivan Ilych*, it is the consciousness and acceptance of death that reveals the significance of life. In this sense, then, we are beginning to see, beginning with this tale, a profound shift in his view of the world. Tolstoy is now saying that the acceptance of the world and the revelation of the complex purity of sensuous things are not enough, because the roots of the sensuous things are deeper than their flowering in this world. Without the consciousness of death, the things themselves become spectral, as indeed they become with Ivan's consciousness of his impending death.

The reasons for this change have to do with a great number of things among which Tolstoy's religious conversion, his advancing age, and the maturing of his philosophical views must count. It is probably impossible to separate cause from effect, nor may it matter. However, his concern with "brotherhood" seems to lie, at least in part, at the heart of the change. Critics have generally taken his concern with

brotherhood as an indication that his view of truth has changed: that
he sees it not as something individual but as something communal.
This is the way, for example, that Janko Lavrin understands Tolstoy's
religious thought in his later years.[2] If one takes individualism to
imply exploitation and selfishness, Lavrin is right. Still, Tolstoy had
always been against these things, and the only difference with the later
works would be one of emphasis and directness. But if one takes
individualism as Tolstoy had defined it, in his early creative works
through *War and Peace*, as the radically concrete at-one-ness with
one's being and with the sensuous flow about one, then he continues
to champion individualism. There is thus consistency and continuity
in his thought and creation. The repeated refrain of his later
works—whatever the collective words of brotherhood, sacrifice, giving—is that one comes to brotherhood by way of individual reason
and consciousness. Tolstoy's Christian anarchism represents in one
sense the most extreme individualism, because it makes one's being
inviolate to the tamperings of secular authority of any kind. Society in
the sense of abstract impositions of others on oneself was opposed to
individualism in the early works, and it continues to be opposed to it
in the later works. The point is that one comes to brotherhood by
being oneself. And one come to "false" brotherhood by being
anti-individual, that is, by way of societies, abstract religious precepts,
governments—in other words, by way of generalized feelings and
choices above the concrete flow within one.

The sacramental moments in the early works had to do with some
enriched individualism: a Natasha swimming in the happiness of her
own being and indifferent to the society about her; a Nikolay cut off
from the social forms of regiment, estate, and possible marriage and
alone with the primal elements of field, sensation, desire, and wolf.
The individual and society are opposed, but after the conversion
Tolstoy needs to find some way to weld religious conviction with
aesthetic and philosophic outlook to bring individual and society
together. He does it on the theological and social levels by his
exhortations to share one's goods, love one's fellow man, and resist no
evil. He can make his exhortations directly in his expository works, but
his artistic conscience works to preserve as well as to deny. Something
of the same changes can be seen to operate in his artistic works, though
in a form that preserves what he had said before the conversion.
Society and the individual are still opposed in *The Death of Ivan Ilych*
as they had been in the early works. It is through himself and his own
suffering that Ivan Ilych comes to the truth about himself, and not

through education, the imitation of others, or indoctrination by others. Natasha, Nikolay at the hunt, Andrey on the battlefield of Austerlitz come to the truth by way of individual consciousness as Ivan Ilych does. But whereas the consciousness of Natasha, Andrey, and Nikolay is one of immediate seizure of some pristine and personal perceptual and sensuous manifold, Ivan Ilych's consciousness is one of personal suffering. Pain and the consciousness of death are now the special conditions of perceiving truth, not happiness and absorption in sense. Death for Tolstoy now, as the supremely shared experience, is the model of all solidarity, and only the profound consciousness of its significance can bring one to the communion of true brotherhood. The sacramental individual moments of the early works brought one to communion with others only by way of the infectious spirit of such happiness: Andrey is drawn to Natasha because she is absorbed in her own immediate being, and Pierre is able to command the interest of the Mamantov sisters and of Villarsky because he looks at things only from his own point of view. Because such absorption in self implies respect for the selves of others, Tolstoy has a theoretical position for the infection of one being upon another. Yet the radical individualism on which these moments are based offer at best a limited communing effect. The consciousness of death, Tolstoy is convinced, is the cement of true brotherhood. Even while he continues to preach brotherhood and to portray the consciousness of it in his artistic works, Tolstoy continues to denounce false brotherhood (society). Such false brotherhood comes about and manifests itself in ways that are similar to those of the early works: by imitation, group control, education, that is, by way of nonindividual experience.

There is both continuity and change in Tolstoy's artistic works beginning with *The Death of Ivan Ilych*. The continuity is preserved in the "form" of experience, which continues as before to be radically individual and given, something prior to the educative influence of others; but the change lies in the character of that "given," which is no longer simply the purity of the instincts. Tolstoy would have said with Dostoevsky and father Zossima that the roots of sensuous things lie in other worlds. What is real and human for him is the consciousness of death; without such consciousness the experiences of this world are spectral. This is precisely what he portrays so magnificently in *Master and Man*.

8   *Master and Man*

None of the later works fits more accurately the requirements that Tolstoy set forth in *What Is Art?* than does *Master and Man*. *What Is Art?* provoked general disapproval when it was first published in 1898. Although the outrage has subsided, the criticism, more distant now and less, is still just as uncompromising. This is not the place for an analysis or defense of *What Is Art?* It should be noted, however, that what Tolstoy was saying in his creative works was of one piece with what he was saying in his religious, political and economic writings. Even more, his later works reflect something of his thinking on art. He was asking in *What Is Art?* for an art that would be understandable by everyone, an art of simplicity against one of sophistication, of ease of understanding against difficulty of understanding, of universal situations against exclusive or special themes—an art for everyone against an art for few people. These seem reasonable goals, but they may be threatening to what has been the exclusionist trend of Western art. It is hard to think of a single Western critic, whatever the country, at least since the Renaissance, who has not held a view of art as something sacred. We may differ as to what constitutes the greatness of art, but we do not question that it has "high seriousness." There are only high views of art in the West, and it was Tolstoy's "low" view of art that was infuriating to the West. But he was not alone in such a view, for he was following fairly closely in the tradition of Chernyshevsky and Pisarev, both of whom questioned the utility of art.

As Russian critical thought has always vacillated between "high" and "low" views of art, so Tolstoy, broad as he was, embodied both views. The West, reacting with fury to his "low" view, did not notice that he had a "high" view also, but even the high view with its anti-elitist thrust was so much at variance with what the West has always thought of art that this too had to be rejected. When Tolstoy fulminated in *What Is Art?* against corrupted art and put forth criteria for a true and universal art, he had in mind a work of the simplicity and beauty of *Master and Man*. The subject matter of this tale is universal, its style is simple, and the technique is immediately accessible to understanding.

Master and Man more clearly embodies the criteria of good art as put forth in *What Is Art?* than does *The Death of Ivan Ilych*. The latter has a density of detail and a complexity of psychology that separates it somewhat from the ideal art that Tolstoy proposed. *Master and Man* has the elements of a morality play. Vassily Brekhunov is a man of this world—selfish, overbearing, rich, rapacious. He is the biblical rich man filling his granaries and neglecting his soul. Nikita is the opposite: he is the poor man who is rich in spirit. Vassily is insensitive and crude, Nikita sensitive and humane. One bludgeons the world and the other meekly accepts his lot. Tolstoy makes no attempt to soften the contrast. Vassily, the rich man, is dressed in two fur coats and expensive leather boots; and Nikita, the poor man, is dressed in a worn, greasy sheepskin and patched felt boots. Tolstoy will have nothing to do with ambiguity; he is determined that no reader, no matter how unsophisticated, will miss the difference between Nikita and Vassily, nor for that matter the significance of the journey they undertake, which is a passing from life to death.

The elements are few, and the disposition of them has the air of a parable. Tolstoy stresses without embarrassment the "everyman" character of the tale. The details that anchor the story in contemporary Russia are few—the names, a few mannerisms, a sprinkling of local color. But once beyond the village and in the snow storm, the journey becomes everyone's journey across life and toward death; Vassily Brekhunov becomes all the rich, overbearing, profit-grasping men of the world, and Nikita all the suffering, gentle, have-nots. This is the tale of the man of flesh and the man of spirit joined together in the journey of life and confrontation with death. The elements of the story are the most enduring of man's experience and understanding: the flesh and spirit and life and death.

The point of the story is largely the effect that the consciousness of death has upon Brekhunov and his relationship to Nikita and, by extension, the effect of death upon the relationship of man to the other. Tolstoy achieves this effect by playing on the symbolic qualities of the snow storm. Much of the power of the tale rests in the way in which he uses the natural setting of the snow storm to communicate the palpable presence of death and its progressive extinguishing of what we normally associate with life. The snow "buries" the travelers and is cold like death. The Russian word for "snowdrift," into which

Vassily and Nikita sink (*sugrob*), contains within it the word *grob*, the word for coffin or in its archaic meaning "grave." The snow joins heaven and earth (we are told that the line between heaven and earth was not visible), and one loses one's bearings in the snow storm so that what one thought substantial becomes spectral and what was spectral becomes substantial. The habitations of men in this great white waste are like small islands of comfort and, as such, islands of illusion that are shelters against the annihilating white. Tolstoy's fulminations in the early works against the corruptions of society have now taken the ghastly form of showing society's irrelevance in the presence of death. Culture, society, history had always been "contrivances" for Tolstoy, obscuring what is essential in man's relationship to life. And what is most essential in the relationship at this juncture in his career is death. He seems intent on confronting a universe of waste, so as to gauge what is left. The snow in the tale erases the scratchings of civilization, the roads and the mile posts; it environs everything that we associate with human life and civilization. Tolstoy is intent on seeing what is left when the illusions are stripped away.

As the story progresses, the sensuous world is progressively annihilated by the snow storm, as it is annihilated by death. Motion becomes stillness; sound, silence; color, the enveloping whiteness; the variety of nature, the uniformity of the bleak snow. Light, sound, heat, motion are progressively extinguished. People become fewer, communication grows sporadic. Nikolay and Vassily are moved relentlessly to a terrifying isolation and dispossession of everything that surrounds them in their normal life, so as to face the presence of death without the illusions of civilization. The opening scene of the story, for example, is characterized by motion, preparations, and noise. Nikita runs to harness the horse, jingles the bit; the horse smacks its lips after drinking, plays with Nikita, and strains to gambol over the yard. Vassily's young boy rushes into the yard, excitedly leaps into the sledge, and then just as excitedly insists on holding the reins while Nikita goes inside to dress more warmly. Vassily, excited by the drink, frowns, compresses his lips, spits, talks loudly and peremptorily. Voices and movement dominate the scene. The wind, harbinger of the storm, is hardly heard in the yard. As the story progresses, the motion, sound, and communication will subside, until they have been totally obliterated by the snow storm. After the second departure from Grishkino, Mukhorty slows down to a walk, trots only while under the sting of the whip, slows down again, and finally comes to a complete stop by the edge of a ravine. The effect—which is achieved gradually and unobtrusively—is one of something giving out, like energy exhausting itself. After Mukhorty stops, Vassily makes one last, desperate attempt to move again by leaping on the horse, leaving Nikita behind. When he slips off the horse, he attempts to make his way through the deep snow, only to return to the point from which he began.

As with the motion, so too with communication. When the journey begins, Vassily attempts to talk to Nikita about the cooper who lives with Nikita's wife, and about the horse he wants to sell to Nikita. But as soon as they leave the village behind them, Vassily's words are carried off by the wind. Nikita has trouble hearing his master, and eventually Vassily lapses into silence. Only when Vassily and Nikita visit briefly the peasant family in Grishkino does the sound of human communication revive. By the time we reach the climactic scene of the novel by the ravine, Vassily is talking to himself, thinking to himself; finally even his thoughts are annihilated by the fear and the cold that penetrate his being. Little by little the snow and its qualities, and its symbolic analogue of death and eternity, obliterate everything that we normally associate with temporal human reality. Light and heat, for example, are similarly extinguished during the course of the journey. It is growing dark when Vassily and Nikita start out from the village; when they get to Grishkino the second time, the lights are on in the village. After the brief respite in the peasant's hut, Vassily and Nikita go out into the darkness again, and the light of the peasant's lantern is promptly blown out by the wind. When they are finally buried in the snow by the side of the ravine, Vassily's last matches flicker briefly before the wind extinguishes them.

The same progressive annihilation of the fixities of the world is at work in the central pattern of the story—the hold that possessions have on Vassily's mind. Having undertaken the journey to increase his possessions, he discovers how futile the possessions are in the face of death. Vassily is an economic man. His relationships to everything and everyone have to do with profit. He is a church elder, but he views the church, like everything else, as something to make profit from. When preparing for the journey, he takes 2,300 rubles of church money in his keeping, adding it to 700 rubles of his own for the down payment he intends to make for the wood. Later we learn that he has been reselling partially used candles. He blatantly exploits Nikita. He values Nikita because he is cheap and works hard; he does not pay him the wages he has agreed to, and what he pays him must be spent at his store, so that Nikita is doubly robbed. Even his relationship to his own family is economic. His wife inspires such disgust in him when she urges him to take Nikita with him that he spits and compresses his lips as he does when he is making a deal. He seems genuinely delighted with his seven-year-old son, but Tolstoy is careful to point out that Vassily always thinks of his son as an heir (that is, not as a person). His wife's insistence that he take Nikita with him appears at first to be genuine concern for his personal welfare. But we learn in her next remark that she is concerned about his traveling alone because he is carrying money.

Vassily grows rich at the expense of others, a relationship that Tolstoy expresses in physical terms. Vassily is rotund, florid, energetic; while both his wife and his son—not to speak of Nikita—are thin and pale. Vassily's inner life is a reflection of his outer life. He can think of nothing but his possessions, his deals, and his plans to increase his possessions. Something like an arithmetical computation seems to go on constantly in his mind. When the chill of death begins to penetrate his being, something of a struggle goes on between the disturbing "cold" and his ability to warm himself with thoughts of his possessions. In the end the fear triumphs, and he makes the desperate attempt to save himself. When he falls off Mukhorty and finds himself alone, half-buried in the snow and face to face with the scraggly wormwood pitilessly driven by the wind, he cannot believe that what is happening to him is real. An authoritative English translation tells us that "he tried to wake up but could not,"[1] but the Russian tells us *on khotel prosnut'sya no prosypat'sya nekuda bylo*. The word *prosypat'sya* contains as a root the verb *sypat'sya*, which means to pour as into a hole. This word and the participial derivative *zasypanny* is used throughout the story for the endless pouring and covering of human reality that takes place during the journey. The use of the word *prosypat'sya* (to awaken) is a reminder—even as he tries to wake up from the dream—that he is being buried by the relentless reality of the snow storm.

What had been real for Vassily—his possessions—in the climactic scene becomes unreal, and what had appeared to him as unreal— "death"—becomes real. Throughout the progress of the journey, those substantial things that formed his world become more and more unreal, until in the climactic wormwood scene his possessions take on a spectral air. During the journey Vassily imagines again and again that he sees Goryachkin Wood, but each time it turns out to be a bush or a stick of wormwood. Even when he can go no further, Vassily imagines that it is getting light and that he has heard cock crow, but each time it is only wish that is projected into reality. One has the feeling in the journey with its circlings, meanderings, straying from the right road, that it is impossible to reach Goryachkin Wood, and that there is no Goryachkin Wood. For Vassily it exists because he wants it to exist and because he insists that it exist. Vassily batters the world about him into doing his will, and he expects the world to follow his wishes. During the journey his control of circumstances and the force of his will to impose itself on reality, as are all the other factors of his temporal life, are progressively thwarted and rendered ineffective. He comes to realize during the journey that he cannot ignore the snow storm or what it represents. At first he disregards the weather and the warnings of others in his eagerness to reach Goryachkin and make his profit. He is boisterously confident that the journey will be simple, braving the storm again and again despite ever more obvious signs that he is being foolish. Each time he takes the reins and pushes forward, he loses his way; each time he permits Nikita to take the reins or he follows Nikita's advice to permit the horse to find the way, he regains the road.

The journey is not without its premonitory signals. Vassily is in a sense repeatedly warned from continuing, but in his pride that life will give itself to him on his own terms, he pushes ahead. His wife attempts to dissuade him, as does the wind which persistently blows in his face. The horse thief they meet in Grishkino advises them to spend the night there, as do the peasants in Grishkino. The sledge they pass with the carousing peasants is probably to be taken as a premonitory signal also, since there are some grounds for considering that they are on their way to "hell," and the drunken Vassily, like them, is in even greater haste to reach it. There is even some evidence that during the course of the journey Vassily is ritualistically reconfronted with himself: the horse thief who advises them to stay in Grishkino is something of a double for Vassily, who in a way is also a horse thief; indeed, shortly before the encounter he had been trying to cheat Nikita by the sale of a horse. The well-to-do peasants in Grishkino mirror in some ways Vassily's own values, and the drunken peasants in the sledge receive Vassily's approval. He is heartened by the encounter.

Vassily's forcing of life and Nikita's acquiescence in his lot, and the foolishness of one and the wisdom of the other are in keeping with what Tolstoy has always championed. Nikita does not question the rightness of going out in the storm; he accepts without anger or irritation the wrong turns, and when they are forced to settle for the night he prepares with patience to wait out the night and possibly to meet death. Nikita is another example of the right relationship to life: a working in consonance with laws greater than one's ability to perceive them; an immersion in unfathomable directions; and a listening and not a dictating of what one should be and what life should be. What had largely been justified on psychological grounds in the early period—on happiness, lack of frustration, and the plenitude of being—is in the later works placed in a Christian, moral context. The world remains unfathomable in its complexities, but it is faith and not sensuous immersion that brings one in touch with the complexities; one continues to accept reality and not to dictate, but it is now the realities of God rather than those of history that one accepts.

Despite the parable-like air of the story and its overt moralism, the story does not violate our sense of what is probable—not, at least, until Vassily gives his life for Nikita. Vassily Brekhunov is made of iron for a life of transactions and accumulations, but there is little in his store house with which to face death. It is probable that he would persevere in the face of premonitory signals, and probable that he would react with panic in the presence of death. He is what he owns and, his security comes from the fear he can inspire in others. But in the stark wastes of the snow, half buried, lashed by the irrational fury of the storm, he is stripped of his possessions and power and alone with his emptiness. There is only a great white waste about him and inside him.

Vassily's unexpected sacrifice, however, is something different; it must strike us as something imposed on the psychological texture of the story. It is not unlikely that someone like Vassily would crave for human companionship when he finally realizes that he has been abandoned to the unreasoning, indifferent power of death. But one can question that this desire for companionship would take such a sacrificial, Christian form. Tolstoy has been careful to show that Vassily, under the pressure of circumstances that he cannot control, continues to be the same Vassily, eager to imagine that things will turn out as he had imagined them to be, clutching onto the material things that have ruled his outer and inner being. We would expect that Vassily would attempt to bludgeon his way toward his goal again and again, that he would warm himself with the mental computations of what he has made and what he will make, that he would cling to the last light and comfort, as he does with the cigarette and empty match box. We would even allow that Vassily might warm Nikita and himself in the physical way that he does. But it is hard to believe in the tears of joy that come to his eyes or in the indifference he feels toward his possessions at that moment. It is hard to believe in the unprepared-for, new Vassily that arises in his consciousness in his last moments of life.

The sacrifice and the tears of joy at the discovery of truth are similar to what Ivan Ilych experiences a few hours before death. Ivan Ilych, however, is led to the decisive change by a series of subtle psychological and spiritual changes. There is no comparable change in Vassily: up to the point that he lies on Nikita, feels the inexpressible joy of the action, and recognizes the truth of that feeling and the worthlessness of his former life, there is no evidence that he had any reservations about the life he had led. Ivan Ilych goes from confidence to doubt, and finally to admission of a badly lived life. Vassily goes from a smug and boisterously confident and righteous life to a terrified clinging to the rightness of his life. He thinks about the profit that the wood will bring him, about what he has accomplished and what he will accomplish, and, when assaulted by doubt and fear, about the pity of leaving all that he has accumulated. But he does not question the way he has lived. There is no preparation whatsoever for the sudden, decisive repudiation of his material life.

The change seems to be neither psychologically nor artistically palatable. Most critics have faulted the ending because of the overt Christian moralizing; those who are committed to Tolstoy's Christian preachings and have attempted to defend the ending have not been convincing. In both cases the critics have accepted the ending as an instance of Tolstoy's Christian principles. But it may be a mistake to read too quickly a Christian or sacrificial motive into Vassily's actions. Vassily's motives show nothing of what we normally associate with sacrifice. The picture of Vassily when he falls off the horse and finds himself alone half-buried in the snow and lashed remorselessly in the storm is one of existential panic, so terrifying that Vassily cannot believe it is reality and for a moment he believes it to be a dream. We look in vain for any thought—spoken or unspoken—that might indicate some spiritual change occurring in Vassily. Even less visible is any explicit Christian act or word. It is a desperate desire not to confront again the terrifying presence of death that drives Vassily to lie on top of Nikita, not a Christian desire to sacrifice himself for his fellow man. Vassily is moved by one thought alone: to allay by whatever means possible the terror (*strakh*). When he returns to the sledge, he moves immediately to fill the terror of the moment, and he does so as he has always met crises—by vigorous practical activity. He loosens his fur coat, shakes out snow from his boots and gloves, busies himself freeing the leg of the horse, and straightens out the saddle and reins. He is not moved initially to help Nikita; in fact, he does not notice him until Nikita awakens and tells him that he is dying. Even then Vassily's reaction continues to be practical, for he first occupies himself with brushing snow from Nikita. Even when he lies on Nikita, no spiritual change appears to be going on. The breathing of Nikita silences the sound of the wind and the panic associated with it, and the tears of joy that Vassily sheds come from the relief he experiences in escaping the terrible fear and in the warm presence of another human being.

Tolstoy has, of course, deliberately misled the reader, for he has structured his tale on the Christian myth, filling it with biblical sayings and Christian references. The name of the town "crosses," the goal of the journey is "Goryachkino" (hot or feverish place); the lad who quotes Paulson's reader and leads Vassily and Nikita out of town and through the storm is an allusion surely to the Old Testament prophecy that "a little child shall lead them": the saying that it is easier for a camel to pass through the eye of a needle than for a rich man to enter heaven: all these and many more are details which evoke for us at every point a Christian atmosphere, suggesting a Christian resolution. The idea that Vassily performs the quintessential Christian act of sacrificing himself for his fellow man corresponds to a pattern Tolstoy has pursued throughout the story. But Tolstoy is consciously or unconsciously distancing himself from such a conclusion by suggesting that it is not Christian principles or faith that moves men to give themselves for others but instincts of another sort.

Master and Man is a very subversive Christian work, and it has been the inability of critics to notice this subversive quality that has led them to condemn the ending. Tolstoy is suggesting that sacrifice and rebirth—central Christian mysteries—may be irrelevant. Vassily is frozen into a grotesque imitation of Christ when he is found the following day, and his imitation of Christ has not led to rebirth or immortality. Even the other world that Nikita imagines as he awakes is an illusion, since the voices are those of this world. Death, as symbolized by the snow, is a pitiless white waste which annihilates everything living. This is Tolstoy's confrontation with what, on one level, he must have feared the universe to be; his celebration of Vassily's "sacrifice" is his answer to such an existentially brutal universe. One clings to one's fellow man and one gives oneself to one's fellow man not because one is promised immortality but because that's all there is to cling to. It is men that give comfort to each other, not words or doctrine and certainly not the church; Vassily finds the prayers he knows useless when he is half buried in the snowdrift, and there is no mention of faith or of things unseen. It is a physical Vassily who lies on a physical Nikita, who gives Nikita bodily warmth. A man's shield against the terror of death is not his property, true; but nor, apparently, is it his doctrine, his church, or his faith. His shield against the terror of death is his fellow man. One fights against the chill of death by doing something, not by thinking something.

Nor is this interpretation of the novel out of keeping with Tolstoy's overt beliefs at this time. He has, as a man, and in his religious writings become fairly convinced that the Christian tenet of immortality is either false or irrelevant. Yet he continues to preach what we and he would call Christian doctrine: that one must love one's fellow man, refuse to exploit him, beg his forgiveness, and practice poverty. The social, political, and religious writings are not wholly in accord with what he has permitted himself in the story, but then one of the functions of fiction is that it permits a writer to be more frank with himself and others than he dares be or knows how to be in expository prose. It is something of a reaffirmation of Tolstoy's basic optimism and conviction in the existence of objective truth—ideals that have motivated him throughout his long life and career—that he confronts a totally brutal and existential universe and refuses to fall into despair. Among the illusions he refuses to entertain is that of organized Christianity. The brotherhood he preaches in his expository writings is a brotherhood that he believes in; but the Christianity which, in his religious writings, he purges of miracles and sacraments, and which exists in the example of Christ, is in this story—and in others too—further attenuated. Yes, men are brothers, or should be brothers, but perhaps only because they are brothers in death. It is the consciousness of death that separates what is real and unreal, that awakens us to the great white waste around us. It is perhaps no accident that it is the body of one man that warms and gives life to the body of another man. There is something grotesque about this deviation from the Christian act of sacrifice, but it is also an accurate representation of Tolstoy's insistence on what remains when one is environed by death. *Men remain*.

What one must keep in mind is that Tolstoy's brutal confrontation with a universe environed by death does not lead him to pessimism. He reaffirms his faith in the value of life in the face of such a universe, somewhat as Albert Camus was to do later. Albert Camus had confronted early in his career a universe that he believed eternally indifferent to man—one in which man was destined to suffer extinction. Yet he continued to believe that life and humanity were beautiful and to champion the unity of man by way of the right kind of "lucidity." It was not for nothing that Camus kept a picture of Tolstoy on his wall.

9 *Resurrection*

By the time Tolstoy had finished *Resurrection* he was more than an author: he was a prophet in search of his crown of thorns. The picture of the noble old man with a white beard, dressed in a linen blouse and Turkish trousers, humbly wielding his scythe, working the fields with his peasants, and persecuted by the autocratic tsar and the orthodox church, was irresistible to the world and to Tolstoy too, who played his part to the full. His fame was disseminated throughout the world in cheap editions of his work in all major languages, and endless streams of pilgrims came to assure him that he had seen the truth and that the truth was needed. Until the 1880s the world honored his art but was indifferent to his preachings; Tolstoy remained the artist first and the teacher second. But by the end of the eighties and certainly by the nineties the world wanted both his art and his truths, and Tolstoy made them the same.

Since the world wanted his opinions on the political and social situation of Russia, he obliged them by scalding rhetoric on the legal system, the prisons, private property, the bureaucracy, and every conceivable institution of contemporary tsarist Russia. There had always been a rhetorical bent in his writings; even the early works are interlarded with pronouncements on marriage, education, agriculture, and various other subjects. But never had Tolstoy's pedagogical bent assumed such gargantuan proportions as in *Resurrection*, nor had it ever posed so grave a threat to his art. George Steiner, among others, has seen the novel as seriously flawed because of the massive intrusions of political and social commentary: "When Tolstoy came to write *Resurrection*, the teacher and prophet in him did violence to the artist. The sense of equilibrium and design which had previously controlled his invention was sacrificed to the urgencies of rhetoric. In this novel the juxtaposition of two ways of life and the theme of the pilgrimage from falsehood to salvation are set forth with the nakedness of a tract."[1] It is easy to see why one would find these denunciatory essays harmful to the aesthetic quality of the novel. They are too many and too long; the person of Tolstoy is found in them too bluntly and directly; they touch too directly on the issues of the time; and they seem to have only the most external and mechanical relationship to the romantic tale of Nekhludov and Maslova's love. Yet the teacher and the prophet had not spoiled such magnificent works as *The Death of Ivan Ilych* and *Master and Man*, and they did not mar *Resurrection*— at least not as seriously as Steiner and others would have us believe.

But if the novel is not spoiled, then the tale and the tracts will have to be joined. The artistic integrity of the novel turns on this question of how one can justify the essays of social commentary—their number, length, the rhetorical anger that pervades them, and the mechanical way in which they are connected with the dramatized tale of love between Maslova and Nekhludov. The novel is structured most visibly on the alternation of visits by Nekhludov from government office to prison and from visits to officials to visits to Maslova. The point of both journeys is the pursuit of justice, and most specifically the pursuit or effort of Nekhludov to right a wrong that he has committed on the person of Maslova. We have Nekhludov's efforts to combat injustice as well as Tolstoy's efforts to combat injustice in the vituperative essays: the tale of personal injustice and the generalized exposition of injustice. One of the functions of the "tracts" surely is to multiply the significance of Nekhludov's perception and recording of the injustices he finds in society. Nekhludov's perception and sense of injustice— not only that which he has committed but also what he sees—would be too small a thing if they were not environed by the magnitude of Tolstoy's perception and wrath. Tolstoy takes what Nekhludov perceives into abstraction; yet at the same time Nekhludov concretizes what Tolstoy surveys. One apparent connection between the essays and the personal tale, then, is "illustrative," and "generalizing": the concretization of what is abstract and intellectual and the multiplication of what is personal and seemingly exceptional. One of the parallels—perhaps the most important—that Tolstoy establishes between tale and tracts by way of the structure of generalizing and illustration is the class nature of the evils that beset contemporary Russian life, a concern that Tolstoy belabors about the same time in *What Is Art?*

Tolstoy's concern with the class nature of contemporary society can be seen in the way he structures both tale and tracts about the problem of the haves and the have-nots. One part of society has arrogated to itself all the privileges, degraded the other half, and then, as protection of its privileges, has punished the other half for degradations that it itself has engendered. Tolstoy does not deal in subtleties in the essays. The representatives of the ruling class are presented as uniformly corrupt, physically and morally repulsive, lacking in human feeling, and uniformly the servants of a monstrous bureaucracy. They are gluttons, philanderers, murderers, liars, and drunkards. Those in prison are also drunkards, murderers, liars and swindlers, but they have been punished for what they have done. The haves are rewarded for it.

The debasement for Tolstoy works both ways: the haves corrupt, but they are in turn corrupted. When we first meet Maslova, she is smoking, drinking, and engaged in prostitution. But Nekhludov, too, drinks, eats, smokes, and engages in prostitution. He has been carrying on an affair with the wife of the Maréchal de Noblesse, and is contemplating the prostitution of himself by marrying Missy Korcha-gin. The differences of corruption between haves and have-nots are those of manner, privilege, and sensitivity. The sensitivity lies with the have-nots. Those in prison are shown to have passively adopted much of the predatory character of the society, but the suffering endured has endowed many of them with dignity and the capacity to feel the suffering of their fellow human beings. As the novel progresses, it becomes clear that by and large the real criminals are outside prison and the martyrs are inside prison.

It is, too, in the light of class privilege and its consequent cruelties that Tolstoy presents the personal injustice that Nekhludov inflicts on Maslova. Nekhludov acts as he does because he has been so taught and formed by the class he belongs to. He is pictured first as pure and innocent—a lover of truth, unsullied by predatory instincts, and a lover of the world and its people. After several years in the army he becomes a drunkard, a gambler, a sensuous, predatory beast. It is the military life that teaches him to drink, to talk coarsely about women and exploit them, to kill what had been true and pure in his being, and to exhalt what is corrupt and unfeeling. For Tolstoy the process of corruption of individual life by social codes is always signaled by the substitution of generalized, mechanical, and impersonal feeling for personal, specific, immediate, and constantly new feeling. One's personal life is obliterated by the general life of society. This is why, during the night of the seduction, Nekhludov moves as if in a dream, mechanically. It is not his own thoughts and feelings that move him to prurience but the voices of his fellow officers. When his love for Maslova was pure, his feelings for her were natural. They were his and not the generalized feelings of his class. Maslova and he had played as equals on that spring day when their lips first touched, but when Nekhludov returns for the Easter visit, Tolstoy is careful to remind us of the class difference of the two: she serves the family, makes beds, brings towels, food, and water. When Nekhludov first puts his arm about her, she is putting a pillow case on a pillow. On the day of his departure, he stands outside the maid's room to give her the hundred rubles. The fall of Maslova is presented as the consequence of the sexual misuse of a servant-ward by a nobleman officer, and that misuse is multiplied many times over, as Maslova is preyed upon by others again and again. The confrontation in the courtroom is between officer and maid, the misuser and the misused, the debaser and the debased; and something of the quintessential mechanism of the society is caught in the irony of the corrupter there to judge the person he has corrupted.

Nekhludov is in the courtroom to complete the fall he began many years before. If there seems little connection between the original seduction and the judicial error, it is there nevertheless. The judicial error which takes place with Nekhludov's inattentive cooperation is an example of that indifference that runs the mechanisms of society. Without the explicit intention of individuals, that indifference results in prison and degradation for many. Nekhludov need only shrug his shoulders, wash his hands, and go to dinner to the Korchagins, which indeed is what he attempts to do, after indulging in the luxury of arranging for a legal appeal. But something had moved in his soul that day, altering his perception. The dinner at the Korchagins and the people present appear to him to be grotesque, a reaction that signals repulsion with himself. Marx said that man is in his essence a social being, but what for Marx was a desirable truth was for Tolstoy only a partial and repulsive truth. Man, for him, begins to reach for his true essence only when he gives up his social being and becomes conscious of his personal being. This is what begins to happen to Nekhludov in the courtroom. It is also the fact that man's true nature lies in the realization of his individual essence that takes the locus of the novel necessarily from the problem of class conflict. Marx saw true consciousness as the awakening of the individual to class consciousness; Tolstoy saw true consciousness as an awakening to individual consciousness. The opposition in the novel between the haves and the have-nots is in the most essential respects an evasion of the real source of corruption, just as Tolstoy's thundering denunciation of the institutions by which Russia is organized is an evasion of the real source of corruption.

The class problem, as all the social and political commentary, are moral hieroglyphics betokening something beyond the institutional framework of the corruption Tolstoy rails against. Tolstoy's rhetoric at the vileness of the institutions and the men who run those institutions would seem to be a call to action. Yet a reading of these vituperations as a call to institutional reform would be grossly in error. To be sure, Tolstoy was in favor of eliminating the degradations of Russian life, was against the lumbering bureaucracy and the spiritually dead rites of the Orthodox church. But to the extent that rhetoric should move one to work for the replacement of vile institutions with better institutions, then it is a call that leads nowhere, just as the presentation of class corruption in such detail does not lead to institutional change. It takes no special emphasis to remind ourselves that it is not "bad" institutions for Tolstoy that corrupt people, but institutions themselves, whether "good" or "bad." The rhetorical wrath is a call to avoid what is the real source of both public and private corruption. In a sense, Tolstoy's "tracts" are a gargantuan misleading of the reader, an evasion he tempts us with, and as such the form of the novel proceeds largely by offering the reader more and more subtle evasions of the truth. If many of the officials in their various roles take their corruptions to be justice, so too does Tolstoy offer us a variety of injustices to be taken as justice and falsities to be taken as truths. Nekhludov is our guide, and he runs the gamut of evasions of truth.

Nekhludov's first evasion is the longest: his attempt to seek justice in the courts that condemn Maslova. He looks for what is not there. The government, offices, lawyers, and civil servants are wrong, but Nekhludov's quest is also wrong. Nekhludov is persuaded that if he makes the proper appeals, sees the right people, takes the right steps, the error in justice will be corrected. The irrelevance of his quest for justice becomes increasingly apparent in the course of the story. Nekhludov seeks what Maslova becomes increasingly indifferent to. When he tells her that he has exhausted every avenue and that everything has fallen through, she hardly hears him and answers perfunctorily and truthfully that none of it matters. She is concerned rather with his reaction to the slander that has been spread about her cavortings with the hospital attendant. What is important to her is what she is in Nekhludov's soul, not what she is in the eyes of the law. It becomes apparent that Nekhludov has sought so earnestly for justice for Maslova because such justice was perhaps another obstacle in his making a complete commitment to the other truth: the truth that he carries within himself.

If he had succeeded in correcting the judicial error and in setting Maslova free, he would have "freed" her to continue the debased, corrupt life she had led and to which he had led her. Nekhludov would have given to the impersonal processes of justice what was his to redeem. He will not buy his redemption at the small price of taking steps to reverse the verdict, nor even at the larger price of giving up his property, alienating his friends and class, leaving his settled, luxurious life, and following Maslova to Siberia. Nor will he buy it at the still larger price, which is to link his life to her irrevocably through marriage. There are even larger prices than that, and near the end of the novel Nekhludov and Maslova are ambiguously aware of them. It is not justice that will free Maslova and Nekhludov, but truth, and truth has nothing to do with judicial error and rectification. It has everything to do with what goes on in the souls of Maslova and Nekhludov. But what goes on there is almost as tangled, complex, and misleading as that which goes on in the labyrinths of officialdom. Some of this tangle is caught in the responses of Maslova to Nekhludov's efforts at redeeming the hurt he has caused her. At first when he seeks her out in prison she has no trouble understanding him: he is one of the predators and she one of those preyed upon, and she meets him with her customary defenses of sexual manipulation. She is interested in the alcohol and tobacco his money will buy and in the judicial steps he is taking to reverse the verdict. But as she begins to grow spiritually, she gives up alcohol, tobacco and faith and interest in the judicial system. She knows that the prison outside is no different from the prison inside. Maslova and Nekhludov meet in evasion of the truth.

The offer of marriage would seem to be a decisive spiritual step beyond the efforts on his part in officialdom to reverse the verdict. It is a personal act of great proportions and consequence for his life. It is too the most appropriate "redemptive" act, because it is what Nekhludov failed to do in the first place, and it is his failure to do so that condemned Maslova to the depraved life she has subsequently led. Yet it is an act that makes Maslova recoil in anger the first time Nekhludov brings it up. She explains this to herself and to him as a reaction against being used by him a second time,—not physically as before but spiritually. There is both truth and blindness in this remark. It is true that then and now Nekhludov is concerned with his feelings: then with the predatory feelings of sex and physical enjoyment and now with the feelings of moral self-cleansing. The offer of marriage is, whatever other significance it may have, threatening to

Maslova. The threat comes from the pain that is recalled from the first experience and the fear of remembering that pain.

As Nekhludov's first corruption of Maslova was his possession of her, so the offer of marriage is another move to possess her. Maslova will be redeemed when she "repossesses" herself, which happens when she begins to believe in herself and realizes that she is not the captive of the society she lives in, nor of past Maslovas and not the captive of Nekhludov's magnanimity. Nekhludov's sacrifice of his name, position, and public esteem is the right journey for him, but not necessarily for Maslova. The efforts at self-cleansing provoke Maslova to remember herself as she was, but Nekhludov's efforts to sacrifice himself for her become a net into which Maslova is gently but persistently drawn. She becomes progressively the object of that magnanimity, sacrifice, self-cleansing, and as such a part of it. What Nekhludov must finally do is divest himself, too, of the self-imposed duty to sacrifice himself for Maslova. *Maslova is not his to ruin or to save*. She belongs to no one but herself, and to the God that is within her. This is why, I am convinced, Tolstoy has Maslova reject his offer of marriage when he repeats it after the reduction of her sentence and the fixing of her official fate. We have very little insight into her motives, and perhaps it doesn't matter, but her rejection of Nekhludov is a sign of her consciousness that she belongs to no one but herself.

It may very well be that Maslova is in love with Nekhludov and even possible that some form of love—other than the redemptive pity that he has pursued and that has pursued him—has grown in Nekhludov for her. There is certainly obligation on both sides: on Nekhludov's part to redeem both himself and her by remaining with her whatever her lot, and on Maslova's part to be grateful for what he has given up for her. But it is a sign of spiritual perfection that Maslova should want to leave that gratitude behind and to leave her benefactor too and tie her life with Simonson. More is involved here surely than Maslova's desire to release him from his promise to link his life with hers, thus sparing him the ruin that would follow. This speculation of Nekhludov's may be looked on as a remnant of the pre-redemptive thinking. For in Tolstoy's moral vision no ruin would come to Nekhludov in continuing to be by her side and abandoning his privileged and corrupt life.

What Nekhludov discovers and what Maslova discovers, although perceived and understood only dimly by both, is that the process of true redemption is a return to what one has been. What Nekhludov and Maslova were at the beginning is preserved in that faded picture that Nekhludov brings Maslova, which she looks at with dismay, hunger, and then affection. He brings her pain in reminding her of what she was, but he also brings her hope. The true love that they enjoyed for a short time as equals and young people with little consciousness of class is caught in the game they play on that thoughtless summer day. There is no doubt that Tolstoy wants us to contrast the image of Nekhludov and Maslova on that day and on the night when he seduces her: to contrast the spontaneity, self-possession, and naturalness of the first love and the premeditated, artificial, abstract, impersonal nature of the second love. The meeting with Maslova behind the lilac bush is "accidental" and not deliberate, and the force that bends her toward his kiss and his toward hers is unpremeditated too. But on the night that Nekhludov seduces Maslova, he forces his way past doors, implorings, and physical resistance. The innocent love is prompted by play and the personal impulses of joy and immediate sensation. The guilty love is prompted by the voices of others and the remembered gestures of others. The innocent love is crowned by sunlight and natural scents and sounds. The guilty love is shrouded by a deep mist and fog, through which Nekhludov moves as if demented and lost.

But as good and true as was the first love, something else is communicated by the flowering of first love in the summer scene, and this something tells us that if the better love is the first, it is not the best. If the lips barely touch, then it would be better if they had not touched at all. If the scene takes place within nature, the nature is not entirely benign: Nekhludov stumbles on nettles, and the blossoms that crown the love are beginning to fall. The true garden of Eden comes before he kisses or even becomes conscious of Maslova. It is when he awakens at dawn and roams the fields alone, and when as "a young man for the first time, without guidance from any one outside, realizes all the beauty and significance of life." The journey toward the purified and redemptive self is a journey toward the self, untouched by and untouching of people.

It is no accident that Simonson's interest in Maslova is not sexual; and if there is no mention of sexuality in Nekhludov's interest in a redeemed Maslova, it cannot be absent, if only in memory and recall. Tolstoy's views on sexuality had come, during the period in which *Resurrection* was written, to the point of seeing chastity as the highest form of spirituality. If such a view is foolish, it is nevertheless in keeping with the dynamism of Tolstoy's moral vision of the world, something that was already implied in *Anna Karenina* and in some of the tales after the conversion. This is not because of some personal distaste of sex—although there were doubtless personal reasons here too—but because such a view is consistent with the way Tolstoy looked upon corruption and redemption. Tolstoy has given us in *Resurrection* a fallen and a redeemed world or a demonic and paradisiacal world, which turns on an axis of self and unself. There is something of Dante's inferno in the journey that Nekhludov takes through official-dom, where every virtue has become a vice, where the natural world has become distorted, and where beasts and madmen rule. In a society where the insane are outside the prisons and the humane are inside, it comes as no great shock that the prophet of redemption is to be found in prison.

The prophet is the old man that Nekhludov first meets by the river and later in prison. He may stand as epigraphic of the novel. In his "mad" words of serving oneself and the God in oneself, he is making a summary statement not only on Tolstoy's moral vision in *Resurrection* but also on Tolstoy's vision before and beyond *Resurrection*. The old man believes in no one but himself and the God in himself, refusing to acknowledge any authority. He has no country, God, or tsar. He says: "Everyone be himself and all will be as one." Nekhludov's interest in the old man is a sign that he is touched by some sympathy, but his silence too is a sign that he does not fully understand his significance. What the old man tells us is what Maslova is beginning to understand and to embody; it is what Nekhludov possessed as a young man but sought in vain in his journey through officialdom and in his impulses of magnanimity, self-sacrifice, and self-denigration. Maslova does not need his sacrifice, for his sacrifice is part of her prison. Maslova does not need Nekhludov, Nekhludov does not need Maslova, and none of us need each other. This is the paradoxical conclusion to which *Resurrection* leads; but if we don't need each other, brotherhood is the consequence of our redemption. For men relate best when they don't relate, just as they love best when they don't love. When they strive for brotherhood by way of conscious ideals and premeditated actions, they take brotherhood into abstraction, coercion, and separation. When they become themselves, they touch others with an immediacy that is not possible otherwise.

This is why Tolstoy's fulminating tracts are a misdirection, for the path to social improvement is no more by way of institutional reform than the path to personal reform is by way of intentional brotherhood. The tracts are the illumination of the demonology that reigns in the contemporary world, shocking us into the consciousness of impersonal, abstract participation in evil, as Nekhludov is shocked into what he has done to another person without meaning to do so. It is doubtful that the demonology could have been adequately expressed without the tracts. Nekhludov, it is true, could have made his journey from no consciousness, to false consciousness, to true consciousness, just as he could have conveyed to us the callous indifference of the officials who administer the machinery of this hell. Yet it would still be a single journey, still fiction. The tracts take the fiction into time and fact; and if this is usually the death of fiction, it is not so this time. Something of the urgency of Nekhludov's agonizing quest, as well as that of Maslova, would be lost if it did not take place in the desperations of contemporary time. We have today left behind, to be sure, that particular demonology, but past facts have a way of fictionalizing themselves and thus preserving themselves. If *Resurrection* has not gone the way of Disraeli's *Sybil*, it is because Tolstoy's facts were already reaching out to fiction and his fiction to facts.

One cannot leave the novel without pointing out once again how optimistic Tolstoy's vision of life is and how it permeates this last major work of his. The title is not to be taken ironically. Although there is hardly to be found on the pages of Russian literature a more scathing attack on the corruptions of contemporary life, there is no despair. For Tolstoy, men have created the hell and misunderstood their true nature, and it is men who, by understanding themselves, can create their redemption. No matter how much men may degrade the earth—and themselves—as the first pages of the novel show, they touch only the surface of the earth and of themselves. Nature pushes forth its healing shoots in the vile air of the corrupted city, as well as in the noxious inner citadel of man. In this sense *Resurrection* is of one piece with the later works. There may be in the lives of men lechery, debauchery, self-deception, and dishonesty, as we have in *Hadji-Murad*, but there are also beautiful flowers and men who lead their lives with grace and beauty as does Hadji Murad. Kautsky in *Father Sergius* may go from the vanities of fashionable life to the vanities of monastic life; he may pursue what seem to be numberless wrong paths, but he finds the right path. The journey of life for men may be across the great wasteland of the universe, fated to end by way of ever smaller circles in death, as in *Master and Man*, but it is also across the space from one heart to another. Men can give comfort to each other. The distance between despair and hope may lengthen in the late works, but it will always be traversable for Leo Tolstoy. There are no irredeemable sins in his world—no Dostoevskian tragic and un-correcting chemistry of the soul. There is *Resurrection*.

Chronicle of Tolstoy's Life and Work[1]

1828	August 28. Tolstoy is born. Mother: Maria Nikolaevna Bolkonskaya, born November 10, 1790. Father: Count Nikolay Il'ich Tolstoy, born June 26, 1794; entered army service in 1812, was with the Russian troops in Europe in 1813; captured by the French and released when the Russians captured Paris in 1814.
1830	August 4. Death of Tolstoy's mother.
1833-34	Tolstoy, five or six years old, announces to his brothers that he knows the secret of universal love, happiness, and harmony for all peoples; and that the secret is written on a green stick, buried on the side of a ravine about a quarter of a mile from the house at Yasnaya Polyana. At his request, Tolstoy was to be buried at that spot.
1837	June 20. Tolstoy's father dies. Tolstoy is nine.
1844	Tolstoy is refused admission to the division of oriental studies of the University of Kazan, but is admitted to the department of Turkish-Arabic studies.
1845	Transfers to the law faculty.
1847	September 14. Leaves the University of Kazan.
1849	Passes an examination in criminal law and legal process at the University of Saint Petersburg.
1851	First mention of *Childhood* in his diary. May 2. Leaves with his brother Nikolay from Moscow for the Caucasus. Participates as a volunteer in Caucasian campaign. August 10. First mention of the living prototype for Eroshka, Epifan Sekhin Epishka. December 23. Writes to his brother that a certain Khadzhi Murad has given himself up to the Russian authorities.
1852	Joins the army. Writes to T. A. Ergol'skaya on December 3 that he is happy to be no longer free, because freedom has caused all his faults.

August 28. Note in the diary: "I'm twenty-four and I haven't done anything yet. I feel that I've been fighting doubts and passions for eight years and to no avail. What am I destined to do? The future will tell."

CHILDHOOD

On July 3, 1852, sends off the manuscript of *Childhood* (*Detstvo*) to the editor of the *Contemporary* (*Sovremennik*). Writes: "In essence this manuscript consists of the first part of a novel to be entitled 'Four Epochs of Development' [*Chetyre epokh razvitiya*]. . . . If it can't be published in one number of the journal because of its size, please divide it into three parts as follows: from the beginning to chapter 17, from 17 to 26, and from 26 to the end." On August 29 Nekrasov assures Tolstoy that he will publish *Childhood* and that the author has considerable talent. "If the subsequent parts have the same vitality and movement, then this will be a good novel." He urges Tolstoy not to hide behind initials but to begin to publish under his full name. *Childhood* is published in the *Contemporary*, no. 9, September 6, under the title of *The History of My Childhood*. Nekrasov writes Tolstoy on September 30 telling him that *Childhood* is better on rereading than on first reading. The first review appears in the next issue of the *Contemporary*, probably by S. S. Dudyshin: "It is a gem from beginning to end" (*Vse ono nachala do kontsa istinno prekrasno*.) On October 21 Nekrasov writes to Turgenev: "Take a look at the novel *Childhood* in the ninth issue—this is a new talent and apparently very promising." Turgenev writes back: "You are right—this is a promising talent. Write to him and urge him to continue writing. Tell him if he is interested that I say hello and applaud what he is doing." Panaev wrote in 1861 in the *Contemporary*, no. 3, of the reception *Childhood* received from its contemporaries: "We welcomed L. N. Tolstoy, the author of *Childhood* and *Boyhood*. His talent seemed genius-like and we were a little timid before it." On November 26, 1852, Tolstoy receives a letter from Nekrasov answering his request for payment for *Childhood* and informing him that in the best of journals there is the tradition of not paying for the first work of an author. He points out that Goncharov, Druzhinin, Panaev, and he himself started their careers in that fashion. He promises to pay Tolstoy the highest rate for future works, that is, 50 rubles in silver for each printer's sheet (signature).

1853   About March 17. "The Raid" (*Nabeg*) is published in the *Contemporary*, no. 3.

July 23. Note in the diary while working on *Boyhood*: "Work, work! How happy I feel when I'm working."

1854   October. In *Contemporary*, no. 10, *Boyhood* (*Otrochestvo*) is published. Critical reception is good. B. Almazov, in *Moskvityanin* 23 (1854), says that the novel "reveals a remarkable capacity for subtle psychological perceptions."

1855   *Notes of a Billiard Marker*, (*Zapiski markera*) published in the *Contemporary*, no. 1.

March 4. Note in the diary: "Yesterday a conversation about theology and faith suggested to me the colossal thought, the fulfillment of which would take a lifetime of devotion. The thought is the following: to establish a new religion in harmony with the development of mankind, the religion of Christ, but purified of belief in mysteries, a practical religion, one that does not promise a future bliss, but one that brings such harmony on earth."

1856   January. In the *Contemporary*, no. 1, "Sevastopol in August, 1855," is published.

Dostoevsky writes to A. N. Maikov, "L. Tolstoy: I like L. Tolstoy very much, but he will not write very much in my opinion (but then maybe I'm wrong)."

March 9. *The Snowstorm* (*Metel'*) is published in the *Contemporary*.

May. *The Two Hussars* is published in the *Contemporary*, no. 5. Botkin calls it a gem.

December. In the *Contemporary*, no. 10, Chernyshevsky's famous analysis of Tolstoy's early works appears in which he characterizes the distinctness of Tolstoy's vision and artistic style as consisting of the following two traits: "dialectic of the soul" (*dialektika dushi*) and "purity of moral feeling" (*chistota nravstvennogo chuvstva*).

The Landowner's Morning (*Utro Pomeshchika*) is published in *Notes from the Fatherland* (1856), no. 12.

1857   January. *Youth* (*Yunost'*) is published in the *Contemporary*, no. 1. In the same issue Chernyshevsky has an article about *A Landowner's Morning* in which he notes "that Tolstoy reproduces with remarkable mastery not only the external conditions of the everyday life of the inhabitants, but what is much more important, their point of view on things. He knows how to put himself into the soul of the peasants."

November. Tolstoy is reading Cervantes' *Don Quixote*.

1858   January 23. Finishes the novel "Three Deaths" (*Tri smerti*).

February. The story *Albert* is published in the *Contemporary*.

March. Hard at work on *The Cossacks*.

July. Hard at work farming. Note in diary of July 19: "From June 16 to July 19, I am not writing, not reading, not thinking. Everything in farm work."

October 30. Sees Valery Arseneva. Note in diary: "I saw Valery. No regret for my feelings."

1859

January. *Three Deaths* is published in *Biblioteka dlya Chteniya*, no. 1. A reviewer for the *Northern Flower (Severnoi Tsvet)* says that Tolstoy "places the reader in a quandary. . . . It is clear that the talented author of *Childhood* and *Boyhood* wanted to express something deep but the thought remained unexpressed. Nevertheless the story is masterfully written." Pisarev in *Dawn (Rassvet)* 4, no. 12, pp. 63-74, writes: "No one has looked into the soul of man so deeply, no one has analyzed the cherished motivations and the transitory and apparently accidental movements of the soul with such intense attention and with such merciless logic."

February 11. Turgenev to Tolstoy: "*Three Deaths* has met with a favorable reception in Saint Petersburg—but people find the ending strange (the death of the tree) and do not understand the link between it and the two preceding sections, and those who do understand it are unsatisfied."

March. Tolstoy is working eight hours a day on *Family Happiness*.

April 5. Finishes *Family Happiness*. Botkin writes Turgenev that *Family Happiness* is "cold and boring" and that everything is "executed with a cold brilliance."

FAMILY HAPPINESS

Family Happiness (Semeynee schast'e) is published in the *Russian Messenger (Russkii vestnik)*, nos. 7 and 8, April 1859. Reviews of the novel are few, probably because the subject matter is remote from the burning issues of the day. A critic in the *Northern Flower* calls it "a nice poetic idyll." A reviewer in *Son of the Fatherland (Syn otechestva)* says that "the thought of the story is not new, but nevertheless interesting and lively; an analysis and understanding of the thought was difficult, but it was beautifully rendered by the author." The *Contemporary* carries no review or even mention of the novel. In 1862, in the journal *Time (Vremya)*, Appolon Grigor'ev calls *Family Happiness* Tolstoy's best work. A. Pyatovsky, writing in the *Contemporary* in 1865, says that Tolstoy is idealizing the landowner's way of life.

End of October. Begins school for peasant children.

November. Writes to B. N. Chicherin that he has chosen to farm for the rest of his life and that he has definitely given up literary activity.

1860

End of January. Writes to his sister: "I am completely occupied with my school and do my writing now among a pack of children."

June 25. Leaves Yasnaya Polyana with his sister for abroad.

July 5. Arrives in Shtettin, Germany.

July 16. Visits a school in Kissingen, Germany. Diary entry: "poor."

September 20. Death of his brother N. N. Tolstoy.
October. Visits eight schools in Marseilles. Negatively impressed.

1861 March. Begins *Polikushka*.
Mid-March. Writes to Turgenev telling him that he has returned to literary work. Gives high praise to Goethe's *Faust*.
March 21–25. Visits Proudhon; they talk about education and abolishing serfdom.
March 28. Speaks to Turgenev of beginning a novel on the Decembrists.
April 12. Returns to Russia.
May 16. Censor grants Tolstoy permission to issue his educational journal *Yasnaya Polyana*.
May 27. Challenges Turgenev to a duel.

1862 March. I. S. Aksakov in *Day* (*Den'*), no. 21, calls the journal *Yasnaya Polyana* a "remarkable literary phenomenon," and "at the same time an extraordinarily important phenomenon in our social life." Chernyshevsky in an article in the *Contemporary* comments on the first two issues of *Yasnaya Polyana*, criticizes Tolstoy's pedagogical ideas, and praises his teaching methods.
May 1. In a letter to Pletnev, Tolstoy says that Turgenev's *Fathers and Sons* is "cold, cold, and does not suit Turgenev's talent. Everything is clever, subtle, artistic. . . ." Tolstoy goes on to say that there is not a single page that "grabs you by the heart."
July 6, 7. Police search Yasnaya Polyana.
August 26. One of the many visits to the Bers family that summer. S. A. Bers (Tolstoy's future wife) reads to Tolstoy a novel she wrote about her sisters and mother, in which Tolstoy plays a part.
August 29. Note in diary: "Not love, as before, not jealousy, not even compassion, but similar to, to something sweet—like a hope (which cannot be). . . . But a beautiful evening, good, sweet feeling. She had me interpret the letter" (apparently the letter of proposal that Tolstoy wrote with first letters of each word).
September 3. Diary: "Never had life with a wife presented itself to my imagination so clearly, joyfully, and peacefully."
September 7. Letter to his sister A. A. Tolstoy: "Old fool that I am, I have fallen in love. I say this and don't know whether or not I have spoken the truth."
September 14. Proposes to Sofia Bers and is accepted.
September 23. Is married.

1863 January 5. Diary: "Domestic happiness has swallowed me completely."

THE COSSACKS

The Cossacks (*Kazaki*) is published in the *Russian Messenger*, no. 1, February 24. Ya P. Polonsky, in an article "about L. N. Tolstoy's latest novel" (Po povodu poslednei povesti gr. L. N. Tolstogo), in *Time* (*Vremya*), 1863, no. 3, praises the fidelity with which Tolstoy renders the atmosphere of the Caucasus; he characterizes Olenin as a "man who has clearly outlived his generation" and faults the novel for a lack of unity in the insertion of such episodes as the killing of Lukashka and the redemption of the body by the Abrek's body. Evgenya Tur, in *Notes of the Fatherland*, 1863, no. 6, gives high praise to Tolstoy's artistic talent, but faults him for poeticizing murder, drunkenness, and thievery. P. B. Annenkov in *The St. Petersburg News*, 1863, nos. 144 and 145, calls it one of the best novels of recent Russian literature and praises it for the fidelity of the ethnographic content.

1863

February 25. Tolstoy's wife writes to her sister that Tolstoy has started a new novel (*War and Peace*).
March 30. *Polikushka* is published in the *Russian Messenger*, no. 2. A reviewer in *Northern Bee* calls the novel a beautiful sketch. But a reviewer in *Notes of the Fatherland*, no. 247, sees in it "lies, unnaturalness, and a slander on life."
April 4. Fet writes Turgenev that *The Cossacks* is a masterpiece.
June 2. A. E. Bers writes Tolstoy that the Cossacks are full of enthusiasm for his *The Cossacks*.
August 3. First son is born.

1864

Turgenev writes to Fet that he has read *Polikushka* and is astonished at Tolstoy's great talent. But he faults him for having the son drowned.
February 24. Tolstoy writes to his sister that he is writing "a long novel from the year 1812."

1865

January 3. Tolstoy sends Katkov a manuscript, "The Year 1805," which contains a description of the life of the Bolkonskys at Bleak Hills, and informs Katkov that the second part, which will be a description of Schongraben battle, will be ready by the end of January. Asks Katkov not to call his work a "novel."

1866

March 25. Turgenev writes to Fet about the second part of "The Year 1805": "Where are the traits of the age here? Weak."
June 16. Fet writes Tolstoy that the character of Andrey is pale and that Andrey cannot be the unifying thread of the episode.
June 27. Turgenev writes to Fet that the second part of "The Year 1805" is poor because the author drags out certain poorly wrought generals of the time in the guise of Kutuzov and Bagration.

WAR AND PEACE

Tolstoy tells in "The Year 1805" that he began work on *War and Peace* in 1856 and that it began as a novel on the Decembrists. There is no mention of this in his diary, nor in any of the rough drafts, so that it is doubtful that he actually wrote anything before 1863 (see 1863, February 25). Tolstoy wrote his Aunt Alexandra Andreevna near the end of October 1863 that he was hard at work on a novel from the 1810s and 1820s. We have Tolstoy's word that he began the novel with the description of the 1820s and worked backward to the War of 1812 and then to 1805, but there is no manuscript confirmation of this order. The rough drafts for the novel (undated) are contained in volumes 13 and 14 of the Jubilee edition (see Bibliography). The first publication of any part of *War and Peace*, "The Year 1805," was in the January and February issues of the *Russian Messenger* for 1865; this corresponds roughly to twenty-four chapters of volume 1, part I. The second part of "The Year 1805" came out in the February, March, and April numbers of the *Russian Messenger* for 1866, corresponding roughly to volume 1, part 2. Tolstoy intended to finish the novel in 1867 and to call it *All's Well that Ends Well*. The first four volumes appeared in 1868 and a fifth and sixth volume in 1869. Much of what we consider final in the novel does not appear in the early drafts. Napoleon is present from the beginning, but Kutuzov and Alexander are not. Prince Andrey is created to satisfy an exigency of situation and plot— Tolstoy needs a young man to carry the standard—and in the early drafts he is killed. The portrait of Kutuzov is negative at first; Napoleon's is not harshly negative. By and large Tolstoy follows conventional opinion in his portrayal of historical personages. The various drafts the novel went through have left a number of contradictions in the novel itself. Princess Marya gives her brother a silver medallion when he goes off to the battle of Austerlitz, but French soldiers take off a golden medallion on the battlefield. In August 1805, Natasha is thirteen; at the beginning of 1806, she is fifteen.

Tolstoy did considerable research for the writing of *War and Peace*, and relied heavily on a number of historians of the period, especially on the work of A. I. Mikhaylovsky-Danilevsky, *Description of the War of 1805 between Alexander and Napoleon (Opisanie pervoi voiny imperatora Aleksandra Napoleonom v 1805 godu)*. Viktor Shklovsky in his 1928 work *Content and Style in Tolstoy's Novel "War and Peace" (Materyal i stil' v romane L'va Tolstogo, Voina i mir)* claims and partially demonstrates that Tolstoy did not hesitate to distort historical sources for dramatic and aesthetic effect. For the 1873 edition of *War and Peace*, Tolstoy eliminated all the French passages in the novel and sharply curtailed the theoretical material. His wife, presumably with his approval, put out an edition in 1886 with the French restored and in all respects the same as the 1868–69 edition, except that it was in four rather than six volumes. Nevertheless, Soviet criticism has conducted a lively argument about the "canonical" text for *War and Peace*. See articles by N. Gudzii and N. Gusev listed below in section VI of the Bibliography.

Most of the early criticism centered on how accurately Tolstoy had portrayed history: the military events of the war of 1812 and the domestic and social life of the years from 1805 to 1812. The novel aroused extraordinary interest during its publication and even then conservative military critics, irritated by the denigration of military leaders, and the radical critics, who saw the novel as lacking in social criticism, mixed praise with reproach. Surviving generals who had served in the campaign of 1812 wrote articles proving that this or that military point was or was not accurately portrayed; but even the most bitter critics admitted that Tolstoy's portrayal of military life and his description of the battle of Borodino was remarkably accurate. A. S. Norov, who took part in the battle of Borodino, acknowledged that Tolstoy had "beautifully and faithfully described the general phases of the battle of Borodino." A. Vitmer bitterly criticized Tolstoy's denigration of Napoleon, his view that the spirit of the common soldiers was the decisive element in the battle, and his neglect of the role of military commanders; but he still grudgingly admitted that Tolstoy was right that there had been no plan to draw Napoleon into the interior, and that the battle of Borodino was fought on positions other than those planned.

Appearing at a time when literature was expected to reflect and to form social consciousness, Tolstoy's *War and Peace* seemed to do neither. His concerns seemed remote from the social realities of the time, his sympathies wholly aristocratic. The radical critic Dmitry Pisarev dismissed the first half of the novel—he died before the second half was published—by calling it a nostalgic tribute to the gentry. The extent to which Tolstoy was stung by criticism on this point can be gauged by his article "A Few Words about *War and Peace*", which appeared in 1868 at the same time as the fourth volume. In this piece he responds with casual contempt to those critics who had regretted that the character of the age had not been better defined in the novel.

Between the conservative military critics and the radical social critics, a great number of critics—of every shade and character—clamored to praise the novel. Almost everyone liked Natasha and Princess Marya. Turgenev did not, however. It is a curious, but not unexpected, cultural coincidence that Turgenev, like James a generation later, was to find the novel lacking. Turgenev did not like the technique, the psychology, the characterizations, the philosophy, and the descriptive detail. Everything was dry, contrived, artificial—"a puppet comedy." Later, when Turgenev had detected which way the winds were blowing, he was to like everything and to praise it with the same vigor with which he had attacked it. In a preface to a French translation of *The Two Hussars* in 1875, Turgenev placed Tolstoy first among Russian men of letters—because of *War and Peace*.

N. K. Strakhov, an important conservative critic and close friend of Tolstoy and Dostoevsky, was much more favorable. In a series of articles in 1869–70, Strakhov wrote the best criticism on *War and Peace* at that time, and possibly the best in Russian since. His praise was perhaps too diffuse: he liked the characters, the portrayal of domestic life, the vividness of detail, the ideas, even the historical chapters. He saw long before Merezhkovsky that Tolstoy's vividness of characterization depended in part on his use of detail, and long before the Soviets that Tolstoy individualized his characters by immersing them in relations to the world about them—to family, class, nation. He gave too much importance to the domestic side of the novel, and his discussion of the emergence of a new "Russian type" carries the flavor of criticism of the sixties and seventies. But he understood the complicated psychology between old Bolkonsky and his daughter better than anyone since; and he anticipates my study by affirming that "among all the various characters and events, we feel the presence of some kind of firm and unshakable principle on which the world of the novel maintains itself." But when he finally asked himself what this principle was, he answered lamely, "The voice raised for the simple and true against the false and rapacious—such is the most important and essential meaning of *War and Peace*."

The Soviets have elevated *War and Peace* above criticism but not beyond interest and critical study, as is amply shown by the 1960 bibliography of more than five thousand pieces on Tolstoy between the years 1917 and 1958 and more than five hundred pieces on *War and Peace* alone. The work on *War and Peace* has been critical, bibliographical, historical, textual; basic scholarly work has been so thorough that Soviet scholars have done even more work on the reception of Tolstoy and *War and Peace* in English-speaking countries than we have.

Soviet critical analysis suffers somewhat from the inevitable litanies to Marxist saints, but much of it is perceptive. It is more varied than Anglo-American criticism with its undeviating structural bias; the Soviets have concerned themselves with history, genesis, psychology of a general sort, and very much with the genre of the novel. They have studied closely the published drafts and variants of the novel, and they have also paid much attention to style, structure, language, and character analysis. Chernyshevsky's brilliant remarks in an early review article of Tolstoy's *Childhood* and *The Sebastopol Sketches* have influenced many studies; his terms "the inner monologue" and "the dialectic of the soul" appear with frequency in criticism on the novel. No one can fail to profit from reading Bocharov's remarkable small book, Bychkov's basic study, some of Saburov's work, and even parts of Ermilov's book (all listed in section VI of the Bibliography). The work of Gudzi and Gusev (also in section VI), both documentary and critical, is of immeasurable importance not only to Soviet scholars and admirers of *War and Peace*, but to readers everywhere.

If Soviet critics have stressed the social and historical problems in the novel, such emphasis is as much Russian as it is Soviet. The Marxist bias is quietly pervasive but seldom intrusive, at least since 1956. Tolstoy himself has had a profound influence on many Soviet attitudes. Before *War and Peace*, the battle of Borodino was considered to be a defeat, but Tolstoy said it was a victory and the Soviets have come to agree with him; Kutuzov was considered to be something of a national embarrassment, but Tolstoy said he was a great general, and the Soviets have made him a national hero. They criticize Tolstoy only for not making him greater. Tolstoy's characterization of Kutuzov as a passive hero is considered to be in error. According to the Soviets, too, Tolstoy proclaimed that the people were the real heroes of the war of 1812, and he did, but not quite in the way the Soviets understand it. Marxist dialectic has permitted the Soviets to find progressive historicism in *War and Peace* and thus to exonerate Tolstoy from the radical critical charges of indifference to history and social realities. By and large, they reject the division that Western critics have often made between Tolstoy the artist and Tolstoy the thinker; some of his ideas, according to them, are true and some are false.

Soviet interpretations of specific characters or aspects of the novel are often perceptive, sometimes at odds with each other, and always serious. Soviet critics generally do not like Platon Karataev, but for reasons other than those advanced by Western critics. He is unreal for us because he is undramatic; he is unreal for them because he is unhistorical. For Soviet critics, Platon Karataev is the product of Tolstoy's subjective and idealistic deflection from historical reality, and an anticipation of his reactionary religious views of the postconversion years. For reasons similar to these, they do not like Andrey's "conversion" and spiritual illumination. Their analysis of character stresses the individuality of people as brought out by their relations to others, and their studies of the language of

War and Peace—studies that do not exist in English criticism except for R. F. Christian's brief chapter—are illuminating. The Soviets have not wearied, unfortunately, of the game of researching and speculating about prototypes for characters in *War and Peace*.

1868   February 14. After reading the first three volumes of *War and Peace*, Turgenev, in a letter to Annenkov, praises certain descriptive passages such as the hunt, but considers the historical chapters to be a puppet comedy. He also finds the repetition of the same detail over and over again (which Mereshkovsky was to praise), such as the mustache on the upper lip of the Princess Bolkonsky, to be insufferable.

1869   January. *Reminiscences of the Year 1812* is published by Vyazemsky in the *Russian Archive*, no. 1.
September 2. In a hotel in Arzamaz, Tolstoy for the first time experiences indescribable terror at the prospect of death.

1870   February 23. First reference to *Anna Karenina*. Tolstoy's wife refers in her diary to a conversation with Leo in which he tells her of imagining a feminine type from the highest society who destroys herself.
December 9. Tolstoy begins to learn Greek.
February 20. Writes to A. A. Tolstoy that he has finished his ABC and that he is beginning another large pedagogical work.
April 18-19. Spends the whole night looking at the stars.
October 28. Tolstoy's wife writes to T. A. Kuzminskaya that her husband has started a new large novel and is happy about his future work. Reference is to work on a novel about Peter the Great.

1873   May 31. Tolstoy writes to N. N. Strakhov that he has translated all the French into Russian for a new edition of *War and Peace*.

1874   June 23. Writes to A. A. Tolstoy that he would like to throw away the novel *Anna Karenina* and that he is not at all pleased with it.
July 8. Writes to P. D. Golokhvasrov that the writing of *Anna Karenina* is repulsive to him.
November 20. Tolstoy's wife writes to S. A. Bers that Tolstoy is completely taken with the educational needs of the people, with schools and educational institutions, which occupy him from morning to night, and that *Anna Karenina* is not getting done.
December 21. Tolstoy sends Katkov, editor of the *Russian Messenger*, first pages of *Anna Karenina*.

ANNA KARENINA

Tolstoy wrote *Anna Karenina* between 1873 and 1876, and the novel was serialized in the *Russian Messenger* from 1874 to 1877. Katkov, the editor, objected to Tolstoy's pacifist views in regard to the Turkish-Serbian-Russian war expressed in the last part and demanded changes, which Tolstoy refused to make. Katkov finished serialization by publishing a summary of the last part, but Tolstoy published the last part as he had written it, in a separate edition of the novel. In 1873 Tolstoy wrote to Strakhov that a fragment from Pushkin, "The guests were getting ready to leave for the country house" (*Gosti sobiralis' na dachu*), suggested the theme of the novel to him, but Tolstoy had already conceived, as recorded in his wife's diary, the theme of the novel in 1870. There is no doubt also that Tolstoy was deeply influenced in 1872 by the fate of the mistress of a nobleman from his district who had committed suicide by throwing herself under a train. The novel was an immediate success, and critical reaction was generally favorable. Radical critics such as Nekrasov and Shchedrin found the novel trivial and remote from the issues of the day. Turgenev wrote Polonsky: "I do not like *Anna Karenina*, despite some truly magnificent pages (the horse race, the hay-making, the hunt). But the whole thing is sour, it smells of Moscow and old maids, Slavophilism and narrow-minded nobility." V. V. Stasov, on the other hand, wrote: "Count Tolstoy has risen to heights which Russia has never seen before. Love and passion have never before been expressed in such depth and with such striking truth, not even in the works of Pushkin and Gogol."

1875   January 29. A French translation of *The Two Hussars* appears in *Le Temps*, with a preface by Turgenev.
February 16. Responding to N. N. Strakhov's letter about the good reception of *Anna Karenina*, Tolstoy says that he had feared a failure and that he clearly sees the weaknesses of the novel.
November 9. Tolstoy to Strakhov: "My God, if only someone would finish *Anna Karenina* for me. Unbearably repulsive." Tolstoy to his brother: "I think it is time to die."

1876   February 29, March 1. To Fet: "The end of winter and the beginning of spring are always my most fruitful time for work, and I have to finish the novel [*Anna Karenina*], which is boring to me."

1877   May 22. In a letter to Strakhov, Tolstoy tells about Katkov's refusal to print the conclusion of *Anna Karenina* without substantial changes.
Early June. The *Russian Messenger* prints a summary of the last part of *Anna Karenina*.

August 25. Tolstoy's wife reports in her diary that Tolstoy says his prayers every day, goes to Mass, fasts, and talks only about his soul and humility.

August. In the July-August issue of the *Diary of a Writer*, Dostoevsky reviews *Anna Karenina*. He has high praise for the novel but takes sharp exception to Tolstoy's disapproval of Russia's participation in the Balkan-Turkish war and Tolstoy's skepticism (as expressed by Levin) of the purity and sincerity of Russian arms and aid to the Serbs.

1878

January. Tolstoy is doing the research for a novel about the Decembrist uprising.

May 8. Turgenev responds warmly to a conciliatory letter from Tolstoy and an invitation from him to renew their friendship. He promises to visit Tolstoy in the summer.

October 1. Turgenev writes Tolstoy about the publication of *The Cossacks* in English and French translations.

1880

May 2-4. Turgenev visits Tolstoy and tries to persuade him to take part in the June celebration in honor of Pushkin. Tolstoy is not persuaded.

May 28. Dostoevsky writes to his wife from Moscow: "About Tolstoy, Katkov reports that Tolstoy has gone completely mad. Yur'ev has been urging me to visit him; but I won't go, although it would be terribly interesting."

1881

March 11 or 17. Tolstoy writes to Tsar Alexander III urging him not to punish the murderers of his father.

1882

October. Learning Hebrew under the instruction of Rabbi S. A. Minor. Reading of Hebrew version of the Bible.

1883

End of June. Deathbed letter from Turgenev urging him to continue writing.

August 24-25. Conversations with G. A. Rusanov about literature. The only novel of Turgenev's that Tolstoy likes is *The Sportsman's Sketches* (*Zapiski okhotnika*). Dostoevsky's *Memoirs from the House of the Dead* is singled out for praise, but he could not finish *The Brothers Karamazov*. *Crime and Punishment* is Dostoevsky's best novel, but after the first couple of chapters the reader knows the rest. Tolstoy does not think much of Shakespeare. He cannot remember when he read *Madame Bovary* but remembers that he liked it.

October. Makes the acquaintance of Vladimir Grigor'evich Chertkov.

1884

April. Note in diary: "I want to start and finish something new. Either the death of the judge or notes of the madman." The first is an early reference to *The Death of Ivan Ilych*.

April. Various entries in his diary about difficult relations with his wife.

Beginning of December. Tolstoy reads aloud to his family a part of *The Death of Ivan Ilych*.

THE DEATH OF IVAN ILYCH

Tolstoy worked on the tale from 1884 to 1886, and it was first published in an 1886 edition of his works (*Sochineniya gr. L. N. Tolstogo*). The prototype for Ivan Ilych seems to have been a member of the Tula court, a certain Ivan Ilych Mechnikov who died in 1881. In her memoirs, T. A. Kuzminskaya reported that "Ivan Ilych Mechnikov served as the prototype of the hero of the novel *The Death of Ivan Ilych*. Tolstoy's wife recounted to me his deathbed thoughts about the fruitless life he had led and later recounted these to Tolstoy." Critical reaction was positive on the whole, even enthusiastic. On April 28, 1886, V. V. Stasov wrote Tolstoy that he had never read anything comparable and that "no people on earth has ever had such a great creation. Everything else is small, petty, weak, and pale in comparison with these seventy odd pages." P. I. Chaykovsky noted the following in his diary on July 12, 1886, after reading the novel: "I have read *The Death of Ivan Ilych*, and I am more convinced than ever that L. N. Tolstoy is the greatest writer on earth."

1887   February 1-8. The drama *The Power of Darkness* (*Vlast' T'my*) is published.
March. Note from Alexander III to the Ministry of Internal Affairs about *The Power of Darkness*: "One must put an end to the disgrace of Leo Tolstoy. He is a pure nihilist and blasphemer. It wouldn't be a bad idea to forbid the sale of his drama *The Power of Darkness*. He has had enough success in selling such trash and diffusing it among the people."
End of September. Tolstoy reads Gogol's *Selected Passages from Correspondence with Friends* and finds the work powerful and impressive.

1888   January 29 (February 10). First staging of *The Power of Darkness* in Théâtres libres in Paris. Enthusiastically received. Zola is in the audience.

1889   April 14. Diary entry: "I wrote about art. Got completely mixed up. Irritating. Have to let it go."
April 20. Diary entry: "Tried to write about art and became convinced that I am wasting my time. Got to give it up. . . . It's not going because it's not clear. When it becomes clear, I'll write it all at once."
July 2. Diary entry (about the *Kreutzer Sonata*). "Finished it all. But have to correct it from the beginning. I have to make birth control the central idea. Without children she is led inevitably to a fall."
June 30: Read Bellamy's *Looking Backwards*. "A remarkable

thing." "Beautiful."
August 31. Tolstoy reads *The Kreutzer Sonata* to his family.
The reading disturbed everyone.
November 1. The publishing house Posrednik runs off 300
lithograph copies of *The Kreutzer Sonata.*
November 6. Strakhov to Tolstoy about *The Kreutzer Sonata*:
"You have never written anything more powerful, nor any-
thing more gloomy."

1890   Jan. 10. First performance in Russia of *The Power of Darkness.*
February 15. Chekhov praises *The Kreutzer Sonata* to Plesh-
chev for its art, and writes that it "stimulates thinking."
June 12. I. Bunin writes to Tolstoy with praise of *The Kreutzer
Sonata* and asks permission to visit him.
September 14. Diary: "Read Coleridge. Much that is beautiful. But he suffers from the English sickness. It's clear that
he can think powerfully, clearly, and freely, but as soon as he
touches on England, then, unaware, he becomes a sophist."

1891   Among the books that Tolstoy lists as having had the
greatest influence on him between the years 1878 and 1891
are the following, with evaluations of influence: The New
Testament in Greek—enormous. Henry George's *Progress
and Poverty*—a great deal. Feuerbach's *Das Wesen des
Christenthums*—much. Pascal's *Pensées*—enormous. Confu-
cius and Mencius—a great deal.
April 14-19. Reads Kipling and finds him weak and straining
for originality. Reads *Madame Bovary* and understands why
the French have valued it so highly.
Oct. 23. Reads Fet's translations of *Faust.*

1893   Dec. 22. Diary entry: "I've been in Moscow more than a
month. I find it hard, disgusting. I can't keep the feelings
down. I want to perform a feat of some kind. I want to give
what's left of my life to the service of God. It's the luxury, the
sale of books, the dirty morality, and the vanity, I can't keep
from feeling down. Most important, I want to suffer, I want
to cry out the truth which is burning inside me."

1894   January 3. Bunin visits Tolstoy.
July 10. After listening to Strakhov read aloud Rozanov's *The
Legend of the Grand Inquisitor*, Tolstoy says of Dostoevsky:
"Dostoevsky is the kind of writer whom you must penetrate
to the depths, to forget for a while the imperfection of his
form, so as to find beneath it the true beauty.... The first
couple of chapters of *Crime and Punishment* are masterful.
But after these chapters, it's all done; after that it's a mess."
July 11. Tolstoy characterizes Chekhov as having artistic
perception but nothing firm in his view of life and as
incapable of teaching anything. "He is always vacillating and
searching."

August 10. Tolstoy's impression of Dante: "Terrible boredom. I tried to read him several times and could never finish him; I read him in Italian when I was learning Italian. Boccaccio was better, at least interesting and lively. I read him in French."

1895

January 4. Tolstoy reads the manuscript of *Master and Man* aloud. He finds the novel disappointing, without definite character, and believes it will have to be thoroughly revised.

MASTER AND MAN

On January 14, 1895, Tolstoy sends *Master and Man* (*Khozyain i rabotnik*) to Strakhov, asking him to send it on to the *Northern Messenger* (*Severny vestnik*). "Look it over and tell me whether it can be published. Or is it a shameful thing? It's been so long since I wrote anything artistic that I really don't know what came out. I wrote it with a great deal of satisfaction, but what resulted, I don't know. If you say that it's no good, I won't be hurt. If you think it's good, well then, you sign the proofs for the press."

Strakhov writes back on January 25 with high praise of *Master and Man*. Tolstoy's wife becomes hysterical with jealousy that *Master and Man* was sent to the *Northern Messenger* and persuades Tolstoy not to publish it there. Tolstoy writes to D. Ya Gurevich, the editor: "My reasons are personal and don't pertain to you, but I can't publish my tale in your journal. I fully understand the difficult position that my carelessness puts you in, and I beg your forgiveness." On February 14 Tolstoy writes to Strakhov: "My story has caused me a lot of grief. Sofya Andreevna was very displeased that I gave my story free to the *Northern Messenger*, and because of that almost went mad with jealousy (without cause) of Gurevich, and we all went through some terrible days. She was close to suicide, and only now is she coming around and becoming normal. As a result of all this, she published an announcement that the story will come out in her edition (affixed to the 18th volume of *The Works of Count L. N. Tolstoy*)." Finally, on March 4, 1886, the novel was published simultaneously in the *Northern Messenger* and in Tolstoy's wife's separate edition. The story received widespread praise. On March 19 *The Week* (*Nedelya*) no 12, carried the following report: "No other literary work in Russia has spread over the country as rapidly as has Tolstoy's new work *Master and Man*. In a few days after publication, it was reprinted in practically every newspaper without exception." On May 3 and 4, A. P. Morozov asked Tolstoy's permission to adapt *Master and Man* for the stage. Tolstoy answered: "I give everyone the right to use my works: to translate them, revise them, abridge them, and republish them, as they see fit, and therefore I can't say anything against the publication or staging of your version, and I wish you full success.''

August 8, 9. Chekhov visits Tolstoy for the first time.

1896   At the Hermitage Theatre Tolstoy sees a performance of Shakespeare's *Hamlet* and *King Lear*. On January 14 he writes P. A. Sergeenko his impression: ''I looked at those distortions and thought: one has to struggle against all that.''

1897   June 19. Tolstoy's wife's diary entry: ''Leo is writing feverishly 'about art' and is close to finishing and busies himself with nothing else.''
        December 28. Permission granted by the Ministry of Internal Affairs for the Dukhobors to emigrate abroad.

1899   End of September. Tolstoy rereads Herzen's *Letters to an Old Comrade* (*Pis'ma k staromu tovarishchu*) and is enthusiastic about the work.

1900   January 16. Diary: ''Gorky was here. The talk went well. I like him. A real man of the people.''

1901   May 29. A. S. Suvorin writes in his diary: ''We have two tsars—Nikolay II and Leo Tolstoy. Which is more powerful? Nikolay II can't do anything with Tolstoy, can't shake his throne, whereas Tolstoy without any doubt can shake the throne of Nikolay and his dynasty.''

1902   Tolstoy is near death. Serious illness endures until the beginning of April.
        September 18. Tolstoy finishes *Khadzi Murad*.

RESURRECTION

Tolstoy spent more than ten years writing *Resurrection*. He got the idea of the novel in 1887 from a lawyer friend, A. F. Koni, who told him about a case of a jury member who recognizes a defendant on trial for thievery as a woman he had previously seduced. She is condemned to Siberia, and the nobleman offers to marry her, but the marriage does not take place because of her death. The novel is referred to in Tolstoy's diaries as the *Konevskii rasskaz* or the *Konevskaya povest'* (the Koni story or Koni novel). The process of writing is carried on in a desultory fashion for most of the nineties, and is speeded to completion in 1899 primarily because of Tolstoy's desire to use the proceeds from the novel to finance the emigration of the Dukhobors from Russia to Canada. The novel goes through a great number of versions and some of the most important episodes are added in the last revisions. The old tramp that Nekhludov meets in Siberia does not appear until the last revision, and the meeting of Nekhludov with Korchagin at the train station similarly appears only in the last revision. Maslova's meeting with the political exiles occurs late in the revisions, and her character continues to evolve and become more complex with every revision. A. B. Gol'denveyzer, who aided Tolstoy in transcribing corrections, spoke of the "unbelievable work" Tolstoy endured in revising the manuscript and said that Tolstoy rewrote passages tens of times. Yet when Tolstoy sent off the last chapters to *Niva* (in which the novel was serialized in 1899), he wrote in his diary on December 18, 1899: "I have finished *Resurrection*. Not good, Not corrected. Fast. But it's done and no longer interests me." The novel was published in England under the editorship of Chertkhov in a separate edition and free of changes by the censorship in 1899, as well as being serialized in *Niva* during the same year. It appeared in a separate edition in Russia in 1900. The novel provoked a torrent of critical reaction, all of it mixed in praise and criticism. Among the most intelligent early reactions is that of N. K. Mikhaylovsky, who said that *Resurrection* was nowhere near the best of Tolstoy's novels and that many of the best parts have nothing to do with the kernal story of the novel. The psychological interest of the novel, for Mikhaylovsky, is contained in the conflict between voices of others in the heroes and their own voice of reason and feeling. On January 28, 1900, Chekhov wrote about *Resurrection* to M. O. Men'shikov: "This is a remarkable artistic work. The most uninteresting part is everything that is said about the relations between Nekhludof and Katusha. The most interesting is all those princes, generals, aunts, peasants, prisoners, and supervisors."

1902	November 14. Tolstoy writes: "Dostoevsky searched for faith, and when he understood so deeply the unbelievers, he was describing his own lack of faith."
1903	February 12. L. O. Pasternak visits Tolstoy.
	October 9. In a letter to his brother Tolstoy says that he wants to prove in his article on Shakespeare that Shakespeare is "not only not a great writer, but a terrible and disgusting falsehood."
1904	February 9. In answer to a query from the Philadelphia newspaper the *North American* whether he was for Russia or Japan, Tolstoy answers: "I am not for Russia or for Japan, but for the working classes of both countries, which have been deceived by their governments and forced to wage war against their own welfare, conscience, and religion."
	September 10. Reads Kant and translates some passages from his work into Russian.
1905	May 24. V. G. Chertkov arrives from England after eight years of absence.
	August 17. Tolstoy on hearing that peace has been concluded

between Japan and Russia: "What important news! I am ashamed but forced to admit that I have had to fight the feeling of patriotism. I kept hoping that the Russians would win."

1906   September 25. Tolstoy learns that there is a possibility that he will receive the Nobel Prize, and he begs A. A. Ernefel't to use his influence in Stockholm to see to it that he does not.
September 30. Diary entry: "I have been reading Goethe and I see all the harmful influence that this insignificant, bourgeois-egotistical, talented man had on my generation—especially on poor Turgenev with all his enthusiasm about *Faust* (a thoroughly bad work)."
December 1-19. Tolstoy reads Upton Sinclair's *The Jungle* and finds it to be a "remarkable book. The author knows the working people."

1907   January 7. Reads Walt Whitman and finds him "bad."
January 11-12. Reads G. Bernard Shaw's *Man and Superman* and finds it artificial and trite, "terribly witty and in bad taste."

1908   February 25. Tolstoy on Leskov: "He has a difficult style, confused, and long-winded, and that's why he has been forgotten, but still there's lots that is good in his works."
July 9 (22) Letter from Edison asking Tolstoy to record on phonograph in one or two sessions, in English or French, some address to all of mankind. Tolstoy did the recordings on December 24 in Russian, English, and French.

1909   July 12. Diary entry: "If only she knew and understood how she alone has been poisoning the last hours, days, months of my life."
July 18. Tolstoy's wife threatens suicide unless he gives her full rights of ownership to his works. Tolstoy definitely rejects this.
December 28-31. Wanda Landowska performs at Yasnaya Polyana, and Tolstoy finds the music boring.

1910   April 19. Tolstoy receives letters from Mahatma Ghandi and his journal *Indian Home Rule*.
April 28. Diary: "I would like to be alone. It is hard to be with people."
June 26. Another outburst of his wife. She demands his diaries for the last ten years, which are being kept by Chertkov.
July 16. Tolstoy puts his diaries in a bank vault.
September 6. Tolstoy writes to Ghandi about the meaning of his doctrine of nonresistance to evil.
September 24. Diary entry about his wife: "She is sick, and I pity her with all my heart."

October 19. Tolstoy looks over the first volume of *The Brothers Karamazov* and says in his diary: "There's a lot of good in it but all so badly done. The Grand Inquisitor and Zossima's farewell." Also: "I understood today why they like Dostoevsky; there are many beautiful thoughts in his work." October 21. Diary: "At night, I thought of going away." October 26. Letter to V. G. Chertkov: "Now for the first time I felt with special clarity, even to the point of sorrow—how I miss you. There is a whole area of thoughts—feelings which I can share easily with no one else—and know that I am completely understood."

October 27, 28. Tolstoy awakens during the night to find his wife rummaging among his papers, and he decides to leave. Diary entry: "I couldn't lie there, and suddenly I made up my mind definitely to go away. I wrote her a letter." In the letter Tolstoy tells her of his decision to find peace and release from the luxury in which he lives, thanks her for the forty-eight years they have lived together, begs her forgiveness, and asks her not to try to find where he has gone. He leaves with his doctor D. P. Makovitsky about six o'clock. About eleven o'clock Alexandra informs her mother of Tolstoy's departure. Tolstoy's wife attempts suicide.

October 28. Tolstoy visits his sister in the Shamordino monastery.

October 31. Tolstoy is ill and is taken off at the rail junction of Astapova.

November 2. Chertkov comes to Astapovo. Tolstoy's wife arrives shortly before midnight. Tolstoy refuses to see her.

November 3. Tolstoy's last diary entry: "The night was hard. I lay in fever two days. C[hertkov] arrived on the 2d. They say that S[ofya] A[ndreevna] 3-rd T[anya]. At night Serezha arrived, touched me very much. Now the 3d Nikit[in], Tanya, then Goldenv[eizer] and Iv[anovich]."

November 6. Church dignitaries arrive in an attempt to bring Tolstoy to repentance and back to the church. They are unsuccessful.

November 6, night. Tolstoy's last words: "Truth . . . I love much. As they . . ."

November 7, about 5 a.m. His wife is permitted to see him. He is in a coma.

November 7, 6: 05. Tolstoy dies.

November 9. Tolstoy's body arrives at Yasnaya Polyana. He is buried at the ravine where he and his brothers played as children looking for the "green stick" on which Tolstoy as a child believed was inscribed the secret of universal happiness and harmony.

Notes

1. INTRODUCTION

1. Boris Eikhenbaum, *Molodoi Tolstoi* (Petersburg, Berlin, 1922); *Lev Tolstoi*, 2 vols. (Leningrad, 1928 and 1930); *Lev Tolstoi, Semidesyatye gody* (Leningrad, 1960).
2. See especially *Molodoi Tolstoi*, pp. 11-28.
3. Peter Chaadaev published the first philosophic letter in 1836 (conceived about 1829), in which he lamented the lack of tradition in Russian national life. The letters were published in French. For an English translation, see *The Major Works of Peter Chaadaev*, trans. Raymond T. McNally (South Bend, Ind., 1969).
4. Danilevsky's *Rossiya i Evropa* was published in 1869. It is a long, aggressive championing of pan-Slavism under Russia's direction and based on a quasi-scientific theory of cultural types and the successive historical prominence of each. There is no translation.
5. Such a faith underlies the reasoning of Chernyshevsky's "The Anthropological Principle in Philosophy" (1860) and the novel *What Is To Be Done* (1863).
6. Isaiah Berlin, *The Hedgehog and the Fox: An Essay on Tolstoy's View of History* (London and New York, 1953). Berlin has taken the line from the poet Archilochus, "The fox knows many things, but the hedgehog knows one big thing," and uses this difference to differentiate between those writers who seek a single truth, "who relate everything to a single central vision," and "those who pursue many ends, often unrelated and even contradictory." Tolstoy was, according to Berlin, a fox who wanted to be a hedgehog.
7. This conflict animates much of what Merezhkovsky has to say about Tolstoy in his *Tolstoi i Dostoevsky* published originally in 1901 and available in English as Dmitri Merejkowski, *Tolstoi as Man and Artist with an Essay on Dostoievsky* (London, 1902).
8. N. K. Mikhaylovsky, "Zhestokii talant," *Dostoevsky v russkoi kritike* (Moscow, 1956). First published in 1882 in *Otechestvenny e zapiski*, nos. 9-10.
9. Kenneth Burke, *The Philosophy of Literary Form* (New York, 1941).

2. CHILDHOOD and THREE DEATHS

1. Merejkowski, *Tolstoi as Man and Artist*, p. 197.
2. Ibid., p. 809.
3. Isaiah Berlin, "Tolstoy and Enlightenment," in *Tolstoy: A Collection of Critical Essays*, ed. Ralph Matlaw (Englewood Cliffs, N.J., 1967), p. 29.
4. "Sdokhnesh' . . . trava vyrastet na mogilke, vot i vse."
5. "vse ego vremya ya vel sebya ne tak, kak ya zhelal sebya vesti."
6. "Ya napisal v drug mnogo pravil i khotel im vsem sledovat'; no sily moi byli slishkom slaby dlya etogo."

7. "Ya tak slab! Nuzhno boyat'sya prazdnosti i besporyadochnosti tak zhe kak ya boyus' kart."
8. "Ya propadu, ezheli ne ispravlyus'"
9. L. N. Tolstoi, *Polnoe sobranie sochinenii*, ed. V. G. Chertkov, vol. 1 (Moscow-Leningrad, 1928), p. 103. In all subsequent references this standard edition "Jubilee Edition" of 90 volumes (1928–1958) will be referred to as JE.
10. Eikhenbaum sees the dominant as an "ustanovka na melochnost'" so as to accomplish a "narushenie psikhologichskikh proportsii." *Molodoi Tolstoi*, p. 77.
11. Eikhenbaum, *Lev Tolstoi, kniga pervaya*, vol. 1, p. 87.
12. R. F. Christian, *Tolstoy: A Critical Introduction* (Cambridge, England, 1969), p. 21.
13. Ibid., p. 33.
14. Ernest J. Simmons, *Introduction to Tolstoy's Writings* (Chicago, 1968), p. 16.
15. N. G. Chernyshevsky, "Detstvo i Otrochestvo. Voennye rasskazy, L. N. Tolstogo," *Sovremennik* 12 (1856): 53–64. Also available in *Tolstoy v russkoi kritike*, ed. S. P. Bychkov (Moscow, 1952), pp. 91–105.
16. Ibid., pp. 99–100.
17. "Vsegda budu govorit' chto soznanie est' velichaishee moral'noe zlo kotoroe mozhet postignut' cheloveka" (July 4, 1851).
18. "Lev Tolstoi, kak zerkalo russkoi revolyutsii," first published in the Bolshevik newspaper *Proletarii* anonymously on September 9, 1908. Widely available in various editions and collections.
19. Letter of 1 May 1858, in JE, vol. 5, p. 301.
20. Claude Lévi-Strauss, *The Savage Mind* (Chicago, 1962), pp. 16–36.
21. Christian, *Tolstoy*, p. 89.

3. POLIKUSHKA and FAMILY HAPPINESS

1. S. Bychov, *L. N. Tolstoi* (Moscow, 1954), p. 73.
2. Eikhenbaum, *Lev Tolstoi, Kniga pervaya*, vol. 1, pp. 93–97.
3. Christian, *Tolstoy*, p. 94.
4. See letters in JE, particularly for the year 1856.
5. Henri Troyat, *Tolstoy*, trans. Nancy Amphoux (New York, 1967), p. 192. Published in France 1965.
6. George Rapall Noyes, *Tolstoy* (New York, 1918), p. 63.

4. THE COSSACKS

1. John Bayley, *Tolstoy and the Novel* (New York, 1966), p. 63.
2. Merezhkowsky, pp. 13–14.

5. WAR AND PEACE

1. Berlin, *The Hedgehog and the Fox*, p. 66. Tolstoy himself wrote of a conception of unity in somewhat similar terms when he wrote Strakhov about *Anna Karenina* that the elements of any work of his existed in a "labyrinth of connections" (*labirint stseplenii*), or, in the critical language of today, in a "context," and that individual elements that were abstracted from this *labirint stseplenii* lost their significance and quality. He went on to say: "Nuzhny lyudi, kotorye pokazyvali by bessmyslitsu otyskivaniya otdel'nykh myslei v khudozhestvennom proizvedeniya i postoyanno

rukovodili by chitatelei v tom bezknonechno libirint stseplenii, v kotorom i sostoit sushchnost' iskusstvo i po tem zakonam, kotorye sluzhat osnovaniem etikh stseplenii.''

2. Matthew Arnold, "Count Leo Tolstoi," *Fortnightly Review*, December 1887; reprinted in *Essays in Criticism, Second Series*. This article is apparently the progenitor of a long tradition of English "exclamatory" criticism about Tolstoy's capacity to render life without the artifice of art. Even in America, Lionel Trilling, in his article "Anna Karenina," in *The Opposing Self* (New York, 1950), continued to say the same untenable things.

3. Havelock Ellis, *Tolstoi: The New Spirit* (London, New York, n.d.), p. 217.

4. Edward Garnett, *Tolstoy: His Life and Writings* (London, 1914), pp. 33-34.

5. Hugh I'Anson Fausset, *Tolstoy: The Inner Drama* (New York, 1928), p. 146.

6. Edwin Muir, *The Structure of the Novel* (New York, 1929), pp. 96-97.

7. Logan Speirs, *Tolstoy and Chekhov* (Cambridge, England, 1971), p. 2.

8. Elizabeth Gunn, *A Daring Coiffeur: Reflections on "War and Peace" and "Anna Karenina,"* (Totowa, N.J., 1971), p. 37.

9. Henry James, "Preface to *The Tragic Muse*," in *The Art of the Novel*, ed. R. P. Blackmur (New York, 1934), p. 84.

10. Percy Lubbock, *The Craft of Fiction* (London [1912], 1924), p. 32.

11. Albert Cook, "The Unity of *War and Peace*," *Western Review* 22 (Summer 1958): 245.

12. R. F. Christian, *Tolstoy's "War and Peace": A Study* (Oxford, 1962), pp. 124-25.

13. John Hagan "On the Craftsmanship of *War and Peace*," *Essays in Criticism* 13 (January 1963): 33.

14. Jerome Thale, "*War and Peace*: the Art of Incoherence," *Essays in Criticism* 16 (1966): 398-415.

15. Bert O. States, "The Hero and the World: Our Sense of Space in War and Peace," *Modern Fiction Studies* 11 (1965): 153-64.

16. Hagan, "Craftsmanship," pp. 22-23.

17. Muir, *The Structure of the Novel*, pp. 88-114.

18. E. M. de Vogüé, *Le Roman russe* (Paris, 1886), p. 311.

19. Romain Rolland, *Vie de Tolstoi* (Paris, 1913), p. 66.

20. Hagan, "Craftsmanship," pp. 28-29.

21. Noyes, *Tolstoy*, p. 188.

22. Fausset, *Tolstoy*, p. 155.

23. Theodore Redpath, *Tolstoy* (London, 1960), p. 62.

24. Ibid.

25. Christian, *Tolstoy's "War and Peace,"* p. 130.

26. Fausset, *Tolstoy*, p. 149.

27. Hagan, "Craftsmanship," p. 27.

28. Merejkowski, *Tolstoi*, p. 207.

29. S. Bocharov, *Roman L. Tolstogo, Voina i Mir* (Moscow, 1968), pp. 75-120.

30. Christian, *Tolstoy*, p. 150.

31. James T. Farrell, "History and War in Tolstoy's *War and Peace*," in *Literature and Morality* (New York, 1945), p. 203.

32. Percy Lubbock, *The Craft of Fiction* (London, 1924), p. 33.

33. Bocharov, *Roman L. Tolstogo*, pp. 5-33.

34. Ibid.

35. N. Akhsharumov, " 'Voina i mir,' Sochinenie grafa Tolstogo," *Vsemirny trud*, 4 (1868), 25-67.

36. Turgenev to I. P. Borisov, 16 March 1865.
37. Flaubert's criticism of the theory was tempered by extravagant praise for the novel itself. He said in a letter to Turgenev: "Merci de m'avoir fait lire le roman de Tolstoi. C'est de premier ordre. Quel peintre et quel psychologue! Les deux premiers [volumes] sont *sublimes*; mais le troisième dégringole affreusement. Il se répète et il philosophise. Enfin on voit le monsieur, l'auteur et Le Russe, tandis que jusque-là on n'avait vu que la Nature et l'Humanité. Il me semble qu'il y a parfois des choses à la Shakespeare. Je poussais des cris d'admiration pendant cette lecture . . . et elle est longue! Parlez-moi de *l'auteur*. Est-ce son premier livre? En tout cas, il a des *boules*. Oui, c'est bien fort, bien fort." Lettre de 21 janvier, 1880. *Correspondance, Supplément* (Juillet 1877-Mai 1880), ed. René Dumesnil, Jean Pommier, et Claude Digeon (Paris, 1954), pp. 298-99.
38. Lubbock, *The Craft of Fiction*, p. 35.
39. Janko Lavrin, *Tolstoy: An Approach* (New York, 1946), p. 27.
40. Noyes, *Tolstoy*, p. 177.
41. Courrière, *Histoire de la littérature contemporaine en Russie* (Paris, 1875), p. 354. Although de Vogüé's work *Le Roman russe* is widely reported to be the source for the earliest Western reaction to Russian literature, Courrière's work antedates it by more than a decade. Courrière's is a work of considerable critical merit. "Mais pourquoi faut-il que l'admiration qu'on éprouve pour ces beautés soit gâtée par les théories philosophiques de l'auteur? Le comte L. Tolstoi n'a vu dans cette lutte gigantesque entre deux mondes, dans ce grand mouvement de l'humanité, que le concours et l'enchaînement de causes accidentelles, indépendantes de la volonté humaine. Napoléon et Alexandre, Koutouzof et Bagration, Les Français et les Russes ne sont que de simples pions mis en mouvement par la main de la destinée sur le vaste échiquier du monde. Le fatalisme de l'auteur est raisonneur, doctrinaire; il rabaisse à sa petite mesure tous les grands événements de cette époque."
42. JE, vol. 15, p. 238. 'no vyskazannoe mnoyu zdes' bez tsitat i ssylok, v epiloge romane, ne est' minutnaya fantaziya mysli, a est' neizbezhny dlya menya vyvod semiletnikh trudov, kotorye ya ne vlasten byl ne sdelat'."
43. Tolstoy to Pogodin, March 21, 1868.
44. JE, vol. 13, p. 56.
45. Berlin, *The Hedgehog and the Fox*, pp. 29-30.
46. JE, vol. 10, p. 231. "Nashe vozzrenie ne tol'ko ne isklyuchaet nashu svobodu, no nekolebimo ustanavlivaet sushchestvovanie ee, osnovannoe ne na razume, no na neposredstvennom soznanii. Kakovy by ni byli obshchie zakony, upravlyayushchie mirom i chelovestvom, beskonechny maly moment svobody vsegda neot' 'emlemo pridnadlezhit mne."
47. JE, vol. 15, p. 290. "Soznanie togo, chto ya esm' svoboden, est' soznanie, kotoroe ne mozhet byt' ni dokazano, ni oprovergnuto razumom."
48. JE, vol. 15, p. 290.
49. Nikolay Ivanovich Kareev, *Istoricheskaya filosofiya gr. L. N. Tolstogo v 'Voine i mire,'* (St. Petersburg, 1888), p. 43.

6. ANNA KARENINA

1. Matthew Arnold, *Essays in Criticism, Second Series, The Works of Matthew Arnold,* vol. 4 (London, 1933), p. 202.
2. Ibid. p. 198.
3. "Seryozha?—vspominala ona—Ya tozhe dumal, chto lyubila ego, i umilyalas'

nad svoeyu nezhnost'yu. A zhila zhe ya bez nego, promenyala zhe ego na druguyu lyubov' i zhalovalas' na etot promen, poka udovletvoryalas' toi lyubov'yu.''
4. W. K. Wimsatt and Monroe C. Beardsley, "The Intentional Fallacy," *Sewanee Review* 59 (Summer 1946). Reprinted in *The Verbal Icon* (Lexington, KY., 1954).

7. THE DEATH OF IVAN ILYCH

1. Maude translates *uzhasnaya* as "terrible," but "terrifying" is clearly closer to the Russian and to the literary context.
2. One of the strongest statements in this regard is to be found—one among many—in Lavrin's *Tolstoy*, p. 114: "His [Tolstoy's] aim to reduce all human beings to the same denominator is one of the most unnatural ideals ever devised by man. If it were possible at all, its result would be a vegetative existence outside history and outside any activities which make life worthwhile."

8. MASTER AND MAN

1. Maude's translation.

9. RESURRECTION

1. George Steiner, *Tolstoy or Dostoevsky* (New York, 1957), p. 92.

10. APPENDIX

1. This chronicle is indebted in part to the superb work of N. N. Gusev, especially the following: *Letopis' zhizni i tvorchestva L'va Nikolaevicha Tolstogo*. 2 vols. (Moscow, 1958, 1960).

Bibliography

EDITIONS OF TOLSTOY'S WORKS

The standard edition of Tolstoy's works is the ninety-volume Jubilee Edition, published between 1928 and 1958. In addition to the texts themselves, this edition includes rough drafts of some of the writings, variants, letters, and diaries. The edition contains more than seven thousand letters (vols. 59–90) and thirteen volumes of diaries (vols. 46–58). It is doubtful that the complete letters or the complete diaries will ever be published in English. Selections from the diaries are to be found in English in *The Diaries of Leo Tolstoy, 1847–52*, trans. C. J. Hogarth and A. Sirnis (London, 1917); *The Private Diary of Leo Tolstoy, 1853–57*, trans. Louise and Aylmer Maude (London and New York, 1927) and *Leo Tolstoy, Last Diaries*, trans. Lydia Weston-Kesich and ed. Leon Stilman (New York, 1960). The letters in the Jubilee Edition are arranged by correspondent (to his wife, Chertkov, various people), and may be supplemented by such editions as *Lev Tolstoi i V. V. Stasov, Perepiska 1878–1906*, ed. V. A. Komarovoi and B. L. Modzalovskii (Moscow, 1929); *L. N. Tolstoi i N. N. Ge, Perepiska* (Moscow-Leningrad, 1930). An edition in English by R. F. Christian of about 600 of the letters is now in press. See also *The Letters of Tolstoy and his Cousin Countess Alexandra Tolstoy, 1857–1903*, trans. L. Islavin (London, 1929), and *Tolstoy's Love Letters, 1856–57*, trans. S. S. Koteliansky and V. Woolf (London, 1923). The best edition of Tolstoy's works in English is the Centenary Edition of Tolstoy, 21 vols., trans. Louise and Aylmer Maude (London, 1929–37). Maude's translations, the best, are also available in various editions, notably the Oxford World Classics, the Norton Critical Editions, and the one-volume Harper *Great Short Works of Leo Tolstoy*. The Jubilee Edition contains rough drafts and variants of many of the works. These may be supplemented by following published sources of manuscript material: *Opisanie izobrazitel'nykh materialov Pushkinskogo doma, III, Lev Tolstoi* (Moscow-Leningrad, 1954). *Opisanie rukopisei khudozestvennykh proizvedenii L. N. Tolstogo*, ed. V. A. Zhdanov et al. (Moscow, 1955). *Opisanie rukopisei statei L. N. Tolstogo. Literatura, iskusstvo, nauka, pedagogika* (Moscow, 1961). Volumes 35, 36, 37,

38, 69 (two books), and 75 of *Literaturnoe Nasledstvo* contain hitherto unpublished materials, as well as reminiscences and critical articles. Volume 75, *Tolstoi i zarubezhny mir* (Moscow, 1965) contains materials of Tolstoy's relations with writers and audiences beyond Russia. Of particular importance are six *obzory* such as "Tolstoy in Germany" and "Tolstoy in Poland." The volume unaccountably does not contain an *obzor* of America and England.

SECONDARY LITERATURE

No bibliography of secondary literature on Tolstoy in Russian can be anything but selective. Soviet secondary literature alone numbers more than eleven thousand pieces, and there is no complete bibliography of pre-Soviet Russian secondary literature on Tolstoy. The bibliography below is particularly selective of Russian materials, but gives considerable secondary literature in English on Tolstoy's major fiction. In England and America, critical interest in Tolstoy has lagged behind that in Dostoevsky. As early as 1958, *Modern Fiction Studies* devoted a special issue to a fairly complete bibliography of secondary materials in English on Dostoevsky; even at this much later date there is nothing comparable available on Tolstoy. There is a scattering of short bibliographies appended to books on Tolstoy, most notably those of Ernest Simmons, *Leo Tolstoy* (Boston, 1946) and R. F. Christian's *Tolstoy, A Critical Introduction* (Cambridge, 1969). The bibliography that follows is fairly representative of secondary materials in English on Tolstoy's fiction. Materials on Tolstoy's expository writings—art, religion, social topics—have been included only if they have general implications for the fiction or are important testaments in themselves. An asterisk before the work indicates a work of exceptional importance.

I. *Bibliographical Aids*

Bibliografiya literatury o L. N. Tolstom, 1917–1958. Ed. N. G. Shelyapin et al. Moscow, 1960. This listing of more than 5,000 pieces has been supplemented by two other volumes with the same title and editors, for 1959–61 and 1962–67. Each volume has as its first section a listing of works by Lenin on Tolstoy. Arranged by years and alphabetically. Much very incidental material.

Bem, A. L., ed. *Bibligraficheskii ukazatel' tvorenii L. N. Tolstogo.* Leningrad, 1926. Of special interest is a listing of translations made by Tolstoy and of articles Tolstoy edited or helped edit.

Bitovt, Yury. *Graf L. Tolstoi v literature i isskustve.* Moscow, 1903. Available in a University of Michigan microfilm edition, 1965. Of interest: list of translations of Tolstoy's works before 1900. Criticism of Tolstoy's works, pp. 99-139. Articles about Tolstoy's fortunes in England and America.

Motyleva, T. L., et al., eds. *Khudozhestvennye proizvedeniya L. N. Tolstogo v perevodakh na innostrannye yazyki.* Moscow, 1961. Listing of translations of Tolstoy's fiction into major languages.

Sorokin, Boris. "Lev Tolstoj in Pre-Revolutionary Russian Criticism." Doctoral dissertation, University of Chicago, 1973. Survey of major prerevolutionary criticism and extensive bibliography.

Zhilina, E. N. *Lev Nikolaevich Tolstoi, 1828-1910.* Leningrad, 1960. A bibliographical aid; includes selective secondary literature on individual works.

II. *Reminiscences and Biographies*

Alexandre, Aimée. *Le mythe de Tolstoi.* Paris, 1960.

Asquith, Cynthia. *Married to Tolstoy.* London, 1960. A defense of Tolstoy's wife in her difficulties with Tolstoy.

*Biryukov, P. *Lev Nikolaevich Tolstoy*, 4 vols. Moscow, 1911-23. Still perhaps the best biography of Tolstoy.

*Brodsky, N. A., et al., eds. *L. N. Tolstoi v vospominaniyakh sovremennikov.* 2 vols. Moscow, 1955. There is also a 1960 edition, ed. S. N. Golubov et al., with some additional material. These are very important volumes. The English edition is considerably abbreviated and awkwardly translated by the Moscow Foreign Publishing House. The 1960 Soviet volume adds some items and drops others, especially of recently published separate books of reminiscences, such as Bulgakov's and Goldenweizer's.

*Bulgakov, Valentin. *The Last Year of Leo Tolstoy.* Trans. Ann Dunnigan. Intro. George Steiner. New York, 1971. Fascinating account (by Tolstoy's male secretary) of Tolstoy's last year and his torturous relations with his wife.

Bulgakov, V. F. *O Tolstom, vospominaniya i rasskazy.* Tula, 1964. Supplementary to his *Poslednii god*, but written after the events, the account does not have the sharply vivid sense of the diary. Often a record of objects in the room and other inconsequential matters.

Bunin, Ivan. *Osvobozhdenie Tolstogo.* Paris, 1937. Draws upon personal recollections, as well as the diary, letters, and reminiscences of others. Beautifully written.

Dole, Nathan Haskell. *The Life of Count Lyof N. Tolstoi.* New York, 1911.

*Eikenbaum, Boris. *Lev Tolstoi, kniga pervaya, 50-e gody*, Leningrad, 1928.

———. *Lev Tolstoi, kniga vtoraya, 60-e gody.* Moscow and Leningrad, 1931.

———. *Lev Tolstoi, semidesyatye gody.* Leningrad, 1960.

*Goldenweizer, A. B. *Talks with Tolstoy*. Trans. S. S. Koteliansky and Virginia Woolf. New York, 1949. This English edition contains about half of the Russian edition *V Blizi Tolstogo*. Ed. S. N. Golubov, Moscow, 1959. The preface to this edition tells us that the original 1922 edition has been supplemented with those passages not published then for the protection of living people, and assures us that nothing has been eliminated (*bez izmenenii*); this is not true. Passages uncomplimentary to socialism have been eliminated or edited. The following, for example, is in the 1922 edition but not in the 1959 one: "Materialism is the most mystical of all doctrines; it makes a belief in some mythical matter, which creates everything out of itself, the foundation of everything. It's sillier than a belief in the Trinity."

Gourfinkel, Nina. *Tolstoi sans Tolstoisme*. Paris, 1946.

*Gorky, Maxim. *Reminiscences of Tolstoy, Chekhov, and Andreev*. New York, 1959. Published earlier in London, 1934. Sensitive recollections of meetings with Tolstoy.

*Gudzii, N. K. *Lev Tolstoi*. Moscow, 1960.

―――, ed. *Lev Nikolaevich Tolstoi*. 2 vols. Moscow, 1955, 1959.

*Gusev, N. N. *Dva goda s L. N. Tolstym*. Moscow, 1912. Gusev worked for Tolstoy from September 1907 to August 4, 1909, when he was arrested and sent to Siberia.

Kubikov, I. N. *Lev Tolstoi*. Moscow, 1928.

*Kuzminskaya, Tatyana A. *Tolstoy as I Knew Him*. New York, 1948. Soviet edition published in 1959. The three-volume Russian 3d edition, 1928, ed. T. Volkov, has corrected previous editions by going back to the manuscripts and including major episodes, such as Strakhov's reactions to *War and Peace* and reminiscences of Fet and Tiutchev, that had not appeared in earlier editions.

Leon, Derrick. *Tolstoy: His Life and Work*. London, 1944. Emphasis on Tolstoy's postconversion life.

*Maude, Aylmer. *The Life of Tolstoy*. 2 vols. New York, 1910. The best biography in English.

―――. *Tolstoy and His Problems*. New York, 1904. Ten essays on biographical and critical subjects. Polemical with critics of Tolstoy.

―――, trans. *The Final Struggle: Countess Tolstoy's Diary for 1910*. London, 1926. Seven essays written by members of Tolstoy's family and two close friends.

Notzel, Karl. *Tolstois Meisterjahre*. Munich and Leipzig, 1918.

Perris, G. H. *Leo Tolstoy: The Grand Mujik*. London, 1898. Representative of early biographical view of Tolstoy. Characteristic passage: "The exquisite sensitiveness which gives us these wonderful psychologies is partly a result of radical traits, partly of the sudden awakening of a people out of barbarism and isolation into power and access to Western ideas."

Philipson, Morris. *The Count Who Wished He Were a Peasant.* New York, 1967.

Polner, T. I. *Tolstoy and His Wife.* New York, 1949. Translation by Nicholas Loredon of *Lev Tolstoi i ego zhena* (Paris, 1928). Documentary treatment of important subject. Polner is on Tolstoy's side.

Porché, François. *Portrait psychologique de Tolstoi.* Paris, 1949.

*Rolland, Romain. *Vie de Tolstoy.* Paris, 1913. A French classic on Tolstoy. Still useful.

Rozanova, S. "Novoe o Tolstom (Po stranitsam uchenykh zapisok GDRO)" *Voprosy literatury* 17, no. 11 (1973): 217-26. Biographical filling out of Tolstoy in Europe, 1857 and 1860-61.

Sarolea, Charles. *Count L. N. Tolstoy: His Life and Work.* London, n.d. Sarolea anticipates, as does Nina Gourfinkel, Isaiah Berlin's long discussion of Joseph de Maistre's influence on Tolstoy.

Sergeenko, P. A. *How Count L. N. Tolstoy Lives and Works.* Trans. Isabel Hapgood. New York, 1898.

Shepeleva, Z. S. *Lev Nikolaevich Tolstoi: Kratkii ocherk zhizni i tvorchestva.* Moscow, 1960.

*Shklovsky, V. *Lev Tolstoi.* Moscow, 1963. Anecdotal, impressionistic, and lacking in organization.

*Simmons, Ernest. *Tolstoy.* Boston, 1946. Standard and established biography. Full and competent.

Soukhotine-Tolstoy, Tatiana. *Sur mon père.* Paris, 1960. Reprints of a long article published in 1928 in *Europe.* Series of memories and impressions.

Sukhotin-Tolstoy, Tatiana. *The Tolstoy Home.* Trans. Alec Brown. London, 1950. Diaries of Tolstoy's second oldest daughter.

Sukhotina-Tolstoiya. *Druz'ya i gosti Yasnoi Polyany.* Moscow, 1923. Reminiscences of Turgenev, Ge, and others.

Tcherkoff, Vladimir. *The Last Days of Tolstoy.* Trans. Nathalie Duddington. London, 1922. Partisan account of Tolstoy's last days and flight by Tolstoy's closest friend.

Tolstoy, Alexandra. *Tolstoy: A Life of My Father.* Trans. Hapgood. New York, 1953. Original published by Chekhov, 1953. A reminiscent biography by Tolstoy's youngest daughter.

————. *The Real Tolstoy.* Morristown, N.J., 1968. Twelve-page critique of Troyat's biography, accusing him of fictionalizing Tolstoy's life.

————. *The Tragedy of Tolstoy.* Trans. Elena Varneck. New Haven, 1933. Unfavorable view of Tolstoy's wife.

Tolstoy, Ilya. *Reminiscences of Tolstoy.* Trans. George Calderon. New York, 1914. Retranslated by Ann Dunnigan as *Tolstoy, My Father: Reminiscences.* Chicago, 1971. Reminiscences by Tolstoy's son.

Tolstoy, Leon. *The Truth about My Father.* New York, 1924.

Arranged topically. Portraits of important visitors to the Tolstoy home, such as Chertkov, Ge.

Tolstoy, Sergey. *Tolstoy Remembered by His Son Sergey Tolstoy.* Trans. Maura Budberg. New York, 1962. Translation of Russian *Ocherki bylogo* (Moscow, 1949) by Tolstoy's oldest son.

Tolstoy, S. L. *Mat' i ded L. N. Tolstogo.* Moscow, 1928. See especially "Ded L. N. Tolstogo kn. N. S. Volkonsky," pp. 7-40, where the prototype for Prince Bolkonsky is discussed.

Tolstoja-Sukhotina, T. A. "Vblizi otsa: Iz dnevnika." *Novy mir* 49, no. 12 (1973): 170-207.

Troyat, Henri. *Tolstoi.* Paris, 1965. An English translation (by Nancy Amphoux) is available in a 1967 Doubleday edition. This biography has been severely criticized for its fanciful reconstruction of Tolstoy's life. For sharp criticism of the book see Alexandra Tolstoy's *The Real Tolstoy* (Morristown, N.J., 1968), as well as Kathryn B. Feuer's "Recent Works of Leo Tolstoy," *Russian Literature* 28 (1969): 217-224.

Volynsky, A. *L. N. Tolstoi: zhizn' i tvorchestvo, 1828-1908.* Saint Petersburg, 1909.

Werth, A., trans. *The Diary of Tolstoy's Wife,* 1860-91. London, 1928.

————, trans. *Countess Tolstoy's Later Diary,* 1891-97. London, 1929.

*Wettlin, Margaret, trans. *Reminiscences of Lev Tolstoy by His Contemporaries.* Moscow, n.d. A selection from the two-volume *L. N. Tolstoi v vospominaniyakh sovremennikov.*

III. *Early Criticism*

1. *Western languages.* A selected chronological listing of works on Tolstoy published through the First World War. For translations of Russian materials, see subsection III,2 below.

*Courrière, C. *Histoire de la littérature contemporaine en Russie.* Paris, 1875. E. M. De Vogüé's work on the Russian novel is often put forth as the earliest source of Western reaction to Russian literature, but Courrière's work appeared even earlier.

*Vogüé, E. M. de. *Le roman russe.* Paris, 1886. English translations: *The Russian Novelists,* translated by J. L. Edmonds. Boston, 1887. Also from the 11th French edition and superior in quality: *The Russian Novel,* trans. M. A. Sawyer. London, 1913. A classic early reaction to important Russian writers, including Tolstoy.

*Arnold, Matthew. "Count Leo Tolstoy!" *Essays in Criticism, Second Series.* London, 1888. First published in December 1887 in the *Fortnightly Review.* Primarily on *Anna Karenina,* but with implications for all of Tolstoy. The work has left its shadow on virtually all of subsequent English criticism on Tolstoy.

Turner, Charles Edward. *Count Tolstoi as Novelist and Thinker*. London, 1888.

Saitschik, R. *Die Weltanschauung Dostojevskijs und Tolstojs*. Leipzig, 1893.

*Howells, William Dean. "The Philosophy of Tolstoy." In *The Library of the World's Best Literature*. Boston, 1897. Howells almost alone in American letters propagated Tolstoy's excellence.

Perris, G. H. *Leo Tolstoy, the Grand Mujik*. London, 1898.

Ellis, H. Havelock. *Tolstoi, a Man of Peace*. Chicago, 1900.

Faguet, Emile. *Propos littéraires*. Paris, 1902.

Norris, Frank. *The Responsibilities of the Novelist*. New York, 1903.

*James, Henry. "Preface to The Tragic Muse" for the New York Edition, vol. 8 New York, 1907-17. Available in *The Art of the Novel*, ed. R. P. Blackmur, pp. 79-97. New York and London, 1934.

Redfern, Percy. *Tolstoy: A Study*. London, 1907. An early statement about the "two Tolstoys."

Chesterton, G. K. *Varied Types*. Pp. 125-144. New York, 1908.

*Maude, Aylmer. *The Life of Tolstoy*. 2 vols. New York, 1910. Still one of the best critical biographies on Tolstoy.

*Rolland, Romain. *Vie de Tolstoy*. Paris, 1913.

Garnett, Edward. *Tolstoy: His Life and Writings*. London and New York, 1914.

Noyes, George Rapall. *Tolstoy*. New York, 1918.

2. Russian. A chronological listing of Russian works on Tolstoy published up to the Soviet revolution, including English translations where available.

*Nekrasov, N. A. "Zametki o zhurnalakh za sentyabr' 1855 g." *Sovremennik*, October 1855. *Polnoe sobranie socahinenii* 4 (1950). Praise of Tolstoy's talent. See also March 1856 issue for second piece (with the same title) on Tolstoy.

Druzhinin, A. B. "O L. N. Tolstom voobshche—'Metel', 'Dva Gusara,' Povesti grafa L. N. Tolstogo." *Biblioteka dlya chteniya* 9 (September 1856): 1-30. Praise of Tolstoy, especially of his objective attitude toward his characters.

*Chernyshevsky, N. G. " 'Detstvo i otrochestvo'. Voennye rasskazy grafa Tolstogo. *Sovremennik* 12 (December 1856): 53-64. One of the best of the early critical writings on Tolstoy. It is in this piece that Chernyshevsky uses the term "vnutrenii monolog"—a term that is obsessive in later Soviet criticism—and praises Tolstoy for his capacity to catch thoughts in their germination. These considerations led Gleb Struve to consider Tolstoy as an early expressor of the "stream of consciousness" technique.

*Pisarev, D. I. " 'Tri smerti', rasskaz grafa L. N. Tolstogo." *Rassvet* 12 (December 1859): 63-74.

Grigor'ev, Apollon. "Yavleniya sovremennoi literatury, propush-chennye nashei kritikoi. Gr. L. N. Tolstoi i ego sochineniya." *Vremya* 1 (January 1862): 1-30; and 9 (September 1862): 1-27. Conflict of artist and the thinker; anticipates Merezhkovsky's thesis.

Botkin, V. P. "Sovremenny e povesti i sovremenny e geroi." *Golos* 21 (April 1863). Analysis centered on *Kazaki.* Tolstoy is criticized for following Rousseau.

Annenkov, P. V. "Sovremennaya belletristika. Graf L. N. Tolstoi. *Kazaki.*"; *Sankt Peterburgskie vedomosti* 27 and 28 (June 1863). The author likes Olenin.

Tur, Evgeniya. "*Kazaki.* Kavkazskaya povest' 1852 g. grafa L. N. Tolstogo." *Otechestvennye zapiski* 7 (July 1863): 242-79.

*Pisarev, Dmitri. "Promakhi nezreloi mysli." *Russkoe slovo*, December 1864, pp. 1-56. On *Childhood, Boyhood, Youth, Landholder's Morning*, and *Lucerne*.

Annenkov, P. V. "Istoricheskie i esteticheskie voprosy v romane gr. L. N. Tolstogo *Voina i mir.*" *Vestnik Evropy* 2 (February 1868): 774-95.

*Pisarev, D. I. "Staroe barstvo. *Voina i Mir* sochineniya gr. L. N. Tolstogo." *Otechesvennye zapiski*, February 1868, pp. 263-91. An extremely interesting reaction by this famous radical critic to the first half of *War and Peace*. Also available—as well as the other two entries here of Pisarev's—in *L. N. Tolstoi v russkoi kritike*, ed. S. P. Bychkov, pp. 207-43. Moscow, 1952.

Leskin, E. *Razbor i isvlechenie iz romana 'Voina i Mir'.* Moscow, 1870.

*Strakhov, N. *Kriticheskii razbor "Voina i Mir."* Saint Petersburg, 1871. These reprints from *Zarya*, 1869-70, are extraordinary early critical essays on *War and Peace*. Very sympathetic but also very perceptive.

*Mikhailovsky, N. K. "Desnitsa i shuitsa L'va Tolstogo." In *N. K. Mikhailovskii; Literaturnye-kriticheskie stat'i.* Moscow, 1957. This classic essay on Tolstoy against himself—anticipating not only Merezhkovsky and I. Berlin but a good part of criticism on Tolstoy—was originally published in 1875. Mikhailovsky wrote a great number of pieces on Tolstoy during a thirty-year period. Of special mention is his "Khozyain i rabotnik gr. L. N. Tolstogo" in 1895 (see section VIII below) and his "O kreitserovoi sonate" in 1890. His criticism is hard to come by in Russian and unavailable in English.

*Dostoevsky, F. M. *Dnevnik pisatelya za 1877 goda.* Paris, n.d. Pp. 268-70 and 275-311. In the July-August 1877 issue of *The Diary of a Writer* Dostoevsky wrote a series of articles on *Anna*

Karenina, especially on Tolstoy's views of the Turkish-Serbian war and his conception of the people.

Leskov, N. S. "Graf L. N. Tolstoi i F. M. Dostoevskii kak eresiarkhi. *Novosti i birzhevaya gazeta* 1 and 3 (April 1883).

*Gromeka, M. S. "*Poslednie proizvedeniya gr. L. N. Tolstogo: kriticheskii etyud.*" Moscow, 1884. Excellent analysis of character, especially of Oblonsky, Vronsky, Karenin, and Anna Karenina. Anna is a failure as a woman, and the real hero is Dolly.

*Strakhov, N. N. *Kriticheskie stat'i ob I. S. Turgeneve i L. N. Tolstom.* Saint Petersburg, 1886. Reprinted in Mouton edition, 1968.

Skabichevskii, A. M. *Graf L. N. Tolstoi kak khudozhnik i myslitel'.* Saint Petersburg, 1887. Tolstoy's heroes are seen as perpetually alienated from the world about them.

*Kareev, N. *Istoricheskaya filosofiya gr. L. N. Tolstogo v 'Voine i Mire.'* Saint Petersburg, 1888. Still the best treatment in Russian of Tolstoy's theory of history in *War and Peace*.

*Leont'ev, K. *O romanakh gr. L. N. Tolstogo. Analiz, stil' i veyanie.* Moscow, 1911. Written in 1890. Reprinted Providence, R.I.: Brown, 1965. Excellent early reading of Tolstoy.

Rozanov, V. V. *Literaturnye ocherki. Sbornik statei.* Saint Petersburg, 1899. Critical of Tolstoy. Erratic.

*Shestov, L. *Dobro v uchenii gr. Tolstogo i F. Nitshe.* St. Peters., 1907. First published in 1900. Excellent and provocative throughout. Translated by Bernard Martin as *Dostoevsky, Tolstoy, and Nietzsche.* Athens, Ohio, 1969.

Ovsyaniko-Kulikovskii, D. N. *L. N. Tolstoi kak kudozhnik.* Saint Petersburg, 1905. Mostly on *War and Peace* and *Anna Karenina*. Proceeds by analysis of characters.

Korolenko, V. G. "Lev Nikolaevich Tolstoi." *Russkoe bogatstvo* 8 (August 1908): 125-243. High praise; Tolstoy is greater than Dostoevsky.

*Lenin, V. I. "Lev Tolstoi kak zerkalo russkoi revolyutsii." *Proletarii*, 11/24. Saint Petersburg, 1908. No essay on Tolstoy has had a greater influence on Tolstoy criticism in the Soviet Union and none is quoted as frequently. Tolstoy anticipated the revolution of 1805, for he mirrored the objective discontent among the people. He was able to transcend his own class and express the deepest consciousness of the peasant class. One can find this essay in many collections but it is probably most accessible in *L. N. Tolstoi v russkoi kritike*, ed. S. P. Bychkov, pp. 57-61.

Plekhanov, G. B. "Tolstoi i priroda." *Zvezda* 4 (1924). Written in 1908 for a special eighty-year jubilee collection, but not published at that time. Tolstoy feared death because of his individualism, which was a social phenomenon of his class. Worth reading, too, is Plekhanov's "Smeshenie predstavlenii. Uchenie L. N. Tolstogo."

Mysl' 1 (1910), and 2 (1911). About Tolstoy's doctrine of non-resistance to evil and Tolstoy's indifference to social conditions.

*Bely, Andrey. *Tragediya tvorchestva.* "*Dostoevsky i Tolstoi.*" Moscow, 1911.

Veresaev, V. V. *Zhivaya zhizn'.* O *Dostoevskom i L've Tolstom.*" Moscow, 1911. Early Marxist critic.

Ivanov, Vyacheslav. *Lev Tolstoi i kul'tura.* Saint Petersburg, 1911.

Ivanov, Razumnik, R. B. "Lev Nikolaevich Tolstoi." In *Istoriya russkoi literatury* 19 veka, Moscow, 1911.

Obnitsky, V. P. and T. I. Polner. *Voina i Mir, sbornik.* Moscow, 1912. Collection of articles including such diverse titles as "Aleksandr i Napoleon" and "Voina 1812 goda i narodnoe khozyaistvo."

Sorokin, Pitirim Aleksandrovich. *L. N. To'lstoi kak filosof.* Moscow, 1914.

IV. *General Criticism*

Abraham, Gerald. *Tolstoy.* New York, 1974. Reprint of 1935 edition; a volume in the Great Lives series. Short, competent, but limited in critical commentary.

Adamovich, George. "Tolstoy as an Artist." *The Russian Review* 19 (1960): 140–49.

Aldanov, Mark. *Zagadka Tolstogo.* Providence, R.I., 1969. First published in 1923. Study of the "contradictions" of Tolstoy. Introduction by Thomas Winner.

Anan'eva, V. P., et al., eds. *Lev Tolstoi. Problemy yazyka i stil'ya.* Tula, 1971. More than fifty articles on language and style.

Anzulovic, Branimir. "Tolstoi and the Novel." *Genre* 3 (1970): 1–16.

Aucouturier, Michel. "Langage intérieur et analyse psychologique chez Tolstoj." *Revue des études slaves* 34 (1948).

*Bayley, John. *Tolstoy and the Novel.* London, 1966. One of the best recent critical works on Tolstoy. Henry James's influence on Bayley's conception of the novel is evident.

Benson, Ruth Crego. *Women in Tolstoy: The Ideal and the Erotic.* Urbana, Ill., Chicago, and London, 1973. Short (141 pp.) study of an important topic. Claims that Tolstoy's attitude toward women is ambivalent and in part hostile.

*Berlin, Isaiah. "Tolstoy and Enlightenment." *Encounter* 16, no. 2 (1961): 29–40. Available in Berlin's *Mightier than the Sword* (London, 1964) and in Ralph Matlaw, ed., *Tolstoy, a Collection of Critical Essays* (Englewood Clifts, N.J., 1967). Excellent.

*———. *The Hedgehog and the Fox: An Essay on Tolstoy's View of History.* New York, 1953. The best book in English on Tolstoy's theory of history and one of the best on Tolstoy generally.

Bialkozowicz, Bazyli. *Lwa Tolstoja związki z Polską.* Warsaw, 1966.

Buyniak, Victor. "Stendhal as Young Tolstoy's Literary Model." *Etudes slaves et est-européennes* 5 (1960): 16-27.

Blagoi, D. D., ed. *Lev Nikolaevich Tolstoi, sbornik statei i materialov.* Moscow, 1951. Includes studies of *Kazaki, Voskresenie.* Of particular importance is N. K. Gudzii, "Ot 'Romana Russkogo Pomeshchika' k 'Utru Pomeshchika,' " pp. 390-424.

Boiko, M. "Vnutrennii monolog v proizvedeniyakh L. N. Tolstogo i F. M. Dostoevskogo." In *Lev Nikolaevich Tolstoi,* ed. N. K. Gudzii, 2:83-98. Moscow, 1959.

Bychkov, S. P. *L. N. Tolstoi, ocherk tvorchestva.* Moscow, 1954.

———, ed. *L. N. Tolstoi v russkoi kritike.* Moscow, 1952. Excellent source of major Russian critics. Most of the selections are from the nineteenth and early twentieth century: Lenin, Chernyshevsky, Pisarev, Annenkov, Dragomirov, Turgenev, Mikhailovsky, Korolenko, Blok, Plekhanov, Gorky, and Lunacharsky.

Chicherin, A. V. *Vozniknovenie roman-epopei.* Moscow, 1958. Tolstoy's works in the context of the development of the novel form in world literature. Particular reference to Zola, Romain Rolland, and Galsworthy's *The Forsyte Saga.*

*Christian, R. F. *Tolstoy: A Critical Introduction.* Cambridge, 1969. Standard work on Tolstoy; solid and helpful; approach is largely by way of sources and influences.

Clifford, Emma. "*War and Peace* and the Dynasts." *Modern Philology* 54 (1956): 33-34.

Crankshaw, Edward. *Tolstoy: The Making of a Novelist.* New York, 1974. Large format, glossy, many pictures, impressionistic.

Davis, Helen Edna. *Tolstoy and Nietzsche.* New York, 1929.

Doerne, Martin. *Tolstoj und Dostojewskij: Zwei Christliche Utopien.* Göttingen, 1969. Emphasis on the later works of Tolstoy. Section on each writer and then a comparison.

*Eikhenbaum, Boris. *Molodoi Tolstoi.* Petersburg and Berlin, 1922. Classic formalist study of Tolstoy's early tales. Translated by Gary Kern as *The Young Tolstoy.* Ann Arbor, Mich., 1972.

*———. *Lev Tolstoi.* 3 vols. Moscow, Leningrad, 1928, 1931, 1960. Classic formalist study of the traditions from which Tolstoy's work arose.

———. "Tolstoi do *Voiny i Mira.*" Introduction to A. Ostrovsky's *Molodoi Tolstoi v zapisyakh so vremennikov.* Leningrad, 1929.

———. "Nasledie Belinskogo i Lev Tolstoi." *Voprosy literatury,* 6 (1961): 124-48. A hitherto unpublished article dealing with the atmosphere and aesthetic problems of the 1850s.

*Ermilov, V. *Tolstoi romanist. "Voina i Mir," "Anna Karenina," "Voskresenie."* Moscow, 1965. Systematic analysis of characters and situations.

Evlakhov, A. M. *Lev Tolstoi. Konstitutialnye osobennosti psikhiki.* Moscow, 1930. Author attempts to prove that Tolstoy was an epileptic. Long introduction by Lunacharsky attempting to justify psychoanalytic investigations such as this one.

Fausset, Hugh I'Anson. *Tolstoy: The Inner Drama.* New York, 1928.

*Feuer, Kathryn. "August 1914: Solzhenitsyn and Tolstoy." In *Aleksandr Solzhenitsyn: Critical Essays and Documentary Materials*, ed. John B. Dunlop, Richard Haugh, and Alexis Klimoff, pp. 372–81. Belmont, Mass., 1973.

―――. "Solzhenitsyn and the Legacy of Tolstoy." In ibid., pp. 129–46. Survey of Tolstoyan models of form and structure used by Solzhenitsyn.

―――. "Recent Works on Leo Tolstoy." *Russian Review* 28 (1969): 217–24. Review article on books by Mooney, Shklovsky, Troyat, and Simmons.

Friche, B. M., ed. *O Tolstom, literaturno-kriticheskii sbornik.* Moscow and Leningrad, 1928. Good collection of Marxist criticism on Tolstoy. Articles by Lenin, Plekhanov, Panov, Roza Luxemburg, L. I. Aksel'rod, V. Friche, A. Martynov, and A. V. Lunacharsky.

―――, ed., *L. N. Tolstoi v svete marksistskoi kritiki.* Moscow and Leningrad, 1929.

Fueloep-Miller, René. "Tolstoy, the Apostolic Crusader." *Russian Review* 19 (April 1960): 99–121.

Gachev, G. "Soderzhatel'nost' formy (epos *Iliada* i *Voina in Mir).*" *Voprosy literatury* 9 (1965): 149–70.

Gibian, George. *Tolstoy and Shakespeare.* The Hague, 1957.

Goldfarb, Clare R. "William Dean Howells: An American Reaction to Tolstoy." *Comparative Literature Studies* 8 (1971): 317–37. Survey of how Howells championed Tolstoy's works against considerable opposition.

Gosse, Edmund. *Books on the Table: Unveiling of Tolstoy.* London, 1921.

Greenwood, B. *Tolstoy: The Comprehensive Vision.* London, 1975. Competent and cursory. Three pages on *Ivan Ilych*!

Grzegorczyk, Piotr. *Lew Tolstoj.* Panstwowy Instytut Wydawniczy, n.p. and n.d. Listing of translations and critical opinion by years.

*Gudzii, N. K. *Kak rabotal L. Tolstoi.* Moscow, 1936. Study of different versions: restricted to *The Kreutzer Sonata*, *The Power of Darkness*, *The Devil*, and *Resurrection.*

―――. *Mirovoe znachenie russkoi literatury.* Moscow, 1944. Comparison of *War and Peace* and Hardy's *Dynasts.*

―――. *Lev Nikolaevich Tolstoi.* Moscow, 1952. Short (110 pp.) study, primarily of *War and Peace*, *Anna Karenina*, and *Resurrection.*

Gunn, Elizabeth. *A Daring Coiffeur: Reflections on Tolstoy's "War and Peace" and "Anna Karenina."* Totwa, N.J., 1971. Eccentric and impressionistic; dependent entirely on translations and secondary sources. "Fictional" criticism.

*Hamburger, Kate. *Leo Tolstoi: Gestalt und Problem*. Bern, 1955. Solid and provocative.

Hemmings, F. W. J. *The Russian Novel in France, 1884-1914*. Oxford, 1950. Written apparently without knowledge of Russian since Tolstoy is quoted in English always and bibliography is entirely in English.

Hendrick, George. "Tolstoy's Quotations from Emerson in *The Cycle of Reading*." *Emerson Society Quarterly* 8 (1957): 29-31.

*Jones, W. Gareth. "George Eliot's *Adam Bede* and Tolstoy's Conception of Anna Karenina." *Modern Language Review* 61 (1966): 73-81. Comparison of Hetty Sorrell and Anna.

Khrapchenko, M. B. *Lev Tolstoi kak khudozhnik*. Moscow, 1963.

Kogan, P. S. *Lev Tolstoi i marksistskaya kritika*. Moscow and Leningrad, n.d.

Knight, G. Wilson. *Shakespeare and Tolstoy*. London, 1934.

Lavrin, Janko. *Tolstoy: An Approach*. New York, 1946.

Lawrence, D. H. *Reflections of the Death of a Porcupine and Other Essays*. Philadelphia, 1925.

Lednicki, Waclaw. *Tolstoy between War and Peace*. London and The Hague, 1965. Tolstoy's relationship to Poland. Very well done.

Lindstrom, Thais E. *Tolstoi en France (1886-1910)*. Paris, 1952. Designed apparently as a corrective to Hemmings's work, but only partly successful.

Lomunov, K. N. *Muzei-Usad'ba, Yasnaya Polyana-50 let*. Tula, 1972. In honor of 100 years of *War and Peace* and 50 years of the Tolstoy museum.

Lossky, N. "*Voina i Mir* Tolstogo i *Doktor Zhivago* Pasternaka," *Novy Zhurnal* 61 (1960): 292-95.

*Lubbock, Percy. *The Craft of Fiction*. London, 1921. This important propagation of James's views on the novel contains several chapters on Tolstoy. Although Lubbock is more sympathetic toward Tolstoy than is James, he is still insidiously critical of the form of Tolstoy's works.

Lukacs, Gyorgy. *Studies in European Realism*. Trans. Edith Bone. London, 1950. Lukacs is an intelligent and sophisticated Marxist with a vast knowledge of European literature. Most of his books touch on Tolstoy. Two chapters in this book from his "orthodox" period: "Tolstoy and the Development of Realism" and "Leo Tolstoy and Western European Literature."

Lunacharsky, A. V. *Tolstoi i Marks*. Leningrad, 1924. Forty-four lectures given in 1924.

————, ed. *O Tolstom, sbornik statei*. Moscow and Leningrad, 1928.

Mann, Thomas. *Goethe und Tolstoi*. Aachen, 1923. Available in

English in his *Essays of Three Decades*. New York, 1947.

Markovitch, Milan. *Jean Jacques Rousseau et Tolstoi*. Paris, 1928.

Marti, Paul. "Tolstois *Krieg und Frieden* und Pasternaks *Doktor Schiwago*." *Schweitzer Monatshefte* 62 (1962): 79–90.

Matlaw, Ralph, ed. *Tolstoy: A Collection of Critical Essays*. Englewood Cliffs, N.J., 1967. A representative selection of essays on Tolstoy not easily accessible elsewhere.

*Motyleva, T. L. *O mirovom znachenii L. N. Tolstogo*. Moscow, 1957. Survey of critical reception and influence in America, England, Germany, France, and Slavic countries. English and American writers discussed: Hardy, Galsworthy, Shaw, Howells, Norris, Crane, Dreiser, Fast. French writers: Flaubert, Zola, Maupassant, Anatole France, Rolland, and others.

Muchnic, Helen. *An Introduction to Russian Literature*. New York, 1964.

*Muir, Edwin. *The Structure of the Novel*. New York, 1929. Excellent on the chronicle form of *War and Peace* and on Tolstoy's fictional use of time.

*Myshkovskaya, L. M. *Masterstvo L. N. Tolstogo*. Moscow, 1958. Study of Tolstoy's style by reference largely to manuscript variants. Most of the book is on *War and Peace* and *Hadji Murad*.

Nal'gieva, Kh. Sh. "Nekotorye osobennosti khudozhestvennogo psikhologizma Tolstogo i F. Dostoevskogo." In *Tolstovskii sbornik*, ed. I. E. Grineva et al., pp. 130–43. Tula, 1970.

Nikolaev, M. P. *L. N. Tolstoi i N. G. Chernyshevskii*. Tula, 1969. This important relationship deserves something better.

Nusinov, I. M. ed. *Lenin i Tolstoi*. Moscow, 1928. A compilation of Lenin's remarks on Tolstoy.

Phelps, Gilbert. *The Russian Novel in English Fiction*. London, 1956.

Plakhotishina, B. M. *Masterstvo L. N. Tolstogo romanista*. Dnepropetrovsk, 1960. Analysis of major novels, proceeding by short selections on individual characters.

Poggioli, Renato. "A Portrait of Tolstoy as Alceste." In his *The Phoenix and the Spider*. Cambridge, Mass., 1957.

———. "Tolstoy as Man and Artist." *Oxford Slavonic Papers*, 1962. Reprinted in *The Spirit of the Letter*. Cambridge, Mass., 1965.

Radionova, N. S. *Lev Nikolaevich Tolstoi, sbornik statei i materialov*. Moscow, 1957.

Rahv, Philip. "Tolstoy: the Green Twig and the Black Trunk." In his *Image and Idea*, pp. 87–104. New York, 1957. Sophisticated and intelligent but also perpetuates some myths about Tolstoy's works. First published in 1949.

Redpath, Theodore. *Tolstoy*. London, 1960.

Rozanova, S. *Tolstoi i Gertsen*. Moscow, 1972.

Rudy, Peter. "Lev Tolstoy's Apprenticeship to Lawrence Sterne,"

Slavic and East European Journal 15 (1971): 1–21.
Sharma, Ranjee. "Tolstoy and India." *Solidarity* 8 (1974): 78–80.
Shifman, A. *Lev Tolstoi i vostok.* Moscow, 1960. Tolstoy's relations (comments, letters etc.) to China, India, Japan, Iran, Turkey, and the Arabian countries.
Shklovsky, Viktor. *Khudozhestvennaya proza: razmyshleniya i razbory.* Moscow, 1959. Tolstoy figures prominently in this collection of more than a hundred short articles. Extensive treatment of *Hadji Murad.*
Simmons, Ernest J. *Introduction to Tolstoy's Writings.* Chicago and London, 1968. Short, readable, factual.
———. "Tolstoy and Chekhov." *Midway* 8, no. 4 (1968): 91–104.
Slonim, Marc. "Four Western Writers on Tolstoy." *Russian Review* 19 (April, 1960): 187–204.
Smith, John Allan. "Tolstoy's Fiction in England and America." Doctoral dissertation, University of Illinois, 1939.
Speirs, Logan. *Tolstoy and Chekhov.* Cambridge, 1971. Divided into two sections with minimal comparison. Based on secondary sources; no knowledge of Russian; derivative and exclamatory.
*Steiner, George. *Tolstoy or Dostoevsky.* New York, 1957. Controversial and provocative.
Struve, Petr. B. *Stat'i o L've Tolstom.* Sofiya, 1921.
Tschizewskij, Dmitrij. "Tolstoi und die Aufklärung des 18. Jahrhunderts." *Archiv* 211 (1974): 45–53.
Tumas, Elena Valiute. "The Literary Kinship of Leo N. Tolstoy and Romain Rolland: A Comparative Study of Epic Dimensions of *War and Peace* and *Jean-Christophe*." Doctoral diss., University of Southern California, 1964.
*Woolf, Virginia. "The Russian Point of View." In *The Common Reader.* New York, 1925. Ecstatic commentary on Russian writers, including Tolstoy.
Zhdanov, V. A. *Ot "Anny Kareninoi" k "Voskreseniyu."* Moscow, 1967.

V. *Studies of the Early Works*

Bursov. B. *Lev Tolstoi, ideinye iskaniya i tvorcheskii period 1847–1862.* Moscow, 1960. Study of early works through *The Cossacks.*
———. "O yazyke L. N. Tolstogo (rannee tvorchestvo). *Neva,* 11 (1960), 199–216. Detailed analysis of "inner monolog" (*vnutrenii monolog*).
Dieckemann, Eberhard. *Erzählformen in Frühwerk L. N. Tolstojs, 1851–1857.* Berlin, 1969. A short work (a little more than 100 pages) on narrative point of view from the earliest fragments, the childhood trilogy and through *The Two Hussars.*
*Eikhenbaum, Boris. "L. Tolstoi na Kavkaze." *Russkaya literatura* 5

(1962): 48-76. Chapter from an unfinished work on Tolstoy's development. Analysis of how the tales written in the Caucasus came into being, especially *Detstvo*, *Nabeg*, *Kazaki*.

Eros, Carol. "Tolstoj's Tales of the Caucasus and Literary Tradition." Doctoral diss., University of Wisconsin, 1973.

Galagan, G. Ya. "Eticheski i esteticheskie iskaniya molodogo Tolstogo." *Russkaya literatura* 17, no. 1 (1974): 136-49. Tolstoy's ethical-aesthetic code was formed in the period 1840-50, and Tolstoy remained faithful to this code to the end of his days. The code is one of "nravstvennoe sovershenstvovanie."

*Hagan, John. "Ambivalence in Tolstoy's *The Cossacks*." *Novel* 3 (1969): 28-47. Tolstoy does not admire the Cossacks in an unqualified way but has some serious reservations about their way of life.

Lee, Nicholas. "Dreams and Daydreams in the Early Fiction of L. N. Tolstoy." In *American Contributions to the Seventh International Congress of Slavists* (Warsaw, 1973), vol 2: *Literature and Folklore*, ed. Victor Terras. The Hague, 1973.

Zaborova, R. "Ob izdaniyakh *Kazakov* L. N. Tolstogo." *Russkaya literatura* 7, no 4 (1964): 206-13.

Zweers, Alexander. *Grown-up Narrator and Childlike Hero: An Analysis of the Literary Devices Employed in Tolstoy's Trilogy, "Childhood," "Boyhood," and "Youth."* The Hague, 1971.

VI. *War and Peace*

One will want to consult volumes 13-16 and the Jubilee Edition for rough drafts and variants to the novel, as well as E. Zaidenshnur's "Istoriya pisaniia i pechataniya *Voiny i mira*, in volume 16, pp. 19-140. The same volume has a list of books that Tolstoy used in writing *War and Peace*, and I. S. Rodionov's "Opisanie rukopisei i korrektur otnosyashchikhsya k *Voine i miru*," pp. 146-211.

Aucoutourier, Michel. "Tolstoi devant Napoleon." *Europe*, 480-81 (1969): 191-98.

Bayley, John, and Binyon, Timothy. "*War and Peace*, an Exchange." *Essays in Criticism* 18 (1968): 100-104. Bayley's criticism of a review by Binyon and Binyon's response, mostly on Tolstoy's theory of military history and the role of commanders.

*Berlin, Isaiah. *The Hedgehog and the Fox: An Essay on Tolstoy's View of History*. New York, 1953. The best book in English on Tolstoy's theory of history and one of the best on Tolstoy generally.

Bezrukova, Z. P. "Formy psikhologicheskogo analiza v romanakh L. N. Tolstogo *Voina i Mir* i Anna Karenina." In *Lev Nikolaevich Tolstoi*, ed. N. K. Gudzii, 1:62-100. Moscow, 1956. Discussion of Chernyshevsky's "inner monologue."

Bier, Jesse. "A Century of *War and Peace*—Gone, Gone with the Wind." *Genre* 4 (1971): 107-41. A devastating criticism of *War and Peace* and especially of Tolstoy's outrageous coincidences and sentimentality.

Bilinkis, Ya. "Mir v *Voine i Mire*." In *O tvorchestve L. N. Tolstogo*, pp. 195-279. Leningrad, 1959. Study of the text against manuscript variants.

Birman, Yu. "O kharaktere vremeni v *Voine i Mire*." *Russkaya literatura* 9 (1966): 125-31.

———. "Nikolen'ka Bolkonsky, budushchii dekabrist." *Russkaya Literatura* 12 (1969): 120-28. Detailed analysis of Andrey's son and the Decembrist theme.

*Bocharov, S. *Roman L. Tolstogo "Voina i Mir."* Moscow, 1963. Short, perceptive, original.

Borisova, I. "Narodnye tseny v *Voine i Mire*." *Voprosy literatury* 3 (1960): 170-91.

Brazhnik, Natal'ya Ivanovna. *Izuchenie romana L. N. Tolstogo "Voina i Mir" v srednei shkole*. Moscow, 1957.

Brian-Chaninov, Nicolas. *"La Guerre et la Paix" de Léon Tolstoi*. Paris, 1931.

*Bychkov, S. P. *Narodno-geroicheskaya epopeya L. N. Tolstogo "Voina i Mir."* Moscow, 1949.

Chappie, Richard L. "The Role and Function of Nature in L. N. Tolstoy's *War and Peace*." *New Zealand Slavonic Journal* 11 (Winter 1973): 86-101.

Cheremisina, M. I. "Sravneniya v romane L. N. Tolstogo *Voina i Mir*." In *Tolstovskii sbornik*, ed. M. P. Nikolaev et al., pp. 163-81. Tula, 1962.

*Chicherin, A. V. *O yazyke i stile romana-epopei "Voina i Mir."* L'vov, 1956.

Chirkov, N. "*Voina i Mir* L. N. Tolstogo kak khudozhestvennoe tseloe." *Russkaya literatura* 9 (1966): 43-65.

*Christian, R. F. *Tolstoy's "War and Peace": A Study*. Oxford, 1962. The only book in English devoted exclusively to *War and Peace*. Largely a study of the rough drafts and variants and some analysis of the language and style.

Cook, Albert. "The Unity of *War and Peace*." *Western Review* 22 (Summer 1958), 243-55.

Debreczeny, Paul. "Freedom and Necessity: A Reconsideration of *War and Peace*." *Papers on Language and Literature* 7 (1971): 185-98. Consideration of Tolstoy's theory of freedom. Tolstoy's position implied a thoroughgoing necessity, but he felt impelled to affirm an irrational freedom.

*Ermilov, V. *Tolstoi khudozhnik i roman "Voina i Mir."* Moscow, 1961. Surprisingly good book by an orthodox Soviet critic—much better than his book on Dostoevsky.

Fadiman, Clifton. "Is *War and Peace* the Greatest Novel Ever Written?" *Holiday* 20 (August, 1956), 6-9, 76.

Farrell, James T. "Tolstoy's *War and Peace* as a Moral Panorama of the Tsarist Feudal Nobility." In his *Literature and Morality*. New York, 1945. One of several essays pertaining to *War and Peace* in this curious volume. Others are: "History and War in Tolstoy's *War and Peace*," "Tolstoy's Portrait of Napoleon," "Leo Tolstoy and Napoleon Bonaparte," and "Historical Image of Napoleon Bonaparte."

Feuer, Kathryn. "The Box that Became *War and Peace*." *Reporter* 20 (May 14, 1959): 33-36. On the early drafts of *War and Peace* and the significance of these drafts for Tolstoy's political opinions.

*Flaubert, Gustave. *Correspondance, Supplément: Juillet 1877-Mai, 1880*. Ed. René Dumesnil, Jean Pommier, and Claude Digeon. Paris, 1945. Includes Flaubert's famous letter to Turgenev dated January 21, 1880, about his reaction to reading *War and Peace* (pp. 298-99).

*Forster, E. M. *Aspects of the Novel*. New York, 1927. Classic statement on *War and Peace* (pp. 38-39).

Gordeeva, Natal'ya Borisovna. *Izuchenie masterstva L. N. Tolstogo v shkole (Voina i Mir)*. Moscow, 1958.

Greenwood, E. B. "Tolstoy's Poetic Realism in *War and Peace*." *Critical Quarterly* 11 (1969): 219-33. Against dividing Tolstoy's art from his ideas.

*Gudzii, N. "Chto shchitat' kanonicheskim tekstom *Voiny i Mira*." *Novy mir* 39 (1963): 234-46. The first of two statements on which edition of *War and Peace* should be considered the definitive text. At issue was the edition from which the French and much of the philosophical material had been eliminated. Gusev took issue with Gudzii.

*————. "Eshche of kanonicheskom tekste *Voiny i Mira*." *Voprosy literatury* 8 (1964): 190-200.

*————. "Snova o kanonicheskom tekste *Voiny i Mira*." *Russkaya literatura* 8 (1965): 98-107.

*————. "O kanonicheskom tekste *Voiny i Mira*." *Voprosy literatury* 8 (1964): 179-90.

Hagan, John H. "A Pattern of Character Development in *War and Peace*." *Slavic and East European Journal* 13 (1969): 164-90. *War and Peace* has shape and structure and is constructed on a sharp contrast of true and false values. Detailed examination of Prince Andrey's development.

————. "On the Craftmanship of *War and Peace*." *Essays in Criticism* 13 (January 1963): 17-49.

Harkins, William E. "A Note on the Use of Narrative and Dialogue in

War and Peace.'' Slavic Review 29 (1970): 86–92.

*Kareev, Nikolai Ivanovich. *Istoricheskaya filosofiya gr. L. N. Tolstogo v "Voine i Mire."* Saint Petersburg, 1888.

Karpenko, M. V. "Razmery predlozheniya v romane L. N. Tolstogo *Voina i Mir.* In *Lev Tolstoi yubileiny sbornik 1910-1960,* ed. N. P. Fatov et al. Chernovtsy, 1961. Statistical and formulaic study of Tolstoy's sentence length.

Krasnov, G. V. "Rabota Tolstogo nad obrazom Tushina." In *Tolstoi khudozhnik,* ed. A. A. Saburov et al., pp. 61–95. Moscow, 1961.

————. "Natasha Rostov: k probleme geroya, *Voina i Mir.*" *Filologicheskie nauki* 5 (1962): 118–28.

————. *Geroi i narod, o romane L'va Tolstogo "Voina i Mir."* Moscow, 1964. Before the Sevastopol Sketches and *War and Peace,* Tolstoy was concerned with self-analysis; after these works, he was concerned with the people (*mysl' narodnaya*). Study of how characters in the novel are linked with qualities of the people (*narod*).

————, ed. *"Voina i Mir,"* sbornik statei. Gorky, 1959.

Lanoux, Armand. "La guerre et la paix." In *Tolstoi,* pp. 151–98. Paris, 1965. Criticism of Tolstoy's theory of history: "Le fatalisme historique n'est pas une doctrine. C'est une intuition brumeuse, la transposition sur le plan militaire du *nitchevo.*"

————. "Pourquoi Tolstoi écrivit *Guerre et Paix.*" *Revue de Paris* 72 (October 1965): 54–66.

Lettenbauer, Wilhelm. "L. Tolstojs Stil in der Sicht der russischen Formalisten." *Stil und Formprobleme* 4 (1959): 396–402.

Leusheva, S. I. *Roman L. N. Tolstogo "Voina i Mir."* Moscow, 1957. A text for school children and as such an introduction to all aspects of *War and Peace*: background, images, character analysis. Representative of official Soviet attitudes.

Lyngstad, Alexandra H. "Tolstoj's Use of Parentheses in *War and Peace.*" *Slavic and East European Journal,* 16 (1972): 403–13. About 700 uses in *War and Peace*; much greater frequency than Dostoevsky and Turgenev. Analysis of range of uses.

Mooney, Harry J., Jr. *Tolstoy's Epic Vision: A Study of "War and Peace" and "Anna Karenina."* Tulsa, Oklahoma, 1968. A thin (88 pp.) volume written with no knowledge of Russian or of nineteenth-century Russian literature.

Naumova, N. "Problema kharaktera v *Voine i Mir.*" *Russkaya literatura* 3 (1960): 100–16.

Neatrour, Elizabeth. "The Role of Platon Karataev in *War and Peace.*" *Madison College Studies and Research,* March 1970, pp. 19–30.

*Ogol'tsev, V. M. "Umen'shitel'nye formy imen sushchestvitel'nykh i prilagatel'nykh kak sredstvo khrakteristiki personazhei v romane L. N. Tolstogo *Voina i Mir.* In *L. N. Tolstoi,* ed. V. P. Rakov, et al., pp. 255-64. Kustanai, 1961. Study of diminutive forms as showing qualities of a character. There are no diminutive forms used for Vera and Ellen, for example.

Potapov, I. A. *Roman L. N. Tolstogo "Voina i Mir": Sovremennoe i i istoricheskoe v romane, problemy kompozitsii, rol' peysazha.* Moscow, 1970.

Ptichnikov, E. M. "Nekotorye nablyudeniya nad priemami sozdaniya obrazov v romane L. N. Tolstogo *Voina i Mir.*" In *Lev Nikolaevich Tolstoi,* ed. N. K. Gudzii, 1:34-61. Moscow, 1955. Division of characters by self-interest and selflessness, those who raise themselves to *obshchechelovecheskie interesy.*

Pugach, S. "Rechevye priemy vyrazheniya vnutrennego mira personazha v romane L. Tolstogo *Voina i Mir.*" *Russkii yazyk v shkole* 23 (1962): 16-22.

Rzhevsky, L. "Ob odnom obraze v romane *Voina i Mir.*" *Novy Zhurnal* 82 (1966): 113-18.

*Saburov, A. A. *"Voina i Mir" L. N. Tolstogo, problematika i poetika.* Moscow, 1959. A 600-page study of the formal elements of *War and Peace*: language, style, genre, character, structure, themes and ideas (*ideinoe soderzhanie*). Heavy to read, but important.

———. *"Voina i Mir* kak natsional'no-geroicheskaya epopeya." In *Tvorchestvo L. N. Tolstogo,* ed. D. Blagoi, pp. 75-163. Moscow, 1959.

Sazonov, P. *"Voina i Mir": filosofiya istorii i obrazy Kutuzova, Platona Karataeva v romane "Voina i Mir" L. Tolstogo.* Przevolsk, 1962.

*Shklovsky, Viktor. *Material i stil' v romane "Voina i Mir" L'va Tolstogo.* Important study during the period of Shklovsky's accommodation of formalism to Marxism. Of special interest is listing of contemporary reviews in the appendix. Basically a study of Tolstoy's use of sources and how he deformed them.

Simonov, Konstantin. "On Reading Tolstoy: An Essay on the Centenary of the First Edition of *War and Peace.*" *Partisan Review* 38 (1971): 208-16.

Skaftymov, A. P. "Obraz Kutuzova i filosofiya istorii v romane Tolstogo *Voina i Mir.*" *Russkaya literatura* 2 (1959): 72-94.

Spence, G. W. "Suicide and Sacrifice in Tolstoy's Ethics." *Russian Review* 22 (1963): 157-67.

*States, Bert O. "The Hero and the World; Our Sense of Space in *War and Peace.*" *Modern Fiction Studies* 11 (1965): 153-64.

Thale, Jerome. "*War and Peace*: The Art of Incoherence." *Essays in Criticism* 16 (1966): 398-415.

Timrot, Aleksandr Dmitrievich. *Geroi i obrazy romane "Voina i Mir," L. N. Tolstogo.* Tula, 1961.

Troitskii, N. N. "*Voina i Mir* i zapadnoevropeiskii istoricheskii roman XIX veka." In *Tvorchestvo L. N. Tolstogo*, ed. D. Blagoi et al. Moscow, 1959. Discusses particularly: Walter Scott, Mérimée, Balzac, Thackeray, Flaubert, Stendhal, and Zola.

Tsapnikov, V. M. "Periody v romane L. N. Tolstogo *Voina i Mir*." In *Tolstovskii sbornik*, ed. M. P. Nikolaev et al., pp. 130–45. Tula, 1902. Study of sentence length and complexity.

Velikodvorskaya, Z. N. "Nablyudeniya nad prisoedinitel'nymi svyaz-yami v romane L. N. Tolstogo *Voina i Mir*." In *Tolstovskii sbornik*, pp. 146–62. Tula, 1962. Study of conjunctive constructions and how they reflect psychology of the characters.

Wasiolek, Edward. "The Theory of History in *War and Peace*." *Midway* 9, no. 2 (1968): 117–35.

Wedel, Erwin. *Die Entstehungsgeschichte von L. N. Tolstojs "Krieg und Frieden*." Wiesbaden, 1961.

Wellek, René. "R. F. Christian, *Tolstoy's War and Peace: A study*." *Slavic Review* 22 (1963): 599–601.

Zaidenshnur, Evelina Efimovna. *"Voina i Mir" L. N. Tolstogo: sozdanie velikoi knigi*. Moscow, 1966.

VII. *Anna Karenina*

*Arnold, Matthew. "Count Leo Tolstoy." *Essays in Criticism, Second Series*. London, 1888. An indispensable essay on *Anna Karenina*. First published in the *Fortnightly Review*, December 1887.

Babaev, E. G. *Roman L'va Tolstogo "Anna Karenina*." Tula, 1968.

Batereau, Brigitte. "Zeit in Lev Tolstojs *Anna Karenina*." *Die Welt der Slaven* 16 (1971): 1–19.

Blackmur, R. P. "*Anna Karenina*: The Dialectic of Incarnation." *Kenyon Review* 12 (1950): 433–56.

Blumberg, Edwina J. "Tolstoy and the English Novel: A Note on *Middlemarch* and *Anna Karenina*." *Slavic Review* 30 (1971): 561–69.

Burkina, N. M. "Esteticheskie iskaniya L. Tolstogo v 70-e gody i roman *Anna Karenina*." In *Tolstovskii sbornik*, pp. 34–43. Tula, 1975.

Call, Paul. "Anna Karenina's Crime and Punishment: The Impact of Historical Theory upon the Russian Novel." *Mosaic* 1 (October 1967): 94–102. Anna's fate illustrates by analogy Tolstoy's view of history in *War and Peace*: the individual is free to act but cannot determine the outcome of his choices.

Comings, Andrew G. *Tolstoy's "Anna Karenina": The Problem of Form*. 13 pp. Occasional Papers in Language and Literature and Linguistics. Athens, Ohio, 1973.

*Dostoevsky, F. M. *Dnevnik pisatelya za 1877 goda*. Paris, n.d. Pp. 268–70 and 275–311.

*Ermilov, V. E. *Roman L. N. Tolstogo "Anna Karenina."* Moscow, 1963. Short and sensible reading by this orthodox Soviet critic. Surprisingly free of polemics.

Flint, Martha M. "The Epigraph of *Anna Karenina.*" *PMLA* 80 (1965): 461-62.

Gibian, George. "Two Kinds of Human Understanding and the Narrator's Voice in *Anna Karenina.*" *Orbis Scriptus* 92 (1966): 315-22. Keystone of the novel is opposition of reason and unreason. Tolstoy approves of instinctive responses and disapproves of intellectualist responses. Analysis of linguistic elements that show this.

Gifford, Henry. "Anna, Lawrence and 'The Law.' " *Critical Quarterly* 1 (1959): 203-6. Argument against Lawrence's criticism of the novel: that Tolstoy betrayed Anna.

————. "Further Notes on *Anna Karenina.*" *Critical Quarterly* 2 (1960): 158-160. A response to Raymond William's "Lawrence and Tolstoy" in *Critical Quarterly* 2 (1960): 33-39, which itself was a criticism of the 1959 article by Gifford. Williams had argued for the complexity of Anna's character.

Greenwood, E. B. "The Unity of *Anna Karenina.*" *Landfall* 15 (1961): 124-34.

*Jackson, Robert L. "Chance and Design in *Anna Karenina.*" In *The Disciplines of Criticism: Essays in Literary Theory, Interpretation and History*, eds. Peter Demetz, Thomas Greene, and Lowry Nelson, pp. 315-29. New Haven, 1968. Detailed analysis of the scene in which Anna first meets Vronsky. This scene is seen as a microcosm of the novel.

Jones, Peter. *Philosophy and the Novel: Philosophical Aspects of "Middlemarch" "Anna Karenina," "The Brothers Karamazov," "A la recherche du temps perdu," and of the Methods of Criticism.* Oxford, 1975.

Jones, T. Robert. "*Anna Karenina* and the Tragic Genre." *Melbourne Slavonic Studies* 4 (1970): 57-67.

Kirpotin, V. "Zlobodnevnoe v *Anne Kareninoi.*" *Voprosy literatury* 9 (1960): 186-92. Contemporary problems played their part in the creation of the novel and particularly in arguments about the Europeanization of education.

Kupreyanova, E. "Vyrazhenie esteticheskikh vorzrenii i nravstvennykh iskanii L. N. Tolstogo v romane *Anna Karenina.*" *Russkaya literatura* 3 (1960): 117-36. Detailed examination of the Mikhailov scene.

*Leavis, R. R. "Anna Karenina." *Critical Quarterly* 2 (1965-66): 5-27. Also available in *Anna Karenina and Other Essays.* London, 1967. Sensitive and sophisticated reading.

*Mann, Thomas. "*Anna Karenina.*" In his *Essays of Three Decades*, trans. H. T. Lowe-Porter, pp. 176-88. New York, 1965. First written in 1939 as preface to a Random House edition of the novel;

published in German the same year.

Prutskov, N. I. "Ob odnoi paralleli *Anna Karenina* Tolstogo i *Dama s sobachkoi Chekhova.*" In *Poetika i stilistika russkoi literatury: pamyati Akademika Viktor Vladimoricha Vinogradova*, pp. 236–46. Leningrad, 1971.

Pursglove, Michael. "The Smiles of Anna Karenina." *Slavic and East European Journal* 17 (1973): 42–48.

Schultze, Sydney P. "The Chapter in *Anna Karenina.*" *Russian Literature Triquarterly* 10 (1974): 351–59. How effective are Tolstoy's minichapters?

Seeley, Frank Friedberg. "La nemesi de *Anna Karenina.*" *Annali Istituto Universitario Orientale, Sezione Slava* 2 (1959): 121–46.

Slade, Tony. "*Anna Karenina* and the Family Ideal." *Southern Review* (Australia) 1 (1963): 85–90. There is a change in marital ideal between *War and Peace* and *The Kreutzer Sonata*, and *Anna Karenina* is the transitional work.

Steward, David D. "*Anna Karenina*: The Dialectic of Prophecy." *PMLA* 79 June 1940): 266–82. Study of how Tolstoy postpones and completes generalization.

*Trilling, Lionel. "*Anna Karenina.*" In *The Opposing Self*. New York, 1969. Originally published by Viking in 1950. A graceful and readable essay—as has been everything by Trilling—but containing unbelievable errors in interpretation, such as the position that Tolstoy did not interfere in the narration of his stories.

*Zhdanov, V. *Tvorcheskaya istoriya "Anny Kareninoi."* Moscow, 1957. Study of the manuscript versions.

VIII. *Studies of the Late Works*

Aikhenvald', N. *Posmertnye sochineniya L. N. Tolstogo*. Saint Petersburg, 1912. Reprint: University of Michigan microfilm.

Azarov, N. "O nekotorykh osobennostyakh povestei Tolstogo 80–90x godov." In *Tolstoi-Khudozhnik, sbornik statei*, ed. D. D. Blagoi et al. Moscow, 1961.

Bilichenko, N. A. "Obraz Simonsona v romane L. N. Tolstogo *Voskresenie*: K voprosu o prototipe." *Russkaya literatura* 15, no. 4 (1972): 161–65.

Dayananda, Y. J. "*The Death of Ivan Ilych*: A Psychological Study on *Death and Dying.*" *Literature and Psychology* 22 (1972): 191–98. A comparison of *The Death of Ivan Ilych* and Elisabeth Kubler-Ross's five stages of dying as outlined in her *On Death and Dying*. New York, 1969. The topic awaits a better treatment.

Giuliani, Ann. "Tolstoi e il clima spirituale della *Sonata a Kreutzer.*" *Ausonia* 12, No. 1 (1959): 26–33.

Hagan, John H., Jr. "Detail and Meaning in Tolstoy's *Master and Man.*" *Criticism* 11 (1969): 31–58. Consideration of Brekhunov (the Master) as "anti-Christ." Many parallels with the Bible.

Halperin, Irving. "The Structural Integrity of *The Death of Ivan Il'ic.*" *Slavic and East European Journal* 5 (1961): 334-40. "The basis of unity of Tolstoj's masterpiece is the increasing intensity and narrowing focus of its 12 narrative parts."

*Hirschberg, W. R. "Tolstoy's *The Death of Ivan Ilich.*" *Explicator* 28, Item 26 (1969). Analysis of the image of Ivan Ilych slipping through the black bag at death and exposition of implications of birth-death symbolism.

Mikhailovsky, N. K. "Khozyain i rabotnik gr. L. Tolstogo," *Otkliki* 1 (1904): 54-63. About "death" in Tolstoy; high praise for *Master and Man*; considerable discussion of *The Death of Ivan Ilych*.

*Myshkovskaya, L. L. *Tolstoi, rabota i stil'.* Moscow, 1939. Language study, mostly on *Hadji-Murad*, some on *Khozyain i rabotnik* and *Kholstomer*.

Olney, James. "Experience, Metaphor, and Meaning: *The Death of Ivan Ilych.*" *Journal of Aesthetics and Art Criticism* 31 (1972): 101-4.

Opul'skaya, L. D. "Psikhologicheskii analiz v romane *Voskresenie.*" In *Tolstoi Khudozhnik, sbornik statei*, ed. D. Blagoi et al. Moscow, 1961.

Pachmuss, Temira. "The Theme of Love and Death in Tolstoy's *The Death of Ivan Ilych.*" *American Slavic and East European Review* 20 (1961): 72-83.

Ronai, Paulo. "A morte de Ivan Ilitch." *Revista do livro* 3 (December, 1958): 71-76.

Rukavitsyn, M. a. "Iskusstvo portreta v povesti L. N. Tolstogo *Smert' Ivana Il'icha.*" *Izvestiya akademii nauk* 23 (1964): 44-48.

Sorokin, Boris. "Ivan I'lich as Jonah: A Cruel Joke." *Canadian Slavic Studies* 5 (1971): 487-507.

Trahan, Elizabeth. "L. N. Tolstoy's *Master and Man*—A Symbolic Narrative." *Slavic and East European Journal* 7 (1963): 258-68. Inspiration of the story is Flaubert's *La légende de Saint-Julien l'hospitalier*.

Turner, C. J. G. "The Language of Fiction: Word Clusters in Tolstoy's *The Death of Ivan Ilyich.*" *Modern Language Review* 65 (1970): 116-21. Focuses on the words *priyatny* i *prilichny* and *lozh'* i *obman*.

Wasiolek, Edward. "Tolstoy's *The Death of Ivan Ilych* and Jamesian Fictional Imperatives." *Modern Fiction Studies* 6 (1960): 314-24.

Woodward, James B. "Tolstoy's *Hadji Murad*: The Evolution of Its Theme and Structure." *Modern Language Review* 68 (1973): 870-82.

Zhdanov, V. A. *Poslednie knigi L. N. Tolstogo.* Moscow, 1971. Much on *Hadji-Murad*.

————. "Iz tvorcheskoi istorii povesti *Kreitserova sonata.*" In *Tolstoi Khudoznik, sbornik statei*, pp. 260–88. Moscow, 1961.

*————. *Tvorcheskaya istoriya romana L. N. Tolstogo "Voskresenie."* Moscow, 1960. Best introduction to the mass of drafts and variants Tolstoy left for the novel. Also criticism and interpretation.

Index